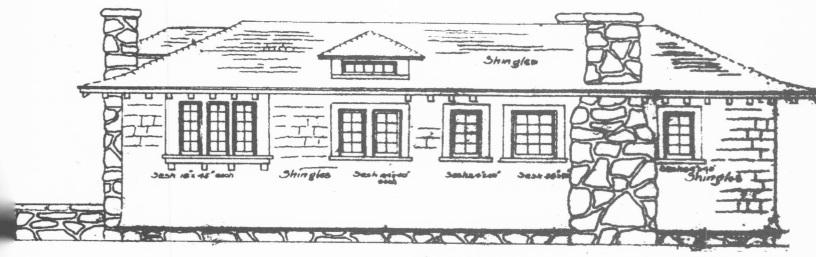

SIDE ELEVATION

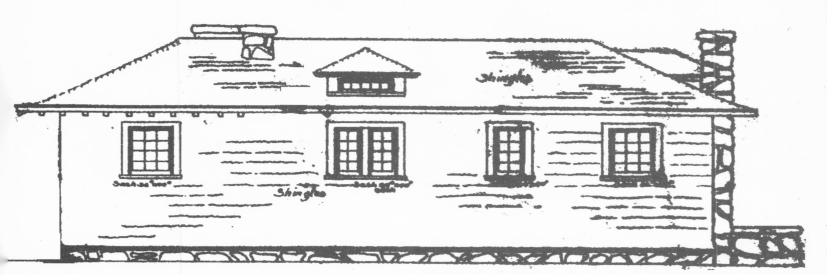

·SIDE ELEVATION

SERIES 1904 - JOLY

CRAFTSMAN BUNGALOW

No. 8

Scale 1/4" = 1'-0"

STICKLEY'S
CRAFTSMAN HOMES

STICKLEY'S CRAFTSMAN HOMES

PLANS
DRAWINGS
PHOTOGRAPHS

Ray Stubblebine

Gibbs Smith, Publisher
Salt Lake City

First Edition
10 09 08 07 06   5 4 3 2 1

Original floor plans courtesy director Gerald Beasley at the Avery Architectural and Fine Arts Library
at Columbia University. Other plans and drawings have been reproduced from original issues of
The Craftsman.

Published by
Gibbs Smith, Publisher
P.O. Box 667
Layton, Utah 84041

Orders: 1.800.835.4993
www.gibbs-smith.com

Interior designed by Rudy Ramos
Printed and bound in Hong Kong

Library of Congress Cataloging-in-Publication Data

Stubblebine, Ray.
  Stickley's craftsman homes : plans, drawings, photographs / by Ray Stubblebine.—1st ed.
    p. cm.
  Includes bibliographical references and index.
  ISBN 1-58685-379-1
  1. Stickley, Gustav, 1858-1942—Criticism and interpretation. 2. Architecture, Domestic—United
States—Designs and plans. 3. Arts and crafts movement—United States. 4. Craftsman (Eastwood,
Syracuse, N.Y.) I. Stickley, Gustav, 1858-1942. II. Title.

NA737.S65S78 2006
328'.37'092—dc22
                                         2005015414

This book is dedicated not only to those Craftsman Home owners who have opened their homes to me, allowing me to share them through this book, but also to all those who unknowingly own a Craftsman Home and have only realized that in some way their homes are unique—and have sought to maintain and preserve them. Perhaps now they may learn what they own and why their homes are so special.

Contents

VOL. XVIII, NO. 5　　　　AUGUST, 1910　　　　25 CENTS

THE CRAFTSMAN

A NEW POLITICAL PARTY FOUNDED ON CONSERVATION AND THE SQUARE DEAL: BY GUSTAV STICKLEY.

FORTY-ONE-WEST-THIRTY-FOURTH-STREET-NEW-YORK

In this view published in *The Craftsman*, the Raymond Riordan house on Silver Lake, near Rolling Prairie, Indiana, is positioned on a slope with the lake visible in the distance. All that now remains of this Stickley-designed home, as interpreted by architect George Maher, is the retaining wall in the foreground.

Preface

I am looking at a worn and chipped white brick that sits collecting dust on my desk. I keep it there as a reminder of the need to document and preserve Gustav Stickley–designed homes while they still survive. The brick is from the ruins of a unique Stickley house. George Maher, a renowned Prairie School architect, interpreted the design of Craftsman Home No. 93 in his own idiom—probably the only time Maher worked with a Stickley house plan. The home was built on the shores of Silver Lake near the town of Rolling Prairie, Indiana, for Raymond Riordan, who was the Superintendent of the Interlaken School for Boys located at that site. Later, Riordan would have an additional connection to Stickley as the two worked together to create a boys' school at Stickley's home in New Jersey—Craftsman Farms.

The photographs from the October 1913 issue of *The Craftsman*, Stickley's monthly magazine and the source for his Craftsman Home designs, show a wonderful home. Yet when I finally located the site in 2003, all that existed was a concrete foundation behind a retaining wall, hidden in eighty years of undergrowth. This house was not the victim of willful destruction—unless scavengers removed most of the useful materials after the home was abandoned—but was destroyed simply because of its remote location.

It appears that after Riordan left Interlaken to work with Stickley in New York, the school could not continue. It was apparently abandoned. Most of the buildings on the site were log structures built by, and for, the boys. Only the house, and what appears to be a boathouse, had concrete foundations. Large old trees now grow out of those foundations. The once well-maintained gardens have grown wild and have thrown up a wall of uncultivated rose bushes to impede the visitor, like the undergrowth around Sleeping Beauty's castle.

This house was one of the many homes conceived and published in *The Craftsman* that have suffered over the intervening years through changing tastes and styles, urban blight, neglect, and the evolution of the location. Yet it is surprising how many of these houses have survived—most through loving and caring ownership.

Gustav Stickley is famous for his furniture designs, but I believe that once his contribution to the promotion and popularization of residential architecture is fully known, he will be equally appreciated for his houses.

I have visited many of his Craftsman Homes, and in almost every case I have met homeowners who realized in some way that they lived in a unique house. Although few knew what it was, they knew their house was something special. Sometimes attempts to "fix" the houses were misguided, but always the intent was to "make it right."

There is much more to know, but there is enough information now—after nineteen years of exploration and study—that I can present what I have found. Hopefully readers will respond, more homes will be found and identified, and some of the many questions that still exist will be answered.

In the case of Gustav Stickley, it is difficult to write anything based solely on available facts. There is so much that is simply not known. After studying what information exists, I find that some speculation is inevitable. I have tried to carefully indicate my sources and to clearly indicate where I am speculating—informed speculation, but speculation nevertheless—and I caution readers to not take my my speculations as gospel. History is often interpretation—authors can view the same facts and come to different conclusions. An example is the recent publication of *Reconfiguring Harvey Ellis* by Eileen Manning Michels, which I eagerly acquired just before publication of this book. The chapters on Gustav Stickley's relationship with Ellis were my concern, and I found myself in disagreement with her assessment of that relationship and of Ellis's house published as "A Note of Color."

Part of the problem with the book is the reliance on Barry Sander's Stickley biography *A Complex Fate* as a resource. That book is well-written but deeply flawed, and its major points have been disproved by both Dr. Mary Ann Smith in her *Gustav Stickley—The Craftsman* (which predates the Sanders book) and David Cather's equally well researched *Gustav Stickley*. Michels' belief is that Ellis's relationship with Stickley was an unhappy one and that in "A Note of Color" he writes a parody of the Arts and Crafts house. I will concede Ellis's article has concerned me because it is somewhat "over the top," but I prefer to interpret the house as an experiment trying to push the envelope of Arts and Crafts design. There is no evidence that I can find to support the idea that Ellis was unhappy working for Stickley, though evidence does indicate that it was difficult for creative people to work for Stickley for extended periods of time. It must be remembered that for Ellis the opportunity to emerge from relative

obscurity and financial distress to work for the most influential publication in America solely devoted to the Arts and Crafts was a tremendous opportunity.

I am not a trained architect or a historian—but I have studied Gustav Stickley and his houses for about twenty years. My wife, Ula, and I began collecting Stickley furniture soon after we were married, long before it was popular and known. In 1982 we began to search for a home to house our growing collection and in 1984 we finally found just the right house. It required an immense amount of sweat equity, including the removal of numerous layers of paint from the downstairs woodwork.

One day while reading through a reprint of Gustav Stickley's *More Craftsman Homes*, Ula showed me a drawing of a house and said, "That's our house!" And it was—our home was Craftsman House No. 104! The floor plans had been reversed (flipped as a mirror image, a practice that I was to find was not uncommon) and other alterations had been made to the design. The roof was Spanish tile and not slate, and the exterior walls were concrete stucco over hollow tile block and not brick veneer over wood-frame construction—but we owned a Stickley home!

About the same time, I had purchased a copy of Dr. Smith's groundbreaking biography. Hers was the first modern biography of Stickley, and even with the passage of time it is still a very accurate and well-researched study of his life. Dr. Smith realized the importance of Stickley's

Craftsman Homes and spent a large part of her book examining the concept and the houses that she was able to locate. She turned me on to the fact that there were other houses like mine, waiting to be "discovered" and documented. She has been a guiding light these many years, and I hope she will accept this book as an extension of her work.

In my job as a photojournalist based in New York City, I began for the first time to study houses as I traveled about. Driving to assignments while working in the New York/New Jersey metropolitan area, I came across several homes I thought might be Stickley designs and thus began my strange journey.

Introduction

Gustav Stickley, drawn when he was about age 40.

Gustav Stickley so synthesized, romanticized, and popularized the Arts and Crafts–style home that today the style is known generally as "Craftsman." He was so successful in promoting his version of the Arts and Crafts–style home that this term has become synonymous with any home in that style. The United States Department of the Interior uses the term *Craftsman* to define the Arts and Crafts–style home in the National Register of Historic Places.

Technically, only a house built from the plans he offered through *The Craftsman* magazine or designed by his "Craftsman Architectural Department" should be called a "Craftsman Home." While Stickley today is known for his furniture, which can command thousands of dollars at auction, a true understanding of his work must include the environment he created for his furniture and other works of the Arts and Crafts movement—the embodiment of his entire philosophy—The Craftsman Home.

Unlike a style based from a design concept, the Arts and Crafts style is derived from a philosophy. Therefore, it can have many derivations that often do not appear all that similar. The work of the French Art Noveau,

the unique architecture of Gaudi in Barcelona, the German Bauhaus movement, the Austrian Wiener Werkstadt, and the American Prairie School all have their roots firmly entwined in the worldwide Arts and Crafts movement that started in England in the 1870s through the writings and promotion of men like William Morris and John Ruskin. This philosophy was summarized in the simple edict urged by Morris— "Surround yourself with nothing that is not useful, and have nothing in your home that is not beautiful. Beauty and practicality should go hand-in-hand."

Therefore, these Craftsman plans offered the average American family a house that was a *home*, based on the bedrock virtues of beauty, simplicity, utility, and organic harmony. Stickley believed that the "nesting instinct . . . was the most deep seated impulse" of humankind. He wrote in *The Craftsman*:

The word that is best loved in the language of every nation is "home," for when a man's home is born out of his heart and developed through his labor and perfected through his

sense of beauty, it is the very cornerstone of his life.

He intended his home designs "to substitute the luxury of taste for the luxury of costliness; to teach that beauty does not imply elaboration or ornament; to employ only those forms and materials which make for simplicity, individuality and dignity of effect." The home served as a key tool in the education of the Arts and Crafts philosophy, the place where the simple life could be fully experienced, a refuge from the unsurly world outside.

Stickley used *The Craftsman*, as a platform to promote his ideas about domestic architecture.

Eventually he decided to publish house designs conceived under his direction—221 numbered homes— with working plans made available to build the houses. These designs ranged from mansions to mountain camps, and most were probably built in the rapidly expanding suburbs at the turn of the nineteenth century.

He claimed that Craftsman Homes were built in every state in the Union as well as overseas.

Stickley is often thought of as a bungalow designer, but less than one half of the houses he created were technically bungalows. In addition to providing plans of those houses in his magazine—free to subscribers—his "architectural department" produced plans for houses on request, for a fee. A total of 254 home designs have been identified, with many more probably waiting to be found.

He expended great effort and expense promoting these homes—he truly believed that he could influence the environment in which Americans lived. In addition to publishing *The Craftsman*, he also released a number of promotional pamphlets and at least two books—*Craftsman Homes* (1909) and *More Craftsman Homes* (1912). According to Stickley, *Craftsman Homes* sold 20,000 copies in two years, leading to the publication of the second volume. Most of

the houses that have been located can be found in these books, leading one to speculate that Stickley published the house designs that were most popular with his readers.

Nearly one hundred years later, it is difficult to determine who created these designs. Gustav Stickley was the owner of a furniture company and a publishing company. He had no design or architectural training. In fact—based on his remaining personal correspondence—he couldn't spell well and his grammar was sometimes rudimentary. But he had practical knowledge based on a lifetime in the furniture business, a great drive to succeed, and vision. He was well read and inquisitive, and he believed in what he was producing and promoting.

In his recent biography *Gustav Stickley,* Arts and Crafts historian David Cathers has identified a number of talented designers who worked for Stickley and helped execute his furniture designs. He has also linked some of them with sketches and

drawings used to illustrate *The Craftsman*'s articles on Stickley's houses, and further research will no doubt show that these men and women were also involved in the design of Craftsman Homes. But these designers worked *for* Gustav Stickley, and it is safe to say that as his furniture is *Stickley* furniture, his houses are *Stickley* homes. As with his furniture (with a few exceptions), Stickley's home designs exhibit certain stylistic traits that are consistent over the twelve-year period that they were published, even as his staff continued to change and evolve. With a few exceptions, it appears that those designers who have been identified rarely achieved the same level of creative accomplishment once they left Stickley's employ.

A fire in Stickley's Syracuse, New York, home on Christmas Eve in 1901 gave him the opportunity to try to put into practice his yet unrealized vision of what a home should be. It gave him the excuse to build a new interior on the two lower floors of his 1900 Queen Anne–style home. What evolved is the quintessential Stickley interior: the cornerstone, so to speak, of everything that followed. In an article in *The Craftsman* one year later, New York City architect Samuel Howe (who was working for *The Craftsman* at the time and may have influenced the design) describes in detail a visit to the home.[1] The article includes a number of detailed drawings of the interior. That interior is

Some of the publications Stickley produced promoting his Craftsman Homes.

the basis of much of what Stickley created and promoted over the next thirteen years. He outfitted his home with his own lighting and furniture creations. Living with his furniture in a setting fully designed for it must have reinforced the ideas already in his head that there was a need for homes designed for his Arts and Crafts style—and while the ideas of designing an open space floor plan and offering house plans through a magazine were not Stickley's alone or necessarily new, the idea of offering house designs in *The Craftsman* may have been planted through his personal living experience.

This book attempts to show where some of the influences on Stickley and his designers may have come from. When this book refers to "Stickley" Craftsman Homes, "his" furniture and "his" designs or plans, it is using the attribution to Stickley in the context of Stickley being the person in charge and control. Today no one seriously believes that Stickley himself sat at the drawing board and drew the elevation drawings and floor plans for each of these houses. The question is how much influence he asserted on the designs. It is the position of this book that he controlled everything in his "empire," that he worked with his designers and architects closely, and that he had input in the creative process from start to finish. There should be no question that he was astute enough to surround himself with talent, and he had the capacity to learn and grow from that association. David Cathers has used the term "design director" to describe Stickley's role in his creations.

An advertisement in *The Craftsman* promoted one of his promotional brochures.

A goal of this book is to make all of Stickley's known designs available in one place for the first time.

Most of the images reproduced here come from *The Craftsman* magazine and well over half appear for the first time since they were published almost 100 years ago. While Stickley's two house books have been reprinted by several companies and are currently available, they show less than half of the homes he designed.

As *The Craftsman* material on each home varies, the presentation of these homes in a book cannot be completely consistent. Each house is presented with an exterior illustration to show the reader how Stickley envisioned it, along with floor plans. As space and material permit, additional illustrations and architectural elevation drawings are presented when it is felt that the house has features of interest. Comparative photographs in

color and historical photographs have been included when existing homes built from the plans have been located.

Based on the number of homes published and the length of time that *The Craftsman* served as a major influence on design in America, I believe thousands of these houses in suburbs and towns are still waiting to be discovered.

Only now is Stickley's profound effect on modern design being recognized. Now it is time to explore his impact on popularizing residential home styles in the twentieth century—for that may be his greatest legacy.

Gustav Stickley, photographed about 1908.

Gustav Stickley,
Arts and Crafts Proponent

Mostly a self-educated man with his formal education ending at age 12, Gustav Stickley (1858–1942) was born Gustavus Stoeckel. His name was changed to Stoeklee, and then later to Stickley as he grew to manhood. His first name also changed, as he used Gustave until about 1903, when he appears to have settled on the spelling of "Gustav."[2]

He grew up in Minnesota, where he apprenticed as a stonemason. When he was 18, his mother, Barbara, took Gustav and five of his brothers and sisters to live with her family near Brandt, Pennsylvania. Left behind were his father, Leopold, and three older sisters.

Stickley found work in his uncle Jacob Schlager's chair factory. He discovered that working with wood was far more enjoyable than working with stone, and before he was 21 he was running the chair factory. By 1883, when brothers Charles and Albert joined Gustav, the name Stickley Brothers and Company was on the factory. In 1884 Albert and brother John George moved to Binghamton, New York, with the intention of expanding the business. About 1887 Gustav, who had married Eda Simmons in 1883, sold the Pennsylvania chair business and joined his brothers in Binghamton, where they had established a retail furniture business named Stickley Brothers.

While in Binghamton he tried his hand at managing various business ventures, including running the local streetcar system. In 1888 he left his brothers (Albert and J. George eventually moved on to start Stickley Brothers Furniture Company in Grand Rapids, Michigan, while brother Charles stayed and ran a furniture business in Binghamton) and joined in a partnership with Elgin A. Simonds. Gustav stayed in Binghamton to run their furniture factory while Simonds ran their New York City showroom and sales operation. In 1891 Stickley

Gustav Stickley, ca. 1905.

and Simonds moved their operations to Auburn, New York, where Gustav, aged 33, along with his younger brother Leopold, aged 22, supervised a chair factory on the grounds of the state prison, using convict labor to cut costs and providing the Stickley and Simonds Company with steady

Gustav Stickley plays with his granddaughter Barbara Wiles on the lawn at Craftsman Farms.

income. Funds were needed, for at about the same time the company also bought land and prepared to construct a factory in Eastwood, a suburb of Syracuse, New York. The prison-made furniture was intended to supply state-run facilities, and the product manufactured in Eastwood would be sold to the retail trade. After years of spending time in both Auburn and Syracuse, Stickley finally moved his family to Syracuse in 1896. Reform in laws regarding prison labor created the opportune time to bolster the Eastwood operations.

Meanwhile Stickley's passion to be more than a routine man of commerce burned like a fire inside him. He had returned from two illuminating trips to Europe in 1895 and 1896, where he was exposed to the growing Arts and Crafts movement in Britain and its offshoot "L' art Nouveau" on the Continent. He had been dreaming of producing work of more substance than the mediocre reproduction furniture he had been producing all his life—work of quality and of a whole new design. These trips, if they were not the result of his already growing interest in the movement, must have planted the seed. Any venture into a new area out of the mainstream entertains some risk. There was no real need to take that risk—Stickley was reasonably successful—and if he did desire more wealth, there were other ways less venturesome to achieve it. Perhaps he saw America as a new market ripe for the ideas in design and architecture that were sweeping Europe at the time. Stickley was a man trying to marry personal ideals and

philosophy into his business.

Stickley, beyond his desire to be successful and influential, was a "believer." He had bought into the philosophy of the Arts and Crafts movement and wanted to create things that would make people's lives better—through the William Morris theories of simplicity in life, by creating a lifestyle surrounded by beautiful but practical things. Beauty was to be found in the expression of an object's form and function.

In 1898 Stickley forced the end of

his partnership with Elgin Simonds and formed the Gustave Stickley Company, which he later operated as "The United Crafts." Within a year he was making what he called "The New Furniture." The furniture was plain and bold, yet had a real sense of style and proportion. Made generally out of American white oak (it could also be bought in mahogany and maple, and occasionally in elm and chestnut) with the wood quartersawn to expose the rays of the natural grain patterns, and darkened with ammonia

Eda Simmons Stickley, Gustav's wife, with their daughter Marion at Craftsman Farms.

fumes and colored stains to emphasize that grain pattern, it was radically different from what was being produced and sold commercially in the United States. Even if some of the designs coming out of Stickley's workshops were influenced by published works of English architects and designers, this furniture was boldly original—the natural wood, darkened by exposure to ammonia fumes and covered by a rich satin-like finish, was all that was deemed necessary for decoration.

While it is not the intention of this book to explore Stickley's furniture designs, for that has been done elsewhere, the Craftsman Home is inescapably entwined in those designs and the philosophy behind them.

At the dawn of a new century, Stickley was positioned to embark on a daring venture that would have "profound influence on American culture, in his own time and in ours."[3]

By 1901, the Arts and Crafts movement was becoming popular in the United States, and Stickley was asserting himself as one of its leaders. As the founder and publisher of *The Craftsman* magazine, which became the bible of the movement, he explored whatever interested him, from philosophy to art, from literature to music, but above all, the way to live a good life. It was only natural that he should eventually explore the design of houses. He was interested in a lot more than furniture—in fact, the furniture was only a means to an end—the dream of the creation of a new and simple lifestyle lived in a Craftsman Home.

Gustav and Eda Stickley canoeing, probably in the Adirondacks, ca. 1900.

The Craftsman Home Idea

Where did Stickley's interest in architecture come from? His training as a stonemason and his involvement as a youth in the construction of buildings certainly played a role. An intelligent, self-taught individual, Stickley was curious and open to new ideas. His interests were broad, and he was concerned with the philosophical as well as with the practical.

He must have assimilated the philosophy of integrating the home with the objects one lived with during his trips to Europe and his exposure to the growing Arts and Crafts movement there. Certainly he benefited from his association with Irene Sargent, a Syracuse University professor who was the first editor of *The Craftsman*. She was probably his tutor in many areas, but it is hard to tell if she merely helped form his ideas or was a guiding force. Probably the former, for Stickley went through many associates and collaborators but stayed a course. Certainly she encour-

aged him to create *The Craftsman* and wrote most of the articles in its formative years. Before his founding of the United Crafts and *The Craftsman*, there is little indication that Stickley's interest in architecture was more than the next man's.

We know that he was enamored with architecture, both public and private, simply by studying his magazine. *The Craftsman* is filled with articles on architecture, written by the luminaries of the day, including Louis Sullivan, Frank Packard, Charles and Henry Greene, Irving Gill, William Purcell, George Elmslie, and William Price. English architect Barry Parker wrote a series of articles over a two-year span on the English House (the series may have been an adaptation in serial form from Parker's book with his partner Raymond Unwin). The magazine features articles on public policy in architecture, illustrations of proposed civic improvements, and park designs.

The idea of city and regional planning is advocated. He even listed himself as an architect in the 1904/5 Syracuse City Directory—not as a company president! [4]

Within five months of the first issue of *The Craftsman* (February 1902), Stickley was advocating good home design with the publication of a home specially conceived for the magazine by Syracuse architect Henry Wilhelm Wilkinson, who was also one of Stickley's first furniture designers. The drawings integrate the interior with Craftsman furniture, something that would be the case throughout the life of the magazine. Gustav's primary income was from furniture, and his Arts and Crafts philosophy was that the living environment should be aesthetically integrated. As a marketing opportunity, if not for aesthetic reasons, his houses would naturally feature his furniture.

Even though his furniture is featured in all the house drawings

In February 1902 *The Craftsman* published an article by architect Henry Wilhelm Wilkinson titled "The Planning of a Home." The article is illustrated with a proposed home (top) that features the typical open first-floor plan that Stickley later embraced for so many of his Craftsman Homes. It had a downstairs "dominated by one vast room; a liberal use of wainscoting, ceiling beams and built-ins."

The Parker house (above) was built not far from Craftsman Farms from Craftsman House No. 157 (page 455). This early photo of the living room shows how some Craftsman homeowners integrated Stickley's furniture into their homes.

published during the life of the magazine, it is not clear that he thought he would sell his wares to the Craftsman homeowner. The evidence indicates that he was happy to have his house designs built, whether or not the owners bought his furniture and fixtures. In later years he was not afraid to publish photographs of his Craftsman Homes filled with family heirlooms and Victorian furniture, and some of the houses built under his own supervision do not feature his light fixtures or hardware.

While he may have pictured the Craftsman Home filled with his factory's productions, he accepted the homebuilder's own tastes—and encouraged them. Here the idealist triumphed over the businessman. The houses offered in the magazine certainly did serve to display his furniture in the best light and must have helped sell it. But the house project was not a loss leader to sell furniture. Far from it—the evidence is in *The Craftsman*. Stickley was committed to the Arts and Crafts philosophy of living, and a house that exemplified those ideals was essential. It was as an idealist that he promoted his homes, of which he proudly said, "The number of homes built from Craftsman plans runs into the thousands each year. They are built in all parts of the world, from Alaska to the Fiji Islands . . . "[5]

The reason that Craftsman furniture met with such a wonderful popular response from the very day that it was first exhibited at the Pan-American

to the combined living and dining rooms, which created a sense of larger space in a small house. This concept was revisited often in Craftsman Houses of later years. As in the later houses, the emphasis on this home was on the interior space and decoration.

English emigrant architect Samuel Howe wrote twelve signed articles in *The Craftsman* between 1902 and 1906, and as a trained architect, he should have had an impact on Stickley's thinking in this formative period. It appears, however, that Gustav used Howe mainly as a writer and illustrator. Howe's article in the November 1902 issue features the magazine's first foray into suburban planning with a plot plan for semidetached houses in a garden community (see page 9)—a movement that was of great interest in England at the time. The elevation

drawing of the interior of one of the proposed houses shows Craftsman furniture—of course! It is possible that Howe may have influenced the reconstruction of the interior of Stickley's Syracuse home in 1902, as he wrote the article in December and appears to have done the drawings that accompanied it.

In February 1903 an article by architect E. G. W. Dietrich titled "A Cottage of Quality" is published and an exterior illustration and two floor plans accompany the article. Dietrich was a known architect, and over the years he published houses in other publications, including *The American Architect* and *House Beautiful*. In April an interior drawing planned for the February article, but excised due to space considerations, is published. Then in May Stickley published a

house concept by Dietrich titled "The Craftsman House," the first use of that term in the magazine. The exterior is derivative of work that Dietrich was publishing as early as 1887 ("Seashore House," *The American Architect*, December 10, 1887),[10] and the interiors are English Arts and Crafts in concept. The design is very similar to some of the work of Baillie Scott. That this article was designed with Stickley, or for Stickley, is shown by the use of Craftsman furniture strategically placed throughout the four interior illustrations accompanying the article. While the illustrations of the interiors appear to be quite unlike the exterior rendering of the house, these drawings have survived in Dietrich's files, indicating he, or his staff, drew them. In fact, in a few of the surviving illustrations, the Craftsman furniture has

This house design by E. G. W. Dietrich, published in the May 1903 issue of *The Craftsman*, is the first to be titled a "Craftsman House," although the plans were never part of the Craftsman Homes series offered to readers and begun in 1904.

been painted or drawn over with more modern substitutes, indicating Dietrich may have recycled the drawings for use with other of his house designs.[11] The floor plans of this home are still in the more traditional form of hall, parlor, and dining room. However the article does take the form of the later "Craftsman House" articles of 1904 by detailing the décor colors and woods—and methods of achieving the desired results. Stickley ends the article with the following editor's note:

> To all subscribers of *The Craftsman* any processes or details incident to the building, finishing, or decoration of "The Craftsman House" will be willingly given, through the correspondence department of the Magazine, or more directly by private letter.[12]

For the first time Stickley offered readers, in a more informal way, the opportunity to build a Craftsman Home. It would take seven more months and the arrival of another architect on his staff for the idea to bear full fruit.

When Stickley hired architectural genius and troubled alcoholic Harvey Ellis, his furniture designs took a new direction—becoming lighter in appearance and with more emphasis on the curve as a design element. Ellis was very much influenced by what the English architects, especially Voysey and Baillie Scott, were producing. Designs by both men were published in both the United Kingdom and America through publications like *International Studio*. Ellis also had studied the work of the Scottish architect Charles Rennie Mackintosh. Certainly the house articles he wrote

and drew in *The Craftsman* in the second half of 1903 were influenced by these architects and molded by his own genius, and they were unlike anything Stickley had published before. They were, and still are, some of the finest domestic architecture designs produced in the early years of the twentieth century, if not quite on the highest level achieved by Frank Lloyd Wright, and it is a great tragedy that it appears that none of the concepts were ever built at least in his or Stickley's time.

In the July 1903 issue, two articles by Ellis appeared, illustrated in his hand: "A Craftsman House Design" and "An Adirondack Camp." The Craftsman house is designed for a city or suburban lot of 50 feet frontage and at least 125 feet deep. It owes a debt to Voysey, but the house is all Ellis. He freely admits that the house is designed

This original illustration of the library from Dietrich's "Craftsman House" was hand-tinted by the architect or one of his staff and shows a palette of earth-toned colors.

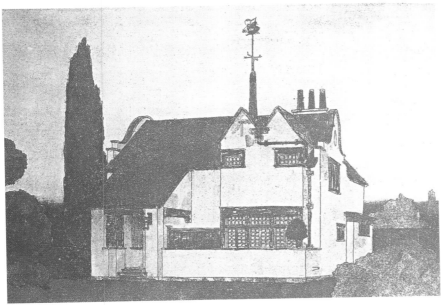

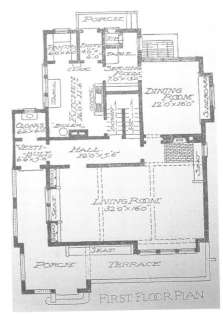

FIRST FLOOR PLAN

The exterior rendition of Harvey Ellis's "A Craftsman House Design" from the July 1903 issue of *The Craftsman* (above left); by using a masonry exterior, minimal eaves, and the quirky peaked dormers, Ellis shows his debt to Voysey.

The floor plan (above right) features a center hall design.

A high-backed seat below high casement windows flanked by matching bookcase/cabinets dominates one end of the living room (left), while a fireplace inglenook flanked by a very large textile wall hanging is tucked away in the other corner (below left). Like the exterior, these rooms show an obvious Voysey influence.

A rare color illustration was used to picture the living room in Harvey Ellis's "Urban House" (top). The use of gold, green, and purple complement the warm wood tones. This illustration, one of two used to illustrate Ellis home designs, indicates that the house illustrations done for the magazine by Ellis were probably in color. The house (above left) is positioned on a city street behind a high wall, and hidden in the rear is a quiet garden (above right). The first-floor plan indicates the house is much deeper than it appears from the street (facing below).

Ellis designed a mountain cabin, or camp, as the second home in July 1903 (above). Stickley revisited this exterior idea many years later for a Craftsman Home (No. 155, page 452) and used some of the design concepts in the plan for his proposed home at Craftsman Farms.

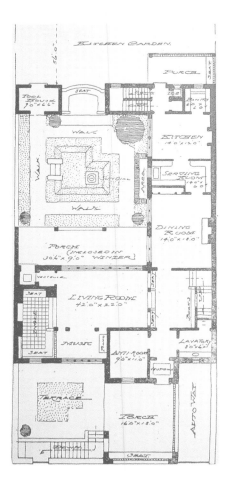

from the inside out: " 'A good plan makes a good elevation'—and this is true, if the designer is honest and frank with himself and his material."[13]

Unlike the Dietrich house designs, this home has a more open floor plan, though it still has a hall/staircase off the entrance, and the fireplace nook divides the living room from the dining room. The long article, with an exterior and three interior drawings, is filled with detailed decorating information. Following "A Craftsman House Design" is a less comprehensive description of a large cabin for the mountains, also with floor plans and exterior and interior illustrations. The busy Ellis also contributes interior illustrations for "A Child's Room" and another article.

"An Urban House" follows in the August issue. This is a wonderful house, designed to create an atmos-phere of quiet and calm in the busy city. Ellis achieves this by using the European model of a home with a high-walled frontage raised above the street and a walled garden to the rear. It is subtitled "No. Three of The Craftsman Series." Behind the wall at the edge of the street, the home is set back 25 feet—allowing for a small garden and a place to park an automobile in the limited space—reducing any noise or disturbances from the street.

In the article, there is an implication that the house has been designed at someone's request for a specific location. If this house was ever built, it has yet to be discovered.[14]

Ellis also drew a series of elevations illustrating a theme of "Puss in Boots" for a youngster's room in a separate article in August, and his hand may be seen in a number of designs for "door draperies" in a third article.

Ellis's design for "A House of Color" is derived more from a study of designs being done in Germany at the time than from Voysey, and certainly is a radical-looking home for its day.

In the September issue Ellis contributed an article and illustrations on "A Summer Chapel," and his protégé Claude Bragdon wrote an illustrated article on "A Simple Dwelling," with floor plans and two drawings of the exterior and living room interior (with Ellis- or Bragdon-designed Stickley furniture). An article on children's furniture is unsigned, but the illustrations appear to be by Ellis. A "Craftsman Yacht" by Ellis is promised for the November issue.

Instead, another house article titled "A Note of Color" appeared, intended (Ellis writes) "simply to advance certain ideas as to the use of color, on the exterior of buildings and, as well, to suggest the desirability of the 'sun parlor' in houses of this class."[15] This house is dominated by a large, high façade that has a stencil-like motif applied to it. The house is built of brick and covered with a coat of cement laid over metal lathe. The cement is colored various tones as it is mixed.

Cement, in its various brands, possesses, within a limited range, colors which may be modified or accentuated as desired by the aid of earth colors, such as yellow ochre, burnt sienna, raw umber and kindred pigments. . . . Let there be applied on the darkest portions of the rough brick skeleton, a cement which, having been lowered to a half tone with raw umber, produces a full olive brown. Those parts which show white in the drawings are covered with pure La Farge cement, which, when set, gives a fine, creamy white. Imbedded in this latter, on the front, is a combination cement inlay in agraffitto work, not at all difficult of execution by the ordinary mason, and absolutely permanent when completed. The body of this decoration is of pale yellow ochre. When it is set and thoroughly hard, the design is . . . deeply traced with a chisel. That portion of the design which has the conventional tree-tops is removed and replaced by a sage green cement, while the deeply incised lines are filled with a cement darkened heavily with lampblack in order to insure a strong outline. The gamut of warm tones is now well begun, but it lacks a note of orange and a cool color to give value to the harmony, which . . . needs vitality to be gained only by opposition. An examination of the design indicates the front door as the focal point for the orange note. This, with the foundation, steps, front door frame, copings, window caps, etc., in Hudson River blue stone, or its equivalent, completes the chord of color.[16]

Ellis, with this vivid description, sets a pattern for the later descriptions of Stickley's Craftsman Homes articles.

Reading the words carefully, with some imagination, the black-and-white sketches of the house burst into color:

The interior . . . is absolutely simple and strictly conforms to the requirements of usefulness and economy. The house is entered at the center, with the main staircase located in front and flanking the front door. Directly opposite is the reception alcove with a fireplace, and on the left of the hall the morning room, which is more than ordinarily important for a residence of this size. This room has for its purely decorative feature a frieze of motifs adapted from the symbolic ornament of the North American Indians. It is formed of asbestos tiles in shades of dull blue, sage green and lemon yellow. The walls of the room, up to the frieze, are covered with Craftsman canvas of pomegranate shade. The facing of the large fire-place is also of asbestos tiles in varying shades of deep French blue and moss green. Here the woodwork, as also in the hall and dining-room, is of fumed oak. . . . The ceiling of this room is finished with plaster with the color of pale lemon yellow.

The hall is treated with extreme simplicity, being wainscoted to the ceiling with wide boards of fumed oak, having vertical semi-beaded joints. The ceiling is beamed, with yellow "butcher's paper" carefully butt-jointed between the same, while the floor is of ebonized cherry. The walls of the dining-room are covered with sand-finished, orange-colored plaster, and decorated at irregular intervals with Craftsman tapestries of varying sizes, illustrating episodes in the life of Sir Gawain, the Green Knight. The ceiling is paneled with wooden beams and is tinted in pale tones of green and old rose, while the floor is of brown fumed oak.

The kitchen and its dependencies are finished in Georgia pine, with the exception of the floors, which are of hard maple, and stained with Prussian blue to the color known as moss-green.

The decoration of the entrance hall is continued up the staircase, and through the hall on the second floor. The bed-rooms, bath-room, etc., are finished in ash, having a warm olive tone; the walls being covered with sand-finished plaster, stained with shellac, tempered with such pigments as may be desired, according to the location of the room. The attic, which is not illustrated, contains a large store-room and an additional servant's bedroom.

The "sun-parlor," located, for privacy, in the second story, has . . . a front and a roof of glass: that of the roof being hammered. . . . The interior walls are finished in Harvard brick; pale yellow for the body of the walls and with a pattern in brown and black for a frieze. The floor is laid in large cement tiles (fourteen by fourteen inches) with two and one-quarter inch joint between: the latter filled with ordinary hard burnt red brick, split lengthwise and set on edge. The glazing of the front of the "sun-parlor" is so adjusted as to be removable in warm weather [and] the space is converted into a quasi roof-garden. This makes it practicable to dispense with the too intimate front porch, which is not only objectionable from an aesthetic point of view, but . . . a positive affront to the passerby.[17]

After all this, he also contributes in that November issue an illustration (at least—the unsigned article is probably his, too) an article titled "What May Be Done to an Ordinary Room," an early attempt by *The Craftsman* to educate readers on what the ideal interior should be—and a prelude to the articles that would accompany every Craftsman Home design for the next few years. An article on floor designs, also by Ellis, follows.

Ellis's last home design, "How to Build a Bungalow," was published in December 1903. This last building— the farmhouse bungalow—was finally re-created in 1999 at Crab Tree Farm outside Chicago, Illinois.

The farm was originally a dairy farm, with buildings built for owner

Pictured are two of the three buildings that flank a central square at Crab Tree Farm—the main barn features the large clock tower (top). The central area was once a large watering pond for livestock.

The front view of C. F. A. Voysey's Prior's Field (above), which may have served as an inspiration for Harvey Ellis's bungalow concept (facing below)—note the similar square tower and deep, flat chimney. The Ellis bungalow, its exterior modified to conform with the existing structures at Crab Tree Farm, was finally built at the end of the twentieth century (facing above).

Grace Durand in 1911 and influenced by the English Arts and Crafts style. The structures were designed by architect Solon Spencer Beman, the Chicago architect of the "utopian" Village of Pullman (designed for Pullman of railroad sleeping car fame) in the 1880s. The buildings of Crab Tree Farm front three sides of a central square. Surmounted by a commanding tower on the eastern

side, all the roofs in Beman's complex are cast from concrete to match the appearance of terra-cotta tile.

The current owner has painstakingly constructed the bungalow to correspond as closely as possible to the original building as featured in *The Craftsman*. The setting at the farm is not a "sylvan" setting as described in *The Craftsman* article, and while the bungalow was planned as a summer residence, this building was planned for year-round use. The Crab Tree bungalow was not completely sheathed in shakes as designed by Ellis, but is a combination of cement and wood shingles in order to help the building fit aesthetically with the surrounding Beman-designed structures. The floor plan is based on the one in the article. Ellis drew his exterior elevation drawings freehand. The hipline of the roof changes with each Ellis elevation and so the final elevation was an extrapolation from those drawings.

The interior rooms have been created to match the drawings of the article, and where there are no illustrations for some of the rooms, drawings from his various other Craftsman designs have been used to create a total Harvey Ellis home design. The color, wall, and woodwork treatments came from a variety of sources. Most were interpreted from written descriptions published in *The Craftsman* and were cross-referenced with period texts on the treatment of rooms and textiles, period wood stains, period linens, wallpaper sample books and periodicals contemporary with *The Craftsman*, colors found through microanalysis in other homes from the period, and, finally, a study of paintings and prints by Harvey Ellis.

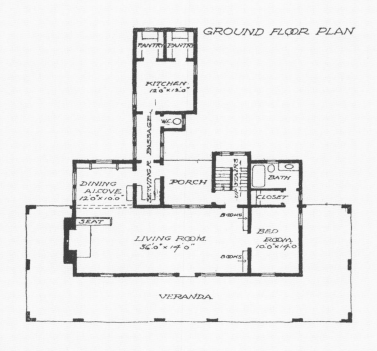

GROUND FLOOR PLAN

PANTRY PANTRY

KITCHEN
12'0" X 12'0"

W.C.

SERVING PASSAGE

DINING
ALCOVE
12'0" X 10'0"

PORCH

UPSTAIRS

BATH

CLOSET

SEAT

LIVING ROOM.
36'0" X 19'0"

BOOKS

BED
ROOM.
10'0" X 19'0"

BOOKS

VERANDA.

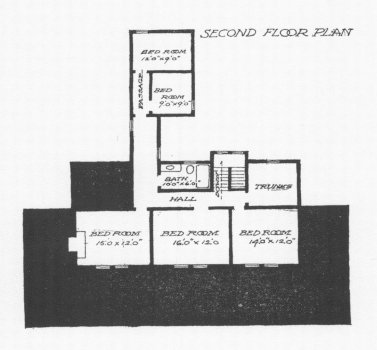

SECOND FLOOR PLAN

BED ROOM.
12'0" X 9'0"

PASSAGE

BED
ROOM
9'0" X 9'0"

BATH
10'0" X 6'0"

TRUNKS

HALL

BED ROOM
15'0" X 12'0"

BED ROOM
16'0" X 12'0"

BED ROOM
14'0" X 12'0"

The interior of the Ellis bungalow (above) is alive with muted colors. The living room is filled with a careful selection of Ellis-designed or inspired Stickley furniture. The dining room is to the right rear, behind the inglenook bench. The Ellis illustration of the same area (left) did not feature much furniture.

The Crab Tree Farm bungalow dining room
(above), while not attempting to match the illustration in every way, is inspired by the color
illustration of the dining room of Ellis's "A
Craftsman House Design" found in the July 1903
issue of *The Craftsman*. An adaptation of the
stained-glass window (right) was used in the
Craftsman Home "Dumblane" (see page 133)
built in Washington, D.C.

Ellis's spartan concept drawing of the other end of the living room (left), which sweeps across the front of the house, is brought to life with furnishings, drapes, and rugs at Crab Tree Farm (above). While the plans indicate a bedroom at the far end of the room, the space has been interpreted as a study or den. The open post-and-panel separation would not allow privacy if the space were a bedroom.

With Ellis working in *The Craftsman* editorial rooms every day, it is easy to imagine Stickley and Ellis working together to develop the idea of producing house plans that could be disseminated through *The Craftsman*. There are no known records or correspondence that prove this, but it is certainly plausible. What we do know is that in November 1903[18] Stickley announced that beginning in January 1904 the first official Craftsman Home would be published, and he set out a program for a house to be published each month, ranging in cost between $2,000 and $15,000. He invited all readers to consider themselves members of "The Home Builder's Club" and to submit ideas and suggestions for homes they would like to see designed. The condition for membership was the purchase of a yearly subscription to *The Craftsman* for $3. Each member of the club was entitled to request blueprints for any one of the twelve houses proposed for 1904. Suggestions for plans were solicited. The announcement ended: "An early correspondence is invited, since the preparation of the designs involves much thought and attention, and at least one month's time is required for the production of one of 'The Craftsman' Houses."

In the December issue there is no editorial mention of "The Home

In this view of the living room (above), hidden behind the portiere is a staircase to the second floor. One bedroom on the second floor (facing) is dedicated to the re-creation of the tapestries designed by Ellis for an article in the August 1902 issue of *The Craftsman* (right) on the story of Puss in Boots.

Builder's Club," but there is a full-page advertisement for the "Club," featuring the illustration of the dining room of Ellis's July 1903 "Craftsman" house. "Complete plans and specifications, along with 'Colored Interiors' and landscaping will be provided for each proposed Craftsman Home. The subjects to be treated are: the Detached City House, the Country and the Farm House, the Artisan's House, the Forest Lodge and the Bungalow." Of the subject houses mentioned, five had already been published in the previous six months—all by Ellis!

The Craftsman Homes project may have been envisioned with Ellis as "chief architect," and that does make sense, for surely Stickley must have recognized he had a genius in his employ. Perhaps the idea was Ellis's and his experiments in house design for the magazine made him enthusiastic about producing real working drawings and seeing his homes built. Examining the Ellis interior illustrations for those six months, it is easy to conclude that those drawings are watercolors. It seems that Stickley and Ellis did intend to provide working drawings of his houses as well as reproductions of the original color drawings for the homes. It is tragic that this never came to fruition, for in the same month that the project was to start, Ellis died.

Another bedroom in the Ellis bungalow (above) features Ellis-inspired furniture designs and an array of Arts and Crafts linens, rugs, and colors. The fireplace area (center) draws its inspiration from an illustration by Ellis from "An Urban House" (right).

When Ellis came to *The Craftsman*, it is apparent through the designs and articles published and the furniture manufactured that he was productive, but at some point his health began to fail. Claude Bragdon wrote his mother in July that he had worked with Ellis and that while Ellis was producing the best work of his life, he looked "worn and old."[19] Ellis was still able to contribute the cover illustration, an article on the Spanish missions of the Southwest, and his last bungalow house design for the December issue of the *The Craftsman*, so he must have been going full-steam through November 1903.

Another bedroom features a sitting "nook" tucked away in a window dormer.

Today, a monthly publication's lead time is sometimes three months or more before it reaches the mailbox at your home, but the production of *The Craftsman*, with a small staff and in another era, was probably faster—perhaps as little as four to six weeks. While it is hard not to believe that some kind of planning was underway for the projected "Home Builder's Club," there is no evidence that Ellis was involved in the design of the first Craftsman Home entry before he became seriously ill in December and died in a hospital on January 2, 1904. One indication of *The Craftsman*'s short production cycle is that the February issue carried a brief eulogy for the architect, probably printed less than four weeks after his death. Based on that possible cycle, the plans published in the January issue were certainly drawn by mid-December, and while certain details are Ellis-like, the home is much too symmetrical—unlike the asymmetrical concept houses previously designed by Ellis. While Mary Ann Smith feels that Ellis might have designed the first published house, the illustrations are certainly not in his hand, and the drawings of the house are crude compared with Ellis's designs from 1903. It may be that Ellis loosely sketched this house before he fell ill.

The cover of the January 1904 issue of the *The Craftsman*—the first cover to be in several colors—used a house illustration that could be argued as in the Ellis style. The cover house is similar in concept to the home published inside as Craftsman Home No. 1, but is only one story and much more modest. It is tempting to speculate that Ellis drew the concept for the first Craftsman Home for the cover, but because of his illness another one of Stickley's designers had to complete the project, and it changed.[20]

If Ellis was the keystone of the project, Stickley certainly did not abandon it. Cathers says that Stickley moved quickly to fill Ellis's shoes. By February he had hired New York City–based architect George R. Nichols, and he turned to his in-house designer LaMont Warner and architect Oliver J. Story. Cathers lists other members of his staff with architectural capability as Harry L. Gardner, Louise Shrimpton, and "draughtsman" Ruth Anne Williams. Architects Carl Sailer and Alfred T. Taylor were also hired on a freelance basis.[21] There is evidence that architect Frank Chouteau Brown also worked for Stickley about this time (his initials appear on illustrations in the March 1904 *Craftsman* magazine). Brown later practiced as an architect in Boston, where he illustrated a series of books on historic Colonial buildings in New England, and later administered the Historic Buildings Survey during the Depression in his capacity as division chief for New England in the Works Progress

The January 1904 issue of *The Craftsman* features what appears to be a one-story version of the first Craftsman Home featured inside, and while the illustration could be argued to be by Harvey Ellis, it is unsigned.

Administration. All this talent contributing to the project may explain why the first two years of house designs lack a consistent overall style.

It is interesting to note that all the linen drawings for the blueprints for the first three homes were dated within one week in March 1904. This indicates that the house elevations and floor plans for the first three houses were not produced until after their publication. A study of the published elevation of Craftsman House No. 1 and the front elevation provided in the set of working plans done later shows that the first drawing needed to be corrected, as the house looked lower (and better) because the second story was not drawn to the proper height. All of these early linen drawings at the Avery Library are signed with a "W" in a circle with the date of the drawings.

So it appears that when "W" did the plans, corrections on the design conception of at least one house had to be made.

Who was "W"? Stickley earlier employed architect Henry Wilkinson, but by 1904 he was apparently no longer working for Gustav. However, designers Ruth Anne Williams and LaMont Warner were in his employ. Architect Ward Wellington Ward lived and practiced in Syracuse after 1908, but he was in New York City in 1904, and there is no evidence of any connection between the two. Since LaMont Warner seems to have signed his drawings "L. A. W.," the choice falls to Williams as the designer, or at least the drafter of the plans.

A study of the plans from 1904 through 1908 indicates at least a dozen or more different hands drawing the detailed sheets on linen, so there is possibly another source for the working drawings. The editor of *The Craftsman*, Irene Sargent, was a professor at Syracuse University. Through her, Stickley could have hired students to draw the plans, and perhaps even design the houses.

Supporting that theory is research on architect Oliver J. Story, who was in Stickley's employ certainly in 1904 and perhaps for several years thereafter. He lived in the Delta Kappa Epsilon fraternity house in Syracuse in 1903 and had an office in that city in 1904 and 1905. He disappears from the city directories roughly the same time that Stickley moves much of his enterprise to New York City. Story does not appear in any New York City directory, but he appears in LaMont Warner's date book as working at least part-time for New York architectural publisher Fred W. Dodge by 1906. By that time, Stickley surely needed supervision of his "architectural department." Story could have filled such a role. Most of the plans of the period have an approval signed, using a symbol that looks like a musical note or a stylized "S." That symbol could be architect Story's monogram. It is certainly possible that he could have become the supervisor of the Craftsman architectural department.

It should be noted that the plans often are also signed by Stickley, using his last name and not an "S," indicating that Stickley insisted on approving each sheet at some point in its creation.

Also with Syracuse University connections (he, too, was a member of Delta Kappa Epsilon) was 1904 fine arts graduate Harry L. Gardner. He was an architectural draughtsman in New York from 1904 to 1908 before establishing a practice in Adams, New York, north of Syracuse. He was hired early in 1904, apparently before he graduated. He died in Syracuse in 1913 of typhoid fever.

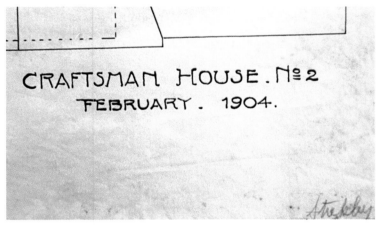

CRAFTSMAN HOUSE. Nº 2
FEBRUARY. 1904.

DINING ROOM FROM A CRAFTSMAN HOUSE—*The Craftsman, July, 1903*

THROUGH MEMBERSHIP
IN THE
CRAFTSMAN HOMEBUILDERS' CLUB

*Anyone can receive, absolutely without
cost, at any time during the year 1904*

Complete Plans and Specifications for a house costing from $2,000 to $15,000, together with Colored
Interiors, Details and Models of Ornament, and projects for simple Landscape Gardening. The
subjects to be treated are: The Detached City House, the Country and the Farm House, the Artisan's
House, the Forest Lodge and the Bungalow. A sample copy of The Craftsman with full explanation of
the conditions of membership in the Homebuilders' Club will be mailed upon receipt of two-cent stamp

GUSTAV STICKLEY
THE CRAFTSMAN BLDG., SYRACUSE, N. Y.

An advertisement in the December 1903 issue of *The Craftsman*
(above) features the dining room of "A Craftsman House
Design" from July 1903 and indicates that full plans of Ellis's
house designs will be offered in 1904, as well as color pictures
from the houses featured.

One of the linen drawings of Craftsman Home No. 1 (top) shows that it was
not drawn until March 12, 1904, more than two months after publication. Also in the
circle in the upper right is the initial of the draftsperson, "W." Stickley approved each
final set of drawings with his signature in pencil on each sheet (above).

Certainly some of the Craftsman Home illustrations printed in *The Craftsman* can be linked to these architects and draftsmen, but that does not mean they necessarily produced the plans. If Stickley used his design staff to produce concepts and drawings for the houses, and then later had the working plans drawn up, he may have contracted out the work to local architectural firms, especially when he moved to Manhattan in 1905.

At the moment, who produced these plans remains a mystery. What is certain is that the guiding hand for this project and the houses that resulted was Gustav Stickley. And as the year 1904 began, he was poised to carry out a project that was as important to him personally as his furniture business was to his financial future.

The Craftsman
Home Evolves

Gustav Stickley was a businessman, and as his business grew, it evolved and changed. How he treated the Craftsman Homes project changed over the years, depending on the time he devoted to it and how it helped him achieve his goals. Thus the space and detail given to each Craftsman Home in his magazine varies.

When the Craftsman Homes project began in 1904, Stickley offered one or more house plans with an accompanying article in each monthly issue of *The Craftsman*. These were detailed descriptions that included an exterior illustration and floor plans; numerous interior illustrations; and often elevation drawings for the front, sides, and rear of the structure. These early exterior designs from "The Craftsman Architects" are all rather eclectic and do not necessarily represent a particular vision or style but rather vernacular styles of the time. It would take several years before Stickley refined his vision into a recognizable style.

Stickley's house designs introduced many ideas that were new to homeowners, so he sought to illustrate them in a comprehensive way. The articles, some running twelve or more pages, included proposed color schemes, fabric choices, and furniture placement for each room. These detailed house plans and descriptions were offered to magazine readers through 1906. These articles, with their many drawings showing the home as it was meant to look, also served the purpose of marketing his new Craftsman products, as his lighting fixtures, cabinet and door hardware, furniture, and

An advertisement in *The Craftsman* offers the Craftsman Home plans for free—with a yearly subscription.

These two advertisements from *The Craftsman* are typical of those from a number of companies that featured Craftsman products in their ads. Both are from Fiske & Company, the New York City–based manufacturer of "Tapestry Bricks." These were decorative bricks that were fired in various colors and could be combined for various effects. They were more coarse and softer than the typical "hard burned" brick and were not used structurally, but as veneer bricks. Stickley promoted these bricks heavily in his homes, one of which is featured in the ad at left.

curtain and pillow designs all were promi-nently featured.

During 1907 Stickley's interests turned to the development of Craftsman Farms, his utopian vision for an Arts and Crafts community and, later, his home and farm. The resources of his drafting department were probably stretched at this time, as they were busy developing the structures for this new venture and simultaneously meeting the demands of clients requesting homes specifically designed for them. It is possible that these new demands and challenges caused Stickley to begin to lose interest in the house plans, as they began to appear irregularly. When they did appear, their presentation was reduced in scope. Besides the exterior illustration and floor plans, only one or two interior illustrations were included—and the elevation drawings disappeared.

Many of the house designs published from mid-1907 to December 1908 related to the Craftsman Farms project or to houses designed for specific clients, which were then reoffered to *Craftsman* magazine readers. At this time it appears that Stickley or his employees also began supervising the construction of a number of Craftsman Homes in the New York metropolitan area; this eventually led to the announcement of the Craftsman Home Building Company. A visual study of a number of homes built in the metropolitan New York area by this division of Stickley's enterprises during this period indicates that what he called at various times "The Craftsman

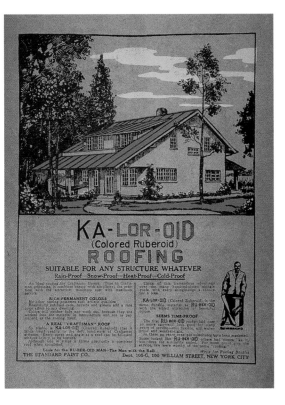

Stickley urged readers to use "Sanitas" wall coverings (above) and designed houses to use "Ka-Lor-oid" and "Ruberoid" roll roofing materials (right). Both companies were heavy advertisers in *The Craftsman*. Stickley does not appear to have suggested products just because they were advertisers, and they may have supported him because he was such an advocate of their products.

Architects" or the "Architectural Department" probably acted as general contractors, as the construction details and quality differ from house to house.

After he was established at Craftsman Farms and began to, as he said, "supervise"[22] the building of houses himself, Stickley appears to have become reinvigorated with the Craftsman Homes project. In October 1908 a full-page advertisement in the magazine announces the "revival of the Home Builder's Club":

> With this issue of *The Craftsman* we are reviving the HOME BUILDER'S CLUB . . . we abandoned the sending out of these plans a year ago because we were aware that our designs, while expressing the theories we held as to house building, were

not always suited to individual needs. For this reason it seemed to us best to rest for a time upon the suggestions we had already given and to confine our attention to reproducing the plans and ideas of other architects working along similar lines. We shall continue to do this, but regret has been expressed by so many of our subscribers at the abandonment of our system of giving out house plans, that we have decided to revive it.[23]

Beginning in 1909 two houses, and sometimes as many as four, were offered to readers every month. This continued through almost seven years until May 1915. The illustrations were routinely one exterior and one interior drawing per house plus floor

plans. A descriptive article that ran perhaps six or seven pages long accompanied the drawings and plans. But in 1912 Stickley decided that he saw no purpose in providing an interior drawing—explaining that those who wanted to build Craftsman Homes were already familiar with the interior designs—and the articles became shorter, with only an exterior illustration and floor plans.

During this period Stickley embraced almost every new development and product in the construction industry. Many of the house designs featured products sold by his advertisers by brand name or generic implication. For the roof he recommended Ludowici-Celadon tile, Ruberoid composite rolls, or Johns-Manville Asbestos shingles; for the structure of the walls he suggested

Natco Hollow Tile (i.e., National Fire Proofing Company hollow tile block), the Van Guilder method of doublewall construction, or Tapestry Brick; and for the home's interior he pushed Grueby Tiles, Morgan doors, Fab-rik-o-na synthetic wall coverings, Sanitas washable wall coverings, cypress and pine wood, Dutch Boy paint, and, again, Tapestry Brick. Naturally, the Northern Pine—and the Southern Cypress—Manufacturing Associations were advertisers in *The Craftsman*. He even used many of these products at Craftsman Farms. The Log House was first covered with roll roofing, probably the Ruberoid brand. When that proved unsatisfactory, Stickley put on tile from Ludowici-Celadon. From 1909 to 1913, if there was a building material or process one wanted to use to build, one could find a Craftsman House designed for it. Thus, the Home Builder's Club brought advertising revenue to the magazine.

Stickley certainly had some relationship with the Morgan Door Company, which was one of the steady advertisers in *The Craftsman*. All the door designs found in Craftsman Homes can be found in various Morgan Door catalogs. The nature of the relationship—whether Stickley embraced the Morgan Door designs or if the company agreed to carry a line of doors he designed for his houses—is not yet known. A study of the doors and jambs removed from one of the Craftsman Home Building Company projects—the Taylor house in Summit, New Jersey—reveals that the doors and jambs were manufactured and pre-assembled in a factory and shipped to the site, but it was not mentioned who manufactured the doors.

In June 1915, publication of the house plans ceased without any explanation or announcement, probably because by this time Stickley was deep in the financial difficulties that eventually led to his bankruptcy and the collapse of his Craftsman enterprises.

One year later, a brief announcement in the magazine said demand from its readers for house plans was still strong, and the house articles would be resumed. Two house plans

Each door in the B. A. Taylor home in Summit, New Jersey, was installed as a unit, pre-hung with a door frame. The frames were stenciled "Craftsman Home Bldg Co Beechwood Park Summit NJ." These doors were probably ordered from the Morgan Sash & Door Company, regular advertisers in *The Craftsman*.

One of the many Craftsman-style Morgan doors is featured in this full-page advertisement from *The Craftsman* (left). A similar door was installed with Stickley hardware in the Francis Knickerbocker home near Hillsdale, New Jersey (right). The Morgan Door catalog featured a number of doors that have been found in Stickley-built Craftsman Homes, and the line may have been designed for Stickley.

Upon Stickley's bankruptcy, *The Craftsman* merged with *The Art World* magazine, and the house plans continued to be offered by that magazine. The advertisement on page 35 for the plans from a 1917 issue (offered free) shows Stickley's name recognition was still important.

per month appeared for the next six months. The final issue of *The Craftsman* in December 1916 contained only one plan—a small country bungalow. Stickley probably was not involved in the design of these final homes as he had by this time lost most of the control over his company. It can be assumed, therefore, that the house articles resumed not because of his passion for the project but for economic reasons. Their resumption, however brief, was testament of the appeal the Craftsman Homes held for many of *The Craftsman*'s readers. The architectural department may have been one of the few remaining

Craftsman operations that still made money for the business during this time.

The architect for these 1916 homes may have been a man named George Fowler, because with the cessation of publication of *The Craftsman*, most of the staff joined a new publication, *The Touchstone*, started by Mary Fanton Roberts, *The Craftsman*'s former editor. A major feature of *The Touchstone* was two Touchstone Homes each month, designed by Fowler.

What was left of *The Craftsman* name and assets was acquired by *The Art World* magazine and that magazine continued to offer the Craftsman

No. 95: Craftsman Cement House Showing Porches, Sleeping Balconies and Terraces

YOU are thinking about a home: the beauty of it: the permanence of it: its special fitness for the lives of those whom it will shelter.

We have prepared TWO HUNDRED HOUSE PLANS designed by CRAFTSMAN ARCHITECTS under the personal supervision of Gustav Stickley, the original craftsman. These plans are complete in every detail and may be yours at a nominal cost. Other plans in various styles of architecture most suitable for the building of truly artistic homes are in course of preparation by leading American architects.

Write to THE ART WORLD and accept the advice of our Home Department which will cheerfully be given without expense to you. Put your own architect in charge.

Build a true CRAFTSMAN home! A shack of logs, bungalow, cottage, or more pretentious house will be *distinctive* if built from CRAFTSMAN HOUSE PLANS.

Address: *Home Department*

THE ART WORLD AND CRAFTSMAN

2 West 45th Street   New York City

Homes blueprints to readers at least into the year 1917, even offering several new designs.

Eventually about half of the original linen drawings for the blueprints of the Craftsman Homes made their way into the drawings collection of the Avery Architectural and Fine Arts Library at Columbia University in New York.[24] Additionally, several sets of original blueprints as well as some of the house drawings are in the collection of the Stickley Museum at Craftsman Farms; also some Craftsman Home owners still possess the original blueprints for their homes. What happened to the other plans and what happened to the rest of the records of the Craftsman Architects remains a mystery.

This close-up of the cover of the April 1917 issue of *The Art World* magazine shows that it merged with *The Craftsman* name but did not give it equal billing.

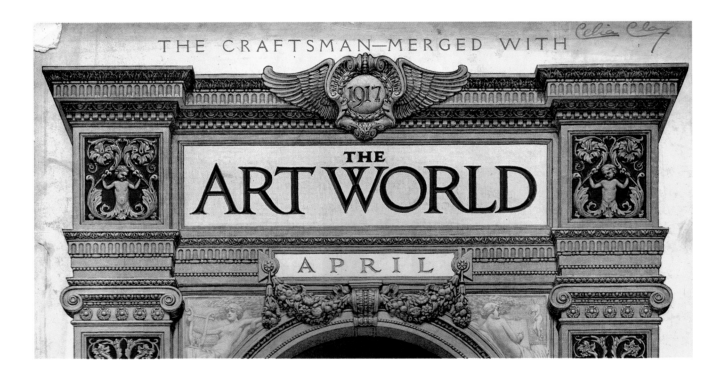

THE CRAFTSMAN—MERGED WITH

1917

THE
ART WORLD

APRIL

The Principles of Craftsman Homes

It is important to understand that the Craftsman Home has roots in all of America. Stickley was not an architect, but a designer. These houses were concepts brought to reality. Ideas from every part of the still-young nation were brought to bear by using buildings already in existence in the American vernacular landscape and by re-creating them through the ideas and ideals of the Arts and Crafts movement. They were not only buildings, but they were, by their design, going to improve the way people lived. Mark Alan Hewitt, in his book *Gustav Stickley's Craftsman Farms*, says,

Social reform would evolve via the transformation of that domestic environment. . . . Stickley designed his houses during a period of significant change in American society and concomitant innovation in the design of middle- and upper-class house types.

Most features of the Craftsman house can be found in earlier prototypes designed by architects, plan-book sources, or in the vernacular types that he admired such as the midwestern farm dwelling or log cabin. Stickley had his aims clearly in mind when he began to design houses . . . and he wrote about them succinctly. But when it came to making architecture he often borrowed what he needed and reassembled features to make a new whole—a synthesis much in keeping with the prevalent eclecticism of the period. He intended to offer middle-income Americans a complete range of domestic solutions tailored to the prevailing needs of the time: economy of construction, durability, family size, functional efficiency and constructional variety (using the full range of available materials and technology).

Stickley . . . set about creating designs to match his concepts. . . . he outlined the characteristics that form the core of all genuine Craftsman houses:

1. Simplicity of form, plan, construction and function;
2. Regularity of outline and plan;
3. A low-profile roof pitch, giving a more "homelike" feel (bungalow-like)[25];
4. Constructed of materials indigenous to site, that is "natural," and durable;
5. Honesty in construction and use of materials (no "useless" ornament);
6. Economy of construction and use of space (no "wasted" space);
7. Maximum potential for indoor-outdoor living, garden spaces, and site views;
8. Open and flexible interiors—multiple-use spaces, minimal partitioning; and
9. Democratic in spirit.

Although there is considerable variety among the . . . designs produced . . . a remarkable consistency is maintained in the adherence to these core principles. . . . Stickley set down the political and social menu for what Americans seemed to want in their post-Victorian dwellings and then sought to serve them a la carte.[26]

Major reform architects of the period were "voicing the same rhetoric" during the period, but Stickley "approached the design problem as a manufacturer, businessman and craftsman: to wit, begin with a small number of basic prototypes (as in his line of armchairs), perfect them, and then expand the line adding features to suit the market."[27] The homes were designed using "different material and constructional forms and revised to fit different climatic and social conditions. In keeping with his shop methods, Stickley began his program by drawing upon a range of houses from the American vernacular landscape: the farmhouse, suburban house, pioneer cabin and bungalow, all popular 'democratic' house types appealing to middle class . . . readers."[28]

Stickley Defends His Trademark

By the year 1913, Gustav Stickley was at the zenith of his career as the Arts and Crafts tastemaker in America. His furniture was sold from coast to coast and *The Craftsman* was arguably the leading voice of the Arts and Crafts movement in America.

He had produced over 174 house designs, with more houses to come. In addition to the free sets of plans he made available to subscribers, he advertised that he would also design homes for the special needs of his readers for an additional fee.

With the bankruptcy of Gustav Stickley and the end of the publication of *The Craftsman* in 1916, all records of the activities of his architectural department disappeared; therefore, any information about this key area of his work is vital.

While the number of people who took advantage of Stickley's offer to design special homes—or to modify homes published in his magazine—is still unknown, a document has come to light that shows people did avail themselves of his service, and reveals more about Stickley's Craftsman Home service—as well as featuring his personal testimony regarding his architectural operations.

A record has been found of sworn testimony given by Gustav Stickley and others in the summer of 1913 in what appears to be a legal action by Stickley against Jud Yoho, a Seattle, Washington, bungalow builder who sold through a magazine/plan book.[29]

Bungalow Magazine was published by Yoho, Seattle's self-proclaimed "Bungalow Craftsman," from 1912 to 1918. It offered a bungalow a month with complete working drawings. The magazine promoted Yoho's construction firm, Craftsman Bungalow Company. His designs, unlike the bungalows of California, were adapted to the hilly topography and cooler climate of the Northwest. Many of the bungalows featured in the magazine were existing Seattle homes.[30]

Yoho was using the name "Craftsman," and Stickley evidently instituted suit, or threatened to, for trademark infringement. The depositions were taken on three days in July and one day in September of 1913, in Stickley's 41 West 34th Street offices.

The document is fascinating as it sheds light on the operation of *The Craftsman*'s architectural department and how its records were kept; it gives an indication of how many plans were sent to readers. It also indicates the type of serious money Stickley was making from the venture and allows a reexamination of Stickley's motives in the creation of the Home Builder's Club. The assumption could be made that since Stickley advertised that subscribers to *The Craftsman* could get one free set of plans with a subscription, he made little money on the creation of these houses. Beyond the idealistic desire to see his homes built across the country, it would seem that he hoped he might expand the sales of his furniture, lighting, and other accessories, and increase his influence as a national tastemaker. However, the testimony indicates that the motives regarding the production of the house plans were not just altruistic.

Under questioning from his attorney, Stickley said, "I do prepare plans and specifications [for houses] that are sold throughout the United States and other parts of the world." When asked to identify the set of plans marked "Series 1904, July Craftsman, bungalow No. 7 1/2" and whether they were "prepared by you or under your supervision?" Stickley replied, "They are plans prepared by *me* [author's italics]." Stickley does not reply *under my supervision*. There is no evidence whatsoever that Stickley had any architectural training beyond the practical seat-of-the-pants type—even in this deposition he states his occupation as "Farmer!"

Further questioning revealed how records of the sales of the plans were kept. There was a separate card for each sale that showed the number of the set of plans sold, their date of preparation, the date of sale, and the name and address of the purchaser. There are indications that the house numbers were at some point changed. The set for Series 1904, No. 7 1/2 was changed to No. 8. When asked why, Stickley replied, "The numbers were afterwards rearranged, for just what purpose I do not know. The magazine would fix the date, as they are always first published in the magazine."

As has been shown, the numbers almost certainly were changed because the plans issued became confusing,

with "Series of 1904, 1905, 1906 and 1907" all bearing the numbers one though twelve or more each year. If each plan set had an individual number, it would be easier and less confusing to order. The houses featured in *Craftsman Homes*, published in 1909, have no numbers at all, while the houses published in the 1912 *More Craftsman Homes* are all numbered with the consecutive system. Did Stickley really not know, or was this the simple answer in what was, after all, a trademark violation case?

The testimony refers to plans that were sold. While he advertised that each subscriber could get a free set of plans for the issues in their subscription, it is apparent that many people ordered plans years after their publication. The testimony says that plans for the 1904 Series No. 7 1/2 home (No. 8) were sold in 1906, 1910, 1912, and 1913. There is no indication that these were the only times they were sold.

As the deposition continues, Stickley's lawyer asks:

Q: "Can you state in a general way to what extent you have prepared plans for houses bearing the trademark 'Craftsman' from 1904 to the present time?"

A: "From one to two each

The cover of the printed record of Gustav Stickley's Patent Interference No. 35725, begun during the summer of 1913 against Seattle bungalow builder Jud Yoho.

month, with very few exceptions."
Q: "State in a general way how many sets of these plans you have sold."

A: "That would be hard to state. They vary of course according to the popularity of the plan. Anywhere from one to one hundred of each set."

Stickley then produced records that proved that Craftsman Home No. 5 of May 1907 (No. 51) "were prepared by me" and sold in November 1907, February 1909, May and October 1910, February 1911, May 1912, and four other times in 1912.

The cover of a plan book issued by Seattle bungalow builder Jud Yoho, using Stickley's "Craftsman" trademark in the title. Stickley sued to stop Yoho from using the term *Craftsman Bungalows.*

With 221 known designs published in *The Craftsman*, even an average of twenty-five homes sold per plan would mean over 5,500 plans sent to clients. And this does not cover free plans sent to subscribers, unless we cannot accept the idea that all the plans discussed in this deposition were sold as claimed, and that free plans were being included, too. Unfortunately there is no indication how much Stickley charged for a "standard" set of magazine house plans, but later testimony on charges for specially designed homes suggests that a figure of $10 to $15 per plan set might be a reasonable guess.[31]

Finally, the issue of specially designed houses for clients is brought up. These were homes commissioned by private clients and generally not featured in the magazine. Some appear in *The Craftsman* after being constructed, with photographs of the completed houses, and some were later offered to readers as featured numbered homes in the magazine after originally being designed for a client. One such house is No. 56, published in September 1908.

The home of W. L. Hicks on Long Island was offered as evidence. Stickley said, "These plans were prepared for Mr. Hicks and charged to him, as appears from our ledger, October 29, 1908. The price charged was $175." While never offered to readers as a numbered house, this stucco-clad home, featured with an illustration and floor plans in a manner similar to the regular house offerings in the magazine, appeared in an advertisement in the January 1909 issue of *The Craftsman* as a home built by Stickley's new Home Building Company. Later it appears in *Craftsman Homes.*

A careful examination of this house and others in the New York metropolitan area, allegedly built by the Home Building Company, shows a wide range of quality in use of wood and in construction techniques. Some of these houses feature Stickley lighting and hardware while others do not. Further statements by Stickley help to explain the differences.

Plans designed for a client in New Jersey were entered in evidence and Stickley continued,

These plans were sold . . . as appears from our ledger, April 12, 1909. The plans in this case also included specifications. The specifications are attached to the blue prints. In this particular instance I sold . . . not only the plans but also the specifications and supervision. It appears . . . that the price . . . was $300.

Other fees are also recorded: $100 for a bungalow in Virginia, $220 for a lodge in Maine, and $200 for a home for E. F. Scheibe in Cambridge, Massachusetts. This testimony supports a theory, as first suggested by Dr. Mary Ann Smith, that Stickley or his firm arranged with various contractors to build homes for clients under their "supervision." This was how the Home Building Company operated, and may explain the differences in the construction of these various homes.

Other testimony at the deposition explained that a Frederick M. Hill, 44, the State Secretary of the YMCA of New York, paid Stickley to redesign a plan he liked—probably the Hicks house. The redesign is cedar-shingled and looks quite different. Hill, who had known Stickley in Syracuse, paid $35 for his plans in September 1909. Finally, Stickley's lawyer called as witnesses several clients of the Home Building Company, including Hill and Earnest Lee Prior. The testimony of these men is interesting in exposing the process by which they came to desire a Craftsman house.

Hill testified that he had lived in his Craftsman Home for almost four years after moving to the New York area from Syracuse. He lived in New York temporarily for three months

while my family were in the west on a visit, while I was prospecting for a home down this way. . . . I came to Gustav Stickley the latter part of August 1909, and asked him to prepare plans and build my house. . . . He prepared the plans in early September, and I paid for them the latter part of September 1909.

Under cross-examination, Hill testified, "I have known Mr. Stickley for at least ten years. We were neighbors in Syracuse . . . ."

Yoho's Attorney: "What do you mean by a 'Craftsman' house?"

Hill: "Well, I have known Mr. Stickley as 'The Craftsman' and manufacturing 'Craftsman' furniture and publishing *The Craftsman* magazine, whose houses were known as 'Craftsman' houses."

Yoho's Attorney: "Then you have used the term 'Craftsman' house as descriptive of a certain type of house?"

Hill: "Yes, and of the type of house that I knew Mr. Stickley was designing and building."

Yoho's Attorney: "Do you know of any trademark used by Mr. Stickley in his business?"

Hill: " . . . Well, I know of his trademark 'Als ik Kan,' and also the trademark 'The Craftsman'—that is, I am not sure that he considers it a trademark, but that is the trademark I have known Mr. Stickley by, that I have known his work by."

Yoho's Attorney: "Did Mr. Stickley design the plans . . . especially for you, or was it a stock design?"

Hill: "Well, it was originally a stock design, but he made quite a number of changes in it. They were practically new plans."

Yoho's Attorney: "Did you pay Mr. Stickley for his services in supervising the construction of your house?"

Hill: "I did."

Stickley's Attorney: "Do you remember what you paid for these plans?"

Hill: "I paid $35 for the changes that were made on the plans. . . . You know what Mr. Stickley's arrangements are, that one who is a subscriber to *The Craftsman* magazine is entitled to a set of plans. Now, that was the original proposition on which I talked about the plans, and then when we found that there were changes that I wanted made, I agreed with Mr. Stickley on the price that he would make these changes for me, that I would pay him $35 for these changes that the *architects* made on the plans [author's italics]."

Yoho's Attorney: "[Did you say that] a subscriber . . . [will] receive a set of plans free if he so desires?"

Hill: "Why, I have so understood."

Yoho's Attorney: "And the $35 which you paid Mr. Stickley was in payment for his services in altering a set of stock plans which you received under such arrangement as a subscriber to *The Craftsman* magazine?"

Hill: "Why, I had no arrangement with Mr. Stickley to receive a set of plans. I knew of a house that Mr. Stickley had built . . . and I liked that house, liked the elevation and the floor plans, and I asked Mr. Stickley to make the changes in the plans that he had used for that other house . . . ."

Merchant Ernest L. Prior offered similar testimony, adding that he "dwelt in the village of South Orange during the building of my 'Craftsman' house, and it is known in the section where I live as the 'Craftsman House.'" Then, in the lawyers' direct examination and cross-examination, several members of Stickley's staff testified as to how the plans were prepared and give an idea of the numbers involved:

Master plans were first made upon tracing linen and blueprints were prepared from these master plans and they were sold. Usually specifications were sold with them.

Q: "State whether or not these plans and specifications were sold extensively throughout various states of the United States."

A: "They were."

Q: "How are you able to identify this fact?"

A: "From the ledger account, namely the sheets of a loose-leaf ledger . . . ."

Q: "Were these all of the loose-leaf sheets from the ledger that you could find?"

A: "No, there are . . . hundreds of others . . . ."

Q: "State to what extent plans and specifications have been sold by Mr. Stickley bearing the trademark 'Craftsman.'"

A: "Hundreds of them to persons in various states of the United States."

Q: "State whether or not you received orders for plans based upon the plans which were published in the magazine, but in which alterations, changes, were required."

A: "Yes."

Q: "A good many of them?"

A: "Well, a good many."

Q: "State whether or not it was quite common for persons to ask to have plans sent them which they had seen in the magazines but in which they desired changes."

A: "Yes."

Q: "And when such plans were changed and prepared for them was an extra charge made for that?"

A: "Yes, invariably so."

Yoho's Attorney: "Were any plans sold . . . which were exactly like some published in *The Craftsman*?"

A: "Yes."

Q. "About what proportion . . . were identical . . . ?"

A: "Why, most of them."

Q: "Then I am correct in assuming that a small proportion only of the Craftsman plans . . . were altered . . . ?"

A: "Comparatively small."

Stickley's lawyer: "[W]ill you state about how many figures or sheets of drawings each set of plans usually numbered?"

A: "In the case of small bungalows there were about three sheets. They ran from that up to twelve, fifteen and seventeen sheets."

Q: "You say that only a small proportion of the plans which were sold were changed? Is it a fact that even this small proportion amounted to hundreds of plans which were sold?"

A: "I cannot say as to that."

Gustav Stickley was finally recalled and asked: "Did you do business under the name of Craftsman Home-Building Company?" He replied: "Yes."

Appended to the document is correspondence between Stickley's lawyers and Yoho dating from September 1913 and ending with a declaration from Mr. Yoho: "I am not putting out any more advertising matter as the proposition has proved a losing one for me and will therefore not want to use the word further."

It therefore appears that Stickley successfully defended his trademarks, and in doing so opened a window for us to look into the past and understand the operations of his architectural department. These voices speak directly to us from the pages of a dusty document. Without the ability to have a tape recording of the proceedings, this is the closest we will get to hearing Stickley and his contemporaries speak.

Merchant Ernest L. Prior had Stickley design and build him this house (top) in Maplewood, New Jersey.

YMCA Secretary Frederick Hill, a friend of Stickley, had him design and supervise the construction of this house (above) in Great Neck, New York.

Stickley's Three Homes

During the period when Gustav Stickley was a major proponent of the Arts and Crafts movement, he owned two homes and planned another that was never built. These three homes are crucial to understanding his ideas about residential architecture. He first built a new home in Syracuse and planned a large home on the site of his "Craftsman Farms" property in New Jersey; when he realized he could not build that house, he converted his planned "Clubhouse" at the Farms into his residence.

In June 1900 he purchased a new home on Columbus Avenue in Syracuse. In the Queen Anne style, the house was rather undistinguished looking and set on a narrow lot. The purchase came just as he was beginning to sell his new line of Arts and Crafts furniture.

In December 1901, just after he began publishing *The Craftsman*, an opportunity to rethink his personal living quarters occurred. On Christmas Eve, a fire broke out in his home. Neighbors helped the family save some of their possessions before city fire companies put out the fire after three hours. What was left in the home was destroyed. "The fire . . . burned holes about eight feet square on the first and second floors and it spread up when it reached the top floor, going up the four walls to the roof . . . the roof was destroyed."[32]

What was not destroyed was Stickley's drive. He determined to remake the house into the ideal American Arts and Crafts home, filling it with his new furniture, metalwork, and linens.

Despite the heavy damage, the building was still structurally sound. Since the house was insured, Stickley may have been forced to keep the lightly damaged exterior intact. What he did do was alter the exterior by building a large bay window and installing a new large Craftsman front door. This door design was repeated on a smaller scale throughout the house. He also completely redefined the floor plans of the first two floors and created a woodwork design that became the signature of the Craftsman style.

The fire damage to the third floor may not have been as extensive as thought, or budgetary considerations may have contributed, but the third floor did not carry through the Craftsman woodwork interior of the other two floors.

While little in architecture is totally new, Stickley's concept differed from other Arts and Crafts interiors of the period. Following ideas that had already been explored in some shingle-style interiors and were being promoted by architects such as Frank Lloyd Wright, the parlor (living room), hall, dining room and rear inglenook-like library were all part of a continuous space—an open floor plan.

More than a hundred years later, the interior still imparts a feel of

44

wonder and excitement. There is a sense of privacy from the point of entry through the massive front door into a vestibule with Grueby tiles[33] laid into the floor, as it is hard to immediately view the whole expanse. But once into the large "living hall," the space opens up. To the left, this hall opens to a smaller living room in the front of the house, with a built-in seat under a large window and a fireplace, while the dining room is straight ahead toward the rear. Beyond the dining room is another fireplace set in a small room (the arrangement of the seating in the room creates an informal "inglenook"— Howe's 1903 article describes it as the "Library") with a settle and another window seat.

This "hall," with a distinctive staircase at one end and a large anchoring window seat on the other side, is directly astride the main axis of the building. From the window seat in the front bay window in the living area, the window seat in the "Library" to the rear of the dining room—at the other end of the house—can just be seen. The beams on the ceiling also run from front to back, taking the eye along the entire open space. Yet the space is divided subtly by the use of post-and-panel dividers and connecting cross-beams that define the "hall." Even though each area's use is clear, they are part of a unified whole. In Queen Anne houses, the hall was the main room for entertaining, while the parlor was reserved for the family. Stickley reverses this idea, creating a hall that becomes overflow space from the living room, and the dining area

flows naturally from the hall. One can envision Stickley entertaining guests in the hall, then in front of the red brick fireplace in the living area, moving naturally to the dining area for dinner, and finishing the evening before the fireplace in the cozy library area.

Not only was Stickley invigorating living space in a practical way, he was also romanticizing the whole Arts and Crafts concept of family life—providing a design rooted in a philosophy of how to live the good life. Central to this philosophy is how the fireplaces are used as key design elements, not only in this house but in all Stickley

home designs. By 1900 central heating was the norm in all but the most remote areas of the country, yet all Craftsman Homes feature a fireplace, and most have several. Stickley certainly accepted the ideas of Frank Lloyd Wright and others that the fireplace was the heart of the home— a place where the family would gather in the evenings to talk and share their experiences of the day.

A horizontal rail wraps around the entire space, capping the window and doorframes. Below it are wide, vertical, tongue-and-groove chestnut boards covering the walls, and above the rail

Gustav Stickley's Queen Anne–style residence in Syracuse, New York, photographed in 2004.

the walls are plastered, as is the ceiling between the oak beams. Built-in window seats, glass-enclosed bookcases, post-and-panel partitions, and two red-brick fireplaces provide visual stimulation to the flat walls. Stickley also used subtle touches to vary those wooden wall surfaces. The V-grooved boards, the slight overhang lines and recesses that occur where the wood boards join beams and baseboards—all provide voids where light and shadow can fall and provide depth and detail.

Seen today, this is an austere, stark look—the woodwork all a warm nut brown throughout and the plaster a uniform white. Since research has shown that the colors in the Log House at Craftsman Farms were unlike what was applied later, it very well may be that the wood stains and wall colors were also very different when these renovations were new. Stickley certainly urged a richer color palette in his Craftsman Homes.

The kitchen, family breakfast room, and a secondary staircase are hidden away behind the broad staircase and the dining room wall.

The second floor features fireplaces faced with Grueby tiles, and the bedrooms have a plate rail above vertical battens. The ceilings are plaster, as is the frieze above the rail. Fabric wall covering was probably installed between the battens. There is a central hall at the top of the stairs that is large enough to use as a sitting room, and unlike the first floor, the wainscoting only reaches about a third of the way up the plaster wall. There is one characteristic touch, perhaps in homage to Baillie Scott

First Floor Plan

Second Floor Plan

The floor plans for the two floors of Stickley's Syracuse home that he redesigned in 1902.

and certainly related to some of Stickley's earlier furniture designs—the use of the corbel to break the severe lines of the plain woodwork. The staircase newel posts reflect a tapered design that Stickley used in most of his Craftsman Homes as well as on the posts of several of his settle designs.

In fact, most of the features that will define later Craftsman Homes are here—the use of post-and-panel; beamed ceilings; the horizontal rail and frieze; the V-joined tongue-and-groove flat boards; board-and-batten panels; built-in bookcases, cabinets, and window seats; fireplaces—all without

ornamentation—a "fine plainness" that owes some to the English architects who influenced him.

David Cathers writes:

This Craftsman residential interior was realized with a somewhat heavy hand, but it was also thrillingly new. Its wooden structure suggested Japanese timber construction, but it was otherwise not quite like anything that had been built before. Stickley had inserted a bold, uncompromising, unified—even radical—interior into his conventional, undistinguished . . .

house and created a whole new world within its walls.[34]

Where did this "thrillingly new" design come from? While it has been established that Gustav Stickley was not a trained architect or interior designer, it appears that he ran his company in every detail. Today he might even be called a "control freak." His daughter Barbara (he had five daughters and a son), who worked for him after about 1905 and was listed in the 1909 New York City directory as Vice President and Treasurer of the company, once described his design process: "He would experiment with a thing until it looked right . . . he had a fine eye for detail, and he always talked about the importance of proportion. He called it 'pro—PAW—tion.' " In the same interview of the ninety-one-year-old daughter, when asked if her father ever employed furniture designers, she asserted that "he designed it all himself."[35] Since we know that he did have designers, are we to disregard her comments? Or, at

the end of the day, did Stickley exercise ironclad creative control over the people who worked for him?

It is probably safe to say that no one person or influence solely created this unique interior. Of the known people who could have participated in its design, only two were in Syracuse the entire time the house was being rebuilt—Gustav Stickley and his head designer LaMont Warner. Henry Wilhelm Wilkinson was off to New York City in February, although he maintained connections with Stickley. The first article in *The Craftsman* by Samuel Howe appears in May 1902. So by April, Howe was probably working for Stickley; but was Howe, based in New York, just writing for the magazine, or was he in Syracuse working on Stickley's new interior? Howe did write the article in *The Craftsman* describing the interior. However the design came about, Gustav Stickley made the final decisions. And Stickley remained true to this basic concept for most of the Craftsman interiors that were created over the next twelve years, despite changing designers and

architects in his employ—and that says more than anything else about who designed this seminal interior.

Stickley lived in this home until he moved his business operations to New York City in late 1905; his family remained there until 1910, when they joined him at Craftsman Farms.

In New York, Stickley lived in a rented apartment during his long absences from Syracuse. Soon after his arrival in New York, he was invited to a party at "Red Gables," the country estate of the Hearst newspaper cartoonist Homer Davenport in Morris Plains, New Jersey, about thirty-five miles by train from the city. He must have liked the area, because by the spring of 1908 he was visiting the Morris Plains area regularly and began buying parcels of land. By March 1909, he had expended over $10,000 purchasing various land plots.[36] His land purchases eventually were consolidated into two separate large plots some distance apart and separated by what is now New Jersey's Route 10, a modern highway that runs roughly on an east-west axis.

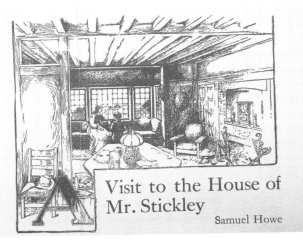

The first page of the 1902 article (above), which appeared in *The Craftsman* on Stickley's redesigned interior by Samuel Howe features a view of the living room. The space was little changed when photographed in 1995 (right).

In Stickley's Syracuse home, the wide and imposing staircase, shown in the 1902 *The Craftsman* article (right), served as a model for a number of similar staircases in Craftsman Homes. By 1995 the house had been divided into apartments and the staircase sealed off (below). The home was purchased by the Stickley Company to prevent it being torn down or dismantled, and while they are maintaining it, no organization with the wherewithal to restore and preserve it has come forward, and the future of the house is uncertain.

The Syracuse dining room, as photographed from the center hall in 1995 (above left), has changed little from the 1902 photograph (above).

Two views of the dining room area from the 1902 *Craftsman* article show the "Library" to the rear of the dining room (left) and the massive sideboard (below left). The staircase can be seen on the left and the door to the kitchen is on the right.

The second-floor hall of the Syracuse house was not only a hall but large enough to be used as a sitting room. The 1902 illustration (right) shows the use of corbels as a decorative trim, a practice that Stickley used in some early Craftsman Homes but later abandoned. The area was photographed in 1995 (below) and, considering its use as apartments, looked very close to its 1902 appearance.

The front room on the second story appears to have functioned as Stickley's home office, as seen in the 1902 illustration (left). The fireplace is revealed to have dark green Grueby tiles in this 1995 photograph (below).

Having a slight debt to Harvey Ellis's mountain camp home, Stickley's proposed home at Craftsman Farms reflected his Arts and Crafts beliefs with simple design and the use of mixed materials. While it was a large home, it certainly was not a mansion, as can be seen from the proposed floor plans (facing).

Through these purchases Gustav began to create his dream of "Craftsman Farms," the farm and boys' school he hoped to establish. In the fall of 1908 he published a series of articles in *The Craftsman* detailing his proposed home, workers' cottages, and a clubhouse that would serve as a social center for his planned school. Originally these were all designed for the southern site, where the ground slopes gradually. However, he later decided to build on the steeper northern property, just north of the present Route 10. From the first announcement of the farm and school plans in October 1908, to the publishing of an article and photos of his finished home three years later in November

1911, the plans changed considerably. Thus the buildings planned and built by Gustav Stickley at Craftsman Farms reflect not only his ideals but also the practical reality of his changing economic circumstances.

All of the structures at the Farms followed his homebuilding philosophy of using the materials at hand, and most of them still exist today. These include three cottages and what might be considered a foreman's house, as well as a horse barn, dairy house, carriage house/garage, chicken coop/barn, and the main Log House. The three cottages are not the cottages pictured in the 1908 illustrations in *The Craftsman* (see pages 240–41), but they do incor-

porate a number of the features published in the articles, including red-tinted poured cement as flooring for the porches, and shingle roofing. All have similar large fireplaces with copper hoods that conceal the Craftsman heating fireplace, one of many products for the home offered by Stickley. The two cottages closest to the main house, probably erected in 1909 and mirror images of the other, each had two bedrooms.

Further up the hill to the northwest of the Log House is the other two-bedroom cottage of stucco that was probably built a few months after the first two, some distance northwest of the Log House. There is now a more recent large addition to this

52

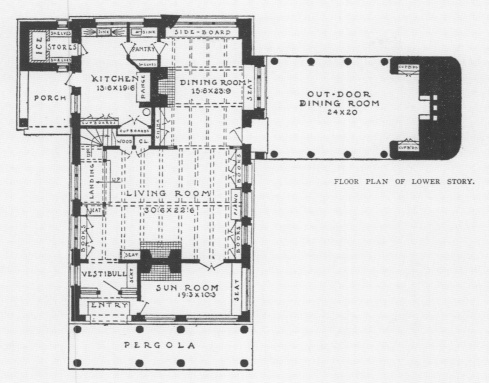

FLOOR PLAN OF LOWER STORY.

ICE · STORES · SHELVES · SINK · SINK · SIDE-BOARD

PANTRY · SHELVES

KITCHEN
13:6 X 19:6

PORCH

RANGE

DINING ROOM
15:8 X 23:9

OUT-DOOR
DINING ROOM
24 X 20

CUP'B'DS

CUP'B'DS

CUPBOARDS · CHINA

WOOD · CL

UP · LANDING · UP

BOOKS

LIVING ROOM
30:6 X 22:6

PIANO

BOOKS

SEAT

SEAT · BOOKS · SEAT · BOOKS

VESTIBULE · SEAT

ENTRY

SEAT

SUN ROOM
19:3 X 10:3

SEAT

PERGOLA

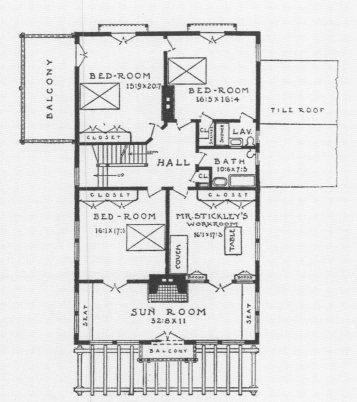

FLOOR PLAN OF SECOND STORY.

BALCONY

BED-ROOM
15:9 X 20:7

BED-ROOM
16:5 X 16:4

TILE ROOF

CLOSET

CL · SHOWER · LAV.

HALL

BATH
10:6 X 7:5

UP

CL

CLOSET · CLOSET

BED-ROOM
16:1 X 17:5

MR. STICKLEY'S
WORKROOM
16:1 X 17:3

TABLE

COUCH

BOOKS · BOOKS

SEAT

SEAT

SUN ROOM
32:8 X 11

BALCONY

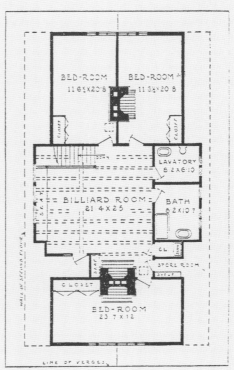

BED-ROOM
11:6½ X 20:8

BED-ROOM
11:5½ X 20:8

CLOSET · CLOSET

UP

LAVATORY
8:2 X 6:10

BILLIARD ROOM
21:4 X 25

BATH
8:2 X 10:7

CL

STORE ROOM

WALL OF SECOND FLOOR

CLOSET

CLOSET

BED-ROOM
23:7 X 12

LINE OF VERGES

building. The Stickley family may have lived in this cottage until the Log House was completed. In one period photograph that survives, there appears to be at least one more cottage located near the Log House, but it no longer exists.

Even before anything was erected, in October 1908 Stickley published an extensive article detailing his proposed home at Craftsman Farms (see page 52). What a wonderful house he conceived! It is striking how similar the first-floor arrangement is to his Syracuse home—but on a grander scale. It might be a case of Stickley using the tried-and-true, but more likely, it is simply the case that there are only so many ways one can design a floor plan. Within a box or rectangle, there are limited ways to design space for a living room, dining room, and kitchen. So while this house cannot be considered unique, it can be considered one of the ultimate Arts and Crafts home designs, for the philosophy is carried out in almost every detail. Stickley titled the article on the home "The Craftsman's House: A Practical Application of all the Theories of Home Building Advocated in the Magazine."

I will not deny that I thoroughly enjoy telling my readers about this practical experiment I am making in the building of my own house. I never before realized how much pleasure was to be found in the building of a dwelling that has completely expressed one's own taste and individuality as the painting of a picture or the writing of a book. In fact, I can think of no creative work that is so absorbingly delightful as this creation of a home to live in for the rest of one's life . . . .

So I give it as an object lesson . . . to others who may find in it some incentive to devote as much thought and care to the building of their own homes instead of . . . entrusting the whole pleasant task to an architect or builder, and so depriving themselves of the interest of sharing with him the work of evolving that which is as personal a possession as one's children or one's friends.[37]

Even though the clubhouse at the Farms was eventually modified to become his home, this proposed

The living room staircase in his proposed home was similar in concept to the one in his Syracuse home.

Two views of the dining room of the proposed home. The drawing gives a sense of space and detail (above) while the elevation shows the spatial relationships. In the tile fireplace surround is an arrangement of tiles that create a "picture" of a Native American spinning a dry stick to start a fire.

DETAIL OF DINING ROOM SHOWING FIREPLACE AND CHINA CLOSET.

The Log House at Craftsman Farms (above), photographed in 2005 after a meticulous restoration,
brought back the original paint colors. Below the
stone retaining wall in the foreground was a large
oval area set aside as a garden, seen in this photo
from a 1913 *Craftsman* article (right).

The proposed clubhouse, pictured in 1908 in
The Craftsman (above), evolved into the Stickley
home, first photographed in 1911 (left).

home expresses different things about Stickley. The proposed house is a real house, much like what he was offering in his published designs. If this home had been built, it would have been an unfettered hands-on example of how Stickley's design ideas, much as we can see Wright's ideas play out in his home and studio, could have been fully worked out—without the compromises so often found in built Craftsman homes. One can get a pretty good idea, though, from the extensive drawings in the article.

The house design was a 31-by-56-foot rectangle covered with a large Spanish tile roof. The eaves extended three feet beyond the sides of the house and four feet at the front and back. A pergola across the front and a second-story balcony broke up the severe lines in front, as did the two balconies off the rear bedrooms and on top of the kitchen porch, and the large pergola-like tile-roofed outdoor dining room that formed an "el" off the right side of the house. Two large shed dormers on the third floor added interest to the rooflines.

The first story was designed to use the split fieldstone and boulders found on the site, while the second and third stories were a veneer of plaster and half-timber, using wood from the chestnut trees growing nearby. Behind this varied surface veneer was ceramic hollow tile block, which also lined the roof under the Spanish tiles—thus, attempting to make the house as fireproof as possible.

Most of Stickley's designs have basements, but he says in the article that he had always had a theory that

The Log House after restoration in 2005 (top) looks as it did in this 1911 photo (above). The extended kitchen wing is visible to the right of the house.

a house should be built without a cellar and rest directly on the ground "with no visible foundation to separate it from the soil and the turf, in which it should almost appear to have taken root."[38] Stickley achieved this by locating the heating plant and laundry in a building "not far away." The article details extensively how Stickley planned to solve the "rising damp" problems that can come from building a structure directly on the ground. Sadly we will never know if some of

those ideas would have worked: excavation to four-foot depth filled with stone rejected from the wall construction, then broken stone, a layer of poured cement covered by "damp proofing" material, and finally a thick layer of tar and sand in which the floor joists were imbedded.

A rough, pebble-dash finish stucco was used on the exterior and given a tone of "dull brownish green," which was brushed off as the mixture set so that the surface was irregular and the

The ca. 1913 photo (above) comes alive in this 2005 view of the restored main room (top). The predominant colors were brown and varying shades of green, from the olive green ceiling to the rich dark green stain applied to the staircase and window and door frames.

Chestnut trees and fieldstone from the property were used extensively in the construction of the clubhouse, which began in August 1910. Sometime between the laying of the clubhouse foundation and its completion in the summer of 1911, Stickley decided to give up the idea of building his ideal house. For unknown reasons, perhaps financial, he had abandoned his idea of a school for boys. Therefore he had less need for a clubhouse. He was already dreaming of consolidating his business operations in New York into one grand structure to be known as "The Craftsman Building." Faced with these expenses, he probably decided he could not afford to build his house in the near future, so he modified the plans of the clubhouse and converted it into his residence while it was still under construction.

Three period photos (right and facing) and a 2005 image (below) show the details of the furnishings in the main room. The furniture of the Log House consisted of one-of-a-kind nonproduction pieces and early examples of his work, most apparently from his Syracuse offices—perhaps conveniently in storage after he moved to New York City. The piano, one of two in the house, is an inlaid version from about 1905. The green-stained elm library table looks like the same one pictured in Stickley's Syracuse offices. The settle facing the north fireplace appears to be a one-of-a-kind leather-covered version of a 1901 production piece. Willow pieces were arranged to provide some lightness and color variation from the mostly dark-stained oak pieces, and the dark-stained chestnut log walls.

illustrations directly from the book and built homes, or took the illustrations to a local architect or draftsman for blueprints. An example of the former is a house (see page 74) in Boardman, Ohio, found while searching for a Stickley home (the Gaither house; see page 327). Oddly enough, both houses were from the same No. 78 design, but one is clearly not built from plans, as the proportions and roofline differ considerably. Considering that this house is located only a mile or so from the Gaither house, it may very well be based on it.

High in the Blue Ridge Mountains in Windy Gap, North Carolina, Royal S. Morrow built a version of No. 96, from August 1910. It is not known if actual plans were used, but the floor plan he sketched on the inside cover of a log cabin building book survives. Since the description of the grounds is so detailed, the sketch may have been made after the home was built. He must have liked the house, because in 1915 he built another Craftsman Home (No. 69, from June 1909; see page 292) in nearby Brevard, where he lived the rest of his life. The Windy Gap home continued to be used as a vacation retreat until it burned down years later.

Architect W. S. Meeker designed a home for his brother Frank D. Meeker in Greenville, Ohio, and Stickley proudly featured the house in *The Craftsman*. The exterior was modified from the No. 78 design (see page 317), with an expanded second floor created by raising and expanding the original shed-roof dormer into a full two-story house. A modi-

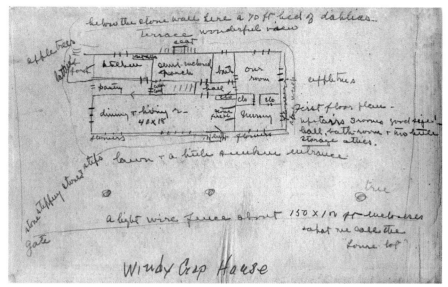

The home built by Royal S. Morrow in Windy Gap, North Carolina (above), was modeled after No. 96 (see page 367). It appears that Morrow sketched the floor plan on the inside cover of a book on constructing log cabins (top), after reading the article in the August 1910 issue of *The Craftsman*.

fied first-floor plan of No. 78 was used, adding about six feet to the rear of the structure across the entire width of the house. The layout of the second floor was altered to add an extra bathroom. However, the interior detailing could be from any Craftsman Home, and Meeker may have used actual plans of No. 78 for the downstairs woodwork and details.[41]

Frances T. Knickerbocker appears to have based her home in Bergen County, New Jersey, (see pages 76–77), on the published plan No. 63 (see page 276), called a "Craftsman farmhouse" (March 1909), and probably an architect was involved. Stickley's downstairs floor plan was followed except that the size of the inglenook was reduced considerably to allow for a larger kitchen, pantry, and dining room. Also the stairs were reversed and the small entrance foyer was not constructed. The upstairs plans were completely changed. On the exterior, the gable-roofed dormer in the front was changed and enlarged while two extra shed-roof dormers were added and the exterior window locations were altered. While Stickley hardware and lighting fixtures were used throughout the first floor (the original lighting was sold before the current owners bought the house—similar designs handmade by the owners have since replaced the lost lights), the significant difference from the Stickley design is in the unexecuted or changed details.

The Walter S. Van Duyn home (see page 78) in Springfield, Illinois, was built from two Craftsman designs

House in Boardman, Ohio, that appears to be built from the illustrations and floor plans in *The Craftsman*, but not the blueprints. No. 78 (see page 317) was illustrated in *The Craftsman* in November 1909 and featured in *More Craftsman Homes*.

married together. The exterior is derived from No. 6 of 1904 (see page 121), but the floor plans are from another house, probably modified from No. 78 (see page 317). Mrs. Van Duyn wrote in *The Craftsman:*

Yes, we built a Craftsman house . . . two of your plans were combined by the architect who used the elevation of one and the

floor plans of another, and we are delighted with the result, which is very generally admired. All of our ideas for fitting were taken from *The Craftsman.* . . . That Mrs. Van Duyn gives *The Craftsman* such generous credit for the inspiration of her beautiful home is a matter of very genuine pride to us.[42]

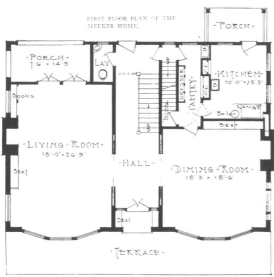

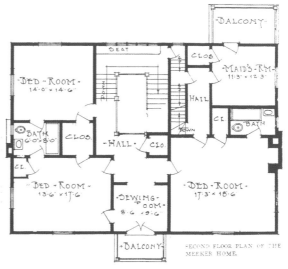

The Meeker house exterior and the floor plans are shown as published in *The Craftsman*. The article and floor plans on No. 78 of November 1909 (see page 317) reveal the differences between the homes.

Ca. 1918 picture of the Frances Knickerbocker home (top). Modeled after Craftsman Home No. 63 (above), the front porch was extended beyond the side wall of the house, and a large billiard room was added to the right side in the 1920s. The staircase features the owner's home-made replacement newel post lamp (right). The original lamp was sold out of the house. The living room (facing above) features an inglenook reduced in size to make other rooms larger. The dining room to the left beyond the inglenook is large and roomy (facing below).

The exterior of the Kakas home, pictured in *The Craftsman* (top), and in 2004 (above).

House," based on one built in Oak Park, Illinois in 1907. The similarities to Stickley's interior designs are striking. Even though the home is not a Stickley design, his influence is very much in evidence. Perhaps Stickley saw Buck's design in *The House Beautiful* and used the floor plan as an inspiration for his own Craftsman plan.

Finally, there is the E. C. Kakas home (left and page 82) in West Medford, Massachusetts. *The Craftsman* says the house is "one of the most charming houses built from Craftsman ideas that has ever come into this office."[43] Kakas, a Boston furrier, was a Stickley admirer, but instead of choosing the Craftsman Architects to design the home, he selected Boston architect Joseph P. Loud. Either Loud was already a reader and follower of *The Craftsman*, or the Kakases were able to show him plainly what they wanted, because the small house that was built could easily have been designed directly by Stickley. This house shows Stickley's influence on local architects and demonstrates his impact on the homes of the period. The interior is fully characteristic of his work, while the exterior uses methods advocated in *The Craftsman*. The design, how-ever, does not have the proportion and balance of most of Stickley's work.

These examples indicate that *The Craftsman*'s influence in home building and home design during the period was more influential than its circulation numbers (over 25,000 in 1908)[44] might indicate. The magazine was readily available in most public libraries across the country.

The first-floor plan of the Kakas house (above left). The original living room as pictured in *The Craftsman* (above right), and in 2004 (above).

Arts and Crafts Colors

One can get a good idea what a Craftsman Home looked like through the drawings and diagrams presented in *The Craftsman*. But more difficult to imagine are the colors of the interiors of these houses because almost all of the illustrations are in black and white. It was difficult and expensive to produce color illustrations in mass printings at the time. Still, Gustav Stickley did try by using two or three spot colors for several magazine covers and on the covers of other promotional publications. A small number of four-color plates of Craftsman interiors, as well as one four-color plate of the exterior of Craftsman House No. 13, were produced in the magazine. Two color plates from Harvey Ellis–designed homes appeared several years after they were first printed in black and white, strongly indicating that the originals all were done in watercolor. *The Craftsman* color plates have been reproduced here accompanying the houses they illustrate. Other color plates also are included from other

period sources, along with catalogs of two of Stickley's competitors: The Limbert Furniture Company and the Stickley Brothers Company. These competitors' Arts and Crafts interiors—concepts from furniture companies and not house builders—also illustrate how different Stickley's approach to house décor was. These other interiors do not approach the Stickley aesthetic in design or quality.

Before "Craftsman" was recognized as a style, restorers of these houses often assumed that their interiors were as monotone as the published illustrations—brown wood and cream-colored or white plaster. The Craftsman Home articles and color illustrations tell us just the opposite—that these houses were filled with color—often bright

and intense, and deep and rich. Varying shades of the same primary color were often used to define space.

The influence of the European Arts and Crafts in America was inevitable, and restorers today sometimes use wallpaper designs, particularly those

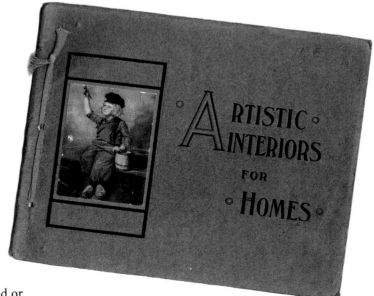

Cover of a set of paint charts "Artistic Interiors for Homes" from the National Lead Paint Company.

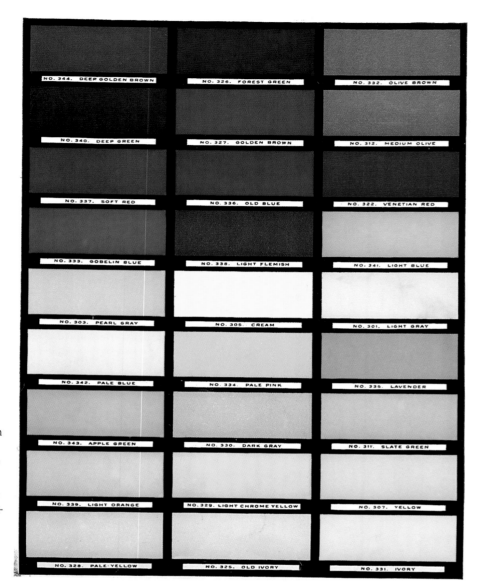

Paint chart (right) of interior colors from the "Artistic Interiors" paint chart set.

Below are some rare interior illustrations from both the Stickley Brothers Company and the Limbert Furniture Company. Although mainly intended to show their furniture in room settings, these color plates show the broad range of colors acceptable in an Arts and Crafts interior. Green is the dominant color in this hall by Stickley Brothers (left), while yellow/gold and light blue dominate this Limbert dining room (right).

of William Morris, in these Stickley-designed homes. However, Morris wall coverings and upholstery fabrics are not appropriate in a pure Stickley-designed house.

Those restoring an Arts and Crafts–style home may shy away from using many of the colors presented here. Few today would dare to paint or stain their walls a forest green or a mustard brown! Although Stickley's earth-toned color palette may be unusual by contemporary standards, it looks wonderful when combined with the accessories such as linens, draperies, rugs and furniture.[45] Of course, some of the colors—particularly the lighter colors of yellows, oranges, and golds—are easier to accept today because they are often used in present-day decorating schemes.

Reading the descriptions of stain and paint colors in the house descriptions that Stickley published often raises the question: What *are* the actual colors mentioned? A visit to the local paint store will not help, as the palette for the modern home is different from that of a hundred years ago.

Reproduced here are original paint charts from several companies active during the publication of Stickley's magazine. There are exterior and interior stains and paints, as well as a chart of masonry coatings. Although even today's modern printing methods cannot reproduce these colors with 100 percent accuracy, the colors here will be close enough to give the reader a good idea of the color palette Stickley was working with, and if duplicating these colors in the home is desired, they should provide a reference.

The use of fabrics as wall coverings and curtains is also addressed in the house descriptions and should not be overlooked, as texture as well as color are vital elements of Arts and Crafts décor. A selection of original curtains and linens from Crab Tree Farm and other sources is included in this section.

A number of photographs of room settings from the buildings of Crab Tree Farm are provided here to show how these colors, together with the Craftsman furniture and furnishings, produced a richly satisfying color palette.

A dining room from a Stickley Brothers furniture catalog (left) features an almost overwhelming amount of red, while the same type of room from Limbert (right) featured sunny yellows and reds.

Samples of Acme Quality Colors
(Continued from inside front cover)

Acme Quality No-Lustre Finish
A lustreless finish for walls and interior surfaces

Acme Quality Kalsomine
A sanitary coating for walls and ceilings

57
53
64
68
25
59

51
64
55
53
59
57

Acme Quality Enamels (Neal's)
Imparts a durable, genuine enamel finish like china to woodwork, walls and furniture. Sanitary and easy to keep bright and attractive. Dust and dirt do not cling to it.

Ivory
Wild Rose
Sea Green
Cabula

Snow White
Blue Tint
Oriental Blue
Vermilion

Acme Quality Carriage and Automobile Paint (Neal's)
For vehicles of all kinds, row boats, iron fences, lawn settees, or any surface—indoors or outdoors—requiring a durable varnish-gloss finish.

Vermilion
Driving Cart Red
Keep Coach Black

Clear Carriage Varnish
Coach Green
Brilliant Blue

Samples of Acme Quality Colors
The selection shown represents but a few of the popular colors in each line. Your dealer will be pleased to show you our *full* line of colors.

ACME WHITE LEAD AND COLOR WORKS, DETROIT, MICH

Acme Quality House Paint
A durable, high-grade paint for protecting and beautifying all kinds of structures. Costs the least because it goes the furthest and lasts the longest. These colors are sold by all Acme Quality dealers. Numbers on labels may not always correspond, but by comparing these colors with dealers' sample cards, the correct shades can be secured.

12
44
18
42
120

211
212
223
225
227

Acme Quality Varno-Lac
A tough, durable, varnish-gloss coating for floors, furniture and woodwork. Stains and varnishes at a single application.

Light Oak
Mahogany
Rosewood
Moss Green

Acme Quality Floor Paint
(Granite)
For floors, steps and all inside surfaces to be walked upon.

French Yellow
Green
Drab
Deep Red

(Continued on inside back cover)

The Acme White Lead and Color Works painting guide book. Color charts for the interior (above left) and for the exterior and floors (above right).

ACME QUALITY
PAINTING
GUIDE
BOOK

ACME WHITE LEAD AND COLOR WORKS
DETROIT MICHIGAN

NINTH EDITION

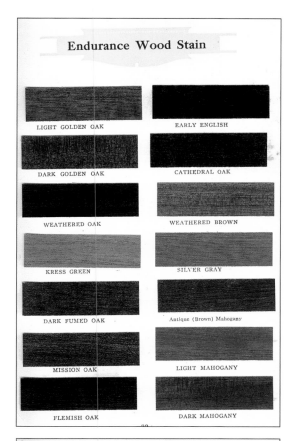

Endurance Wood Stain

LIGHT GOLDEN OAK

EARLY ENGLISH

DARK GOLDEN OAK

CATHEDRAL OAK

WEATHERED OAK

WEATHERED BROWN

KRESS GREEN

SILVER GRAY

DARK FUMED OAK

Antique (Brown) Mahogany

MISSION OAK

LIGHT MAHOGANY

FLEMISH OAK

DARK MAHOGANY

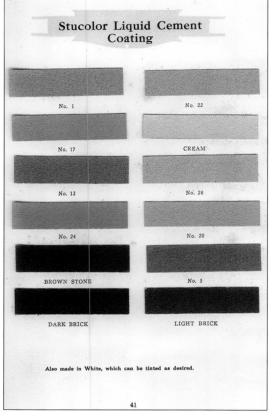

Stucolor Liquid Cement Coating

No. 1

No. 22

No. 17

CREAM

No. 13

No. 26

No. 24

No. 20

BROWN STONE

No. 5

DARK BRICK

LIGHT BRICK

Also made in White, which can be tinted as desired.

41

PATTON'S TOR-ON SHINGLE STAIN

For description, see page 40

RUSSET 362

MAROON 360

IVY GREEN 342

ROOF GREEN 353

INDIAN RED 343

WALNUT 363

MOSS GREEN 354

SLATE 366

Tor-on Shingle Stain will make this type of building last many years longer by warding off sun and rain, thus preventing warping and splitting of the shingles.

Color charts from the Glidden Company show exterior shingle stains, interior wood stains, and masonry coatings.

The following set of photographs of one of the guest cottages at Crab Tree Farm shows how the colors of the walls, rugs, curtains, and upholstery come together to create a harmonious whole.

A sitting room (above) has a unique nook with a shower of Stickley light fixtures. One of the bedrooms is at the rear of the hall to the left. The opposite wall of the room frames a doorway into a large room (facing above) with both sitting and dining areas. In all the rooms the color has been mixed in the plaster coating instead of being applied like a paint. The front living room (facing below) features an original English Arts and Crafts rug with bright colors. In the corner of the front living room (right) is a Stickley tall case clock and a rare desk in front of period curtains of a printed pattern.

The sitting and dining room features a number of beautiful Gustav Stickley pieces in a setting of complementary colors (facing above). The pump house has a Gustav Stickley furnished office (facing below).

The two bedrooms of the cottage display different styles of wood trim. One room (above) features natural wood trim and wallpaper with a stencil above the frieze, while the other (left) shows painted wood trim dividing the wall spaces with a wall covering of rose-colored grass cloth material.

The cottage kitchen (top) is based on two drawings from the September 1905 issue of *The Craftsman*, one of which is reproduced here (above). The dining area is visible through the doorway. The cottage has a period bathroom, too (facing). Linens were a key component of the Arts and Crafts house décor—both in color and in texture. Reproduced on the following pages are a number of period curtains, bedspreads, portieres, and pillowcases, mostly from Crab Tree Farm.

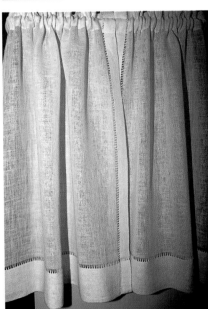

A Glasgow-style bedspread pillow and collar graces one of the beds at Crab Tree Farm. Period bedcovers were often medium linens with a conventionalized center medallion design in appliqué and hand embroidery, sometimes with motifs along the sides, as in this example (above). Another variation of Stickley's block-printed grape design hangs in the dining room of the Harvey Ellis bungalow at Crab Tree Farm (right). This design was offered in four color combinations printed on Mandarin silk casement fabric and was one of the more expensive fabrics the Craftsman Workshops offered.

Preceding page:
The Crab Tree Farm cottage bathroom features linen curtains with an acorn and oak leaf appliqué (top left), designed by John Scott Bradstreet. Offered by the Craftsman Workshops as design number 7, these filet net curtains with hand-darned border (top right) were listed as "the most popular of all we sell." A similar sheer linen scrim fabric curtain, with hand-hemstitching drawn-thread work, was also available (center right). The Craftsman also offered curtains with a block-printed grape design in several color combinations ca. 1912 (below left). The source is unknown for this commercially produced curtain (below right), but it is quite appropriate for a Craftsman Home.

Library. In September 1908 a large home designed for a client is published, and again the plans do not exist at Avery. Three small bungalows published in November 1908 are numbered 53 through 55 in both *More Craftsman Homes* and at Avery. So there remain two houses published without numbers. No. 52 can be assigned to the October 1907 house because it follows in date sequence with No. 51. But the September 1908 house should be No. 53 because it precedes, by date, the three bungalows. Since they are already numbered at both Avery and in *More Craftsman Homes*, the only number left to assign is No. 56. It may be that when this house was published, the intention was not to make it available to readers, and that

later the client allowed the house to be offered.

Why does this matter? A system that corresponds with the numbering of the Avery Library plans is important because readers desiring to build homes in this book will naturally want to obtain copies of the plans at Avery. Also, it is important to see how these house designs developed and changed over time, and this can be best seen if they are presented in the order they were published. Although the final house number in the December 1916 issue of *The Craftsman* is No. 221, there were actually 225 designs published (remember the 1904 3A, B, and C homes and the arbitrary number 49A)—but not all were houses! Of the designs, there were three

schools, one playhouse, and one doghouse that received numbers. There was also a boathouse and one garage, but since they contained living quarters, they can be considered Craftsman Homes. Therefore, there were actually 220 Craftsman Homes published in the magazine.

The houses are presented here in the order in which they were published. Homes specially commissioned from the Craftsman Architects but never offered to readers are listed in the year they were published or constructed, if known. Commentary on each house is offered where appropriate, as well as details about the owners and the existing houses that have been located.

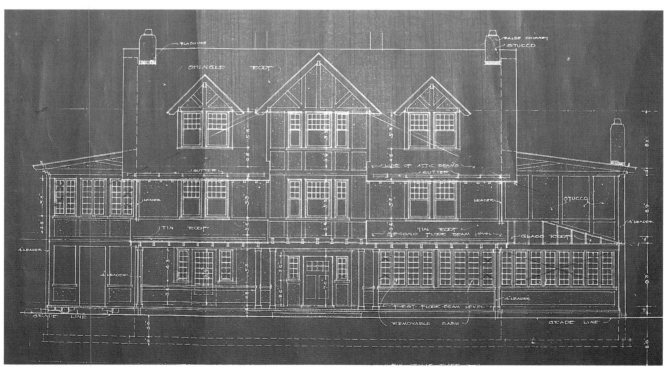

The blueprints for the Peer House in Ithaca, New York (see page 286), show that the builder of a Craftsman Home received full working drawings of elevations and floor plans that any contractor could use to build the house. These drawings, still in the possession of the owners of the home, show the original three-story proposal that was modified later.

The Stickley Craftsman Home Designs

One of the joys of reading the descriptions of Stickley homes found in *The Craftsman* is the enthusiastic and detailed way that they are expressed. The idyllic and romantic heart of the Arts and Crafts movement is caught in the wording of these descriptions. Colors, wood tones, construction materials, are all given a fanciful, naive, and simple interpretation that captures the spirit of the times.

Therefore the following descriptions rely on the original text. There are some direct quotes, but they are mostly a condensation and rearrangement of the text due to space limitations, with some additional comment where needed. All quotes are from the appropriate article of *The Craftsman* unless otherwise noted. Where space permits, the comments on color and accessories have been retained, but since the reader has a floor plan, the descriptive comments on the relationships of the rooms have not. Elements of the text that capture how Stickley "romanticized" these homes have been retained. The

The porch of Craftsman Home No. 41, 1906, exhibits many of the Stickley design elements usually found in Craftsman Homes: the use of mixed materials (stone, wood, and stucco), round wooden support columns, exposed rafters and joinery, the Craftsman-style door and casement windows.

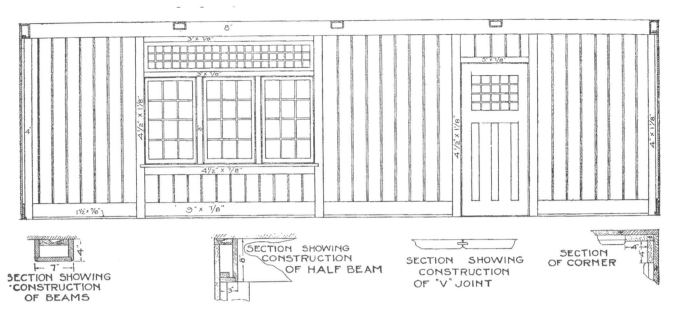

SECTION SHOWING CONSTRUCTION OF BEAMS

SECTION SHOWING CONSTRUCTION OF HALF BEAM

SECTION SHOWING CONSTRUCTION OF "V" JOINT

SECTION OF CORNER

Stickley made suggestions of various ways wood could be used in an interior. In this illustration, one of a series of three elevation drawings of various wall arrangements published in *The Craftsman*, he offers the way a wall could be done in a typical Craftsman scheme.

turn-of-the-century spellings and phraseology have also been retained as much as possible. And of course, by using the name Stickley as in "Stickley says . . . ," this does not mean that Gustav Stickley wrote each word. The terms "Stickley," "Craftsman Architects," "*The Craftsman*," etc., are all used interchangeably to signify what was said in the magazine.

In the beginning of the article describing Craftsman House No. 41, published in the October 1906 issue of *The Craftsman*, Stickley makes a clear summation of the principles of Craftsman Home design:

Houses planned to meet individual needs must necessarily differ from one another as persons do, but houses planned in accordance with the same general principles of construction and arrangement show a strong family resemblance under all the differences. Craftsman houses differ widely in form, according to the locality, climate, material used or required cost, yet all alike are designed after the same fundamental principles of strength and simplicity of construction, convenience and economy of space in the arrangement of rooms, and the gaining of a sense of freedom and restfulness by omitting all unnecessary partitions on the lower floor. The plans as illustrated and described here admit of endless minor modifications if such are desired by the person building the house, and yet the principle remains the same. For instance, we may publish plans of a house to be built of plaster, because to us that material seems the most desirable for gaining the best effect in that particular style of house, and shortly afterwards receive a letter from some member of the Home-Builders' Club, saying that the plans as published suit him in every particular, but that he wants a brick house. In nine cases out of ten it does not seem to occur to him that the house in question can be built of brick quite as well as of plaster, and still remain exactly the Craftsman house that he wants to have. The same applies to wood construction. Our plans may call for shingled walls, and some one may prefer clapboards. If so, the change is easy to make, only we should recommend that the clapboards be wide and rather thick, and left unplaned, as the ordinary thin, smooth clapboard looks too finikin and "dressed up" to be in harmony with the rugged strength of the design.

The same liberty of modification applies to the arrangement of the interior. A family may be able to fit itself into almost any rented house that is big enough to hold it, for there is always the feeling that it is a temporary arrangement after all, but in building a home there must be nothing to "put up with" in the shape of a plan that may be good in itself, but is not quite suited to the requirements of that particular family. The whole secret of creating a home atmosphere . . .

lies in the restful sense of permanence that leaves no room for a desire to change. And much of that peaceful attitude toward the home environment is due to the fact that the house fits the life that is lived in it— fits so perfectly that after the first adjustment there is no further thought about it, only the subconsciousness of peace and comfort and the enjoyment of now and then adding the little touches that are part of the growth of the home. In the descriptions accompanying the published plans of Craftsman houses we have given many suggestions as to color schemes, interior decoration and furnishings. We have given them in detail, describing each

room as we would furnish it according to Craftsman ideas. Naturally these decorative schemes vary as do the plans, and yet any one of them would suit any house, as the underlying principles are changeless throughout all variations.

We believe that no house is satisfying unless it is designed as a whole. We believe that if this is done each room will be a complete thing before a picture, a piece of furniture, or an article of bric-a-brac is put into it, and, being complete, there will be no desire to put in useless things that are only an addition to the cares of the housekeeper, and that after all fail to satisfy because they are needless and therefore out of place. In the

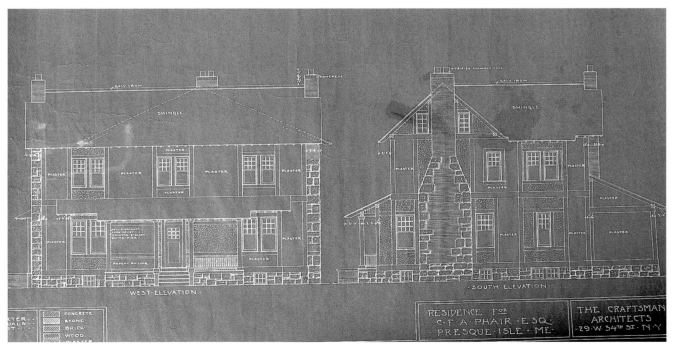

The front and side elevations from the set of blueprints for the C. F. A. Phair home in Presque Isle, Maine (see page 178), are in the possession of the owner.

Craftsman houses, the keynote of each scheme of decoration is the woodwork. The friendliness of wood is unfailing, if only it is given a chance to keep its beauty of color, texture and grain, and is not made to look like something else. There is no sense of the kindly wood in woodwork that is covered with a smooth coat of paint or enamel, or is filled and varnished to a glassy smoothness of surface in which there is no possible chance for the interest that lies in the many variations of grain and in the surface play of changing tones.

In some places, especially bedrooms done in delicate tints, and in bathrooms, the best treatment of the woodwork is the white enamel that gives it the smoothness and mellow tone of ivory, but in the family living-rooms the wood should always be allowed the full value of its own character. If natural wood is used in a bedroom, it should be one of the finer-grained varieties, such as birch, maple or gumwood, all of which lend themselves to light and delicate effects such as belong to intimate personal surroundings. For example, nothing could be daintier than a bedroom done in soft tones of old rose, in the dull gray-blues, or in either the peach or straw shades of yellow, where the woodwork would be of maple so treated as to produce in it a pure tone of soft, silvery-gray, clouded like the color in a hornet's nest. By the same fitness of things, the sturdier woods belong to the rooms that are in general use—rooms

In this detail of a wall at Crab Tree Farm, the plaster has been given a rough surface for light to play on, and the color has been stained into the plaster, giving the color depth and a slightly varied tone, hallmarks of a well-done Craftsman interior.

in which wainscots, beams and all manner of structural features make the woodwork the foundation and background of everything. Any one who has ever lived in a house where the living-rooms are generously paneled with oak or chestnut or cypress, treated so that the mellow darkened color which suggests the ripeness of age shows under the light surface tone of green, gray or luminous brown, and the strong, irregular markings of the grain form the only decoration of the plain surfaces, need not be told of the sense of restfulness and home comfort that belongs to such a room. The soft greens and browns are the natural forest tones, and, given these as a basis, the whole scheme of decoration falls into the same key, the wall surfaces covered with fabric or paper in some contrasting tone that yet keeps the feeling of quietness, or simply left in rough plaster that may be given any desired color or left in the natural gray. In such a room the color accents and highlights belong naturally to the small things—to the curtains, cushions and the treasured little movables that give here and there a splash of color or the gleam of metal, but it is astonishing how few of these are needed, and how the furnishings tend to reduce themselves to what is absolutely necessary. In fact, the furniture of such a room is largely built into it, and right here is the never-ending charm of individuality in each house.

A dining-room where the sideboard, perhaps flanked by china closets, is built into a recess lighted by a high row of small-paned casement windows, has a central point of interest in its very structure that could be given in no other way. The same charm is felt when a window-seat or bookcase is built into the room in exactly the right place, or when a fireplace, nook, or some cunningly contrived recess gives just the little touch of seclusion that intensifies the sense of coziness. It is the feeling of "unalterableness" that gives its individuality to a room, the knowledge that one could be away for years and come back to find it unchanged, and in this lies the very essence of home. [Generally, in all our houses] the whole lower floor is open, with the exception of the kitchen rooms, and while the different rooms are named for the sake of convenience, they are all parts of one very large room. The detailed description of any one of our houses will suggest color-schemes and decorations, and to give them here would be only to repeat what we have so often said before. So these general principles obtain in all our Craftsman houses.

1904

Stickley begins his home design odyssey by initially picturing and describing one house in great detail each month. Since these concepts are new to many readers, every detail must be described and explained. By July he begins to offer an average of two houses a month. The house designs are drawn from many vernacular styles, but consistent design elements begin to feature prominently as the series progresses: large exposed beams (he calls them purlins) that support wide overhanging eaves and wonderful proportion and balance to the exterior elevations. A total of eighteen homes are offered in the inaugural year.

No. 1 (Series of 1904, No. 1) January 1904

Roof: Hipped *Bedrooms:* 6 *Baths:* 1 1/2 *Cost:* $6,500 *Avery Plans:* 12 sheets (4 sheets dated 3/12/04)

The first Craftsman Home is a simple building that is essentially a foursquare house, with a kitchen "el," or extension, to the rear. Its hip roof pulls the structure together visually and the roughcast stucco and recessed windows and porch provide relief from the mass of the home by allowing light to play with the texture and voids created. It exemplifies the Arts and Crafts mantra that "less is more."

This house was conceived in the last two months of 1903. The drawing could be said to be somewhat in Harvey Ellis's style, but compared to Ellis's already-published homes, this one is awkward and very plain.

With its red tile roof, the home is drawn from the vernacular Spanish Mission style of the Southwest part of the United States and it would blend in with any home of this region and also in Florida and California; yet it is suitable for any locale in the United States.

The house is "balloon-framed" wood and sheathed with metal lath covered with a coat of cement. The interior features a traditional center hall. The first floor is finished with chestnut woodwork stained in a brown-gray tone with the plaster ceilings left "under the trowel" and coated with brown shellac, which continues into the upper hall. The floors are white oak stained nut-brown. The upstairs rooms are mostly trimmed in hazelwood, in a gray-green stain, with pine being used in the two small servants' bedrooms to the rear. The floors are Georgia pine, stained yellow-green.

Craftsman Home No. 1 (top), as published in the January 1904 issue of *The Craftsman*, and as built not far from Stickley's Craftsman Farms in developer Charles Hapgood's planned community of Mountain Lakes, New Jersey, about 1912. It is unclear how much Stickley had to do with this construction, but Hapgood offered several of Stickley's designs in modified form. The interior fittings are less elaborate than the plans called for, and the plans for this example are reversed, or flipped in a mirror image. The small dormer in the front was probably a later addition.

GROUND FLOOR PLAN

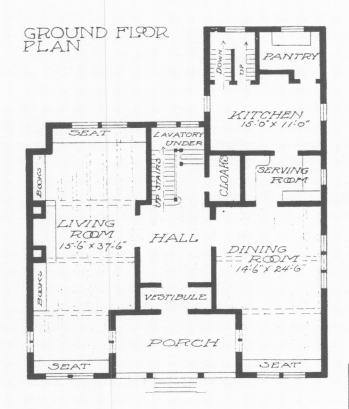

SEAT

BOOKS

LAVATORY UNDER

UP STAIRS

CLOAKS

PANTRY

KITCHEN
15'-0" x 11'-0"

SERVING ROOM

LIVING ROOM
15'-6" x 37'-6"

HALL

DINING ROOM
14'-6" x 24'-6"

BOOKS

VESTIBULE

PORCH

SEAT

SEAT

SECOND FLOOR PLAN

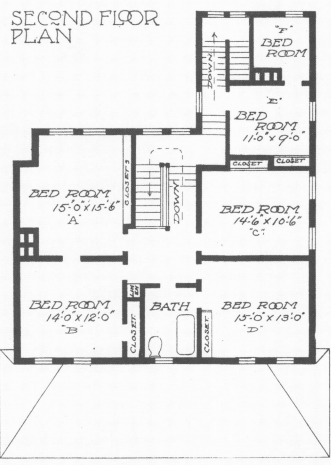

"F" BED ROOM

DOWN

"E" BED ROOM
11'-0" x 9'-0"

CLOSET

CLOSET

CLOSET 3

DOWN

BED ROOM
15'-0" x 15'-6"
"A"

BED ROOM
14'-6" x 10'-6"
"C"

BED ROOM
14'-0" x 12'-0"
"B"

CLOSET

LINEN

BATH

CLOSET

BED ROOM
15'-0" x 13'-0"
"D"

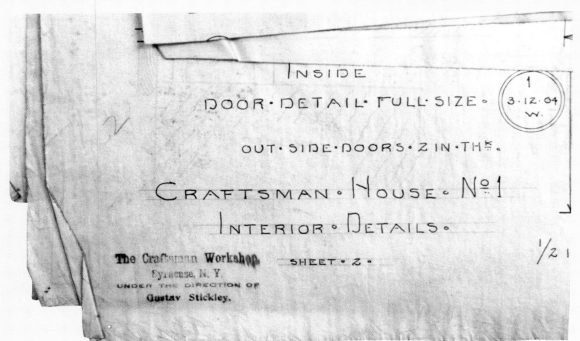

INSIDE

DOOR·DETAIL·FULL·SIZE·

1
3·12·04
W.

OUT·SIDE·DOORS·2·IN·THE·

CRAFTSMAN·HOUSE·N° 1

INTERIOR·DETAILS·

The Craftsman Workshop
Syracuse, N.Y.
UNDER THE DIRECTION OF
Gustav Stickley

SHEET·2·

1/2

The floor plans from *The Craftsman* (top). The linen drawings (left) from the Avery Library reveal that working drawings were not ready when the house was published, as they are dated March 1904.

The living room in *The Craftsman* (top) features walls that are covered with moss-green canvas, reaching up to a frieze of the same fabric in tan color, and stenciled with a Zuni Indian "feather design" motif. The cushions on the window seats are "pomegranate red canvas, and the pillows the same color with gray-green appliqué. The rugs are in warm reds and browns with green accent. The curtains are unbleached linen stenciled with a rose, blue and green poppy motif. The fireplace is red Harvard brick that is not of uniform color, while simply cut corbels of gray stone hold the chestnut mantel." The home in Mountain Lakes (above) does not feature the Stickley details, and the original plans are reversed.

It is interesting to note that the final working drawings were not produced until early March, and the elevation drawings as published in *The Craftsman* are slightly different in the Avery drawings. The height of the home had to be increased as there was not enough headroom on the second floor of the "concept" drawing.

The dining room (left) has chestnut woodwork, dull peacock-blue fabric above it, with blue linen curtains. The Hapgood home (below) eschews the beamed ceiling and built-in furniture but keeps the idea of the high wainscoting.

Roof: Gambrel with gable dormers *Bedrooms:* 6 (or 4 and a study and an upstairs den) *Baths:* 1 1/2 *Cost:* $3,000
Avery Plans: 12 sheets dated from 3/19/04 to 3/21/04, after publication of the house in February

This home is similar to the previously published 1903 designs by E. G. W. Dietrich, and, if not designed by him, is influenced by his work. It also appears to be derivative of much of the work of Maine architect John Calvin Stevens. From the outset it was designed as a vacation home, specially prepared for a client on the island of Martha's Vineyard. It is thus the first home that was prepared for a client and then offered to readers—and the first of many not to be built as proposed.

The exterior is shingled in the New England seaside manner. The shingles are 20 inches long and at least 1/2 inch thick at the butt, and they are left natural except for the roof, which is stained red.

All the rooms get light and air from at least two sides. The living room walls are wainscoted to six feet high above which is "rough-coat" plaster. The cypress ceiling beams continue into the dining room, where the wainscoting is lower and the walls above are finished in plaster covered with a decorative canvas. The bedroom walls are covered with various dyed fabrics.

It is worth noting that within a month of the publication of the house the interior was altered as Stickley rapidly refined his "style." The designs dated March 1904 in the Avery Library, prepared a month after the article was published, show changed interior details. The interior drawings as published later in 1904

Within a year of the published article (illustration, top), an advertisement plate (above) from the February 1905 issue of *The Craftsman* shows that the house was built as a vacation rental, and the published photo plainly shows a stripped-down version of the house. The exterior design has been modified with balconies above either porch wing and rearranged dormers.

A CRAFTSMAN HOUSE : SERIES OF 1904 · NUMBER TWO·

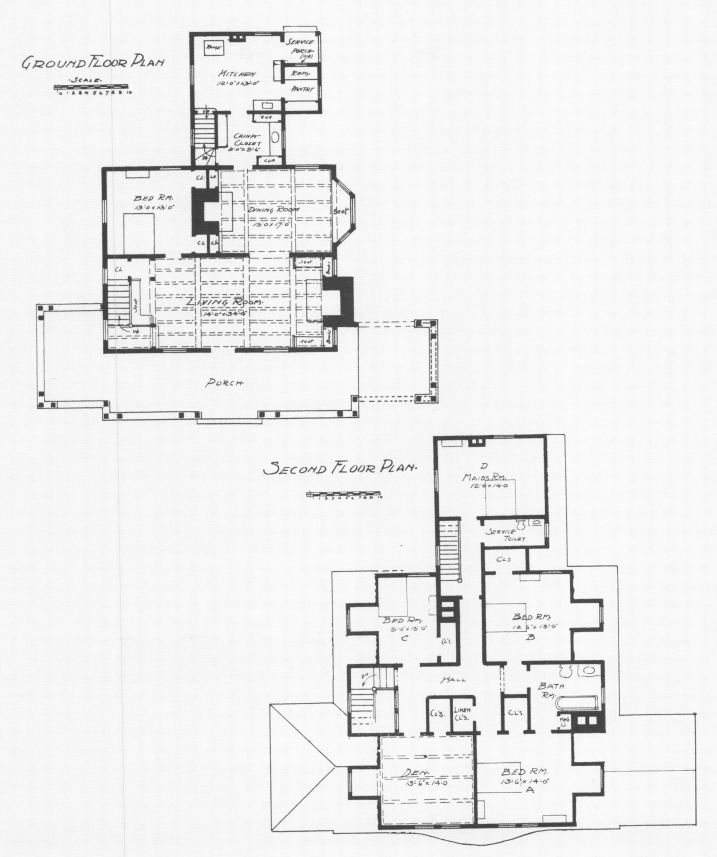

GROUND FLOOR PLAN

·SCALE·
0 1 2 3 4 5 6 7 8 9 10

SERVICE PORCH (1¼)

RANGE

KITCHEN
12'·0"×13'·0"

REFG.

PANTRY

CUP.

CHINA CLOSET
8'·0"×9'·6"

CUP.

UP

DN.

CL. UP

BED RM.
13'·0"×13'·0"

DINING ROOM
13'·0"×17'·0"

SEAT

CL.

CL. ch

CL

SEAT

SEAT

LIVING ROOM·
14'·0"×34'·0"

UP

SEAT

PORCH·

SECOND FLOOR PLAN·

1 2 3 4 5 6 7 8 9 10

D
MAIDS RM.
12'·0"×14'·0"

SERVICE TOILET

CL'S

BED RM.
9'·0"×13'·0"
C

CL'S.

BED RM.
12'·6"×13'·0"
B

DN.

HALL

BATH RM.

CL'S.

LINEN CL'S.

CL'S.

MED CL.

DEN·
13'·6"×14'·0"

BED RM.
13'·6"×14'·0"
A

in the brochure *Things Wrought in the Craftsman Workshops* reflect these changes. The original illustrations owe some debt to Baillie Scott, but the new interior has simpler lines and fits Stickley's emerging style.

A search of the island of Martha's Vineyard did not result in the discovery of this home. Although it may be hidden down one of many narrow roads, it is more probable the house was destroyed or torn down, as the photos indicate a prominent location near the ocean.

The corresponding interior designs from the same house as published in *The Craftsman* (above), and then published in *Things Wrought in the Craftsman Workshops*, a promotional brochure published later in 1904 (center), show a more streamlined and simple interior. The Avery drawings indicate the change was made in the time between the publishing of the article in February and the drawings done in March. The published photo of the same space (right) indicates that the builder paid no attention to the details anyway, although the finished room appears closer to the February concept.

No. 3 (Series of 1904, No. III) March 1904

Roof: Hip *Bedrooms:* 4 (plus 2 more, if needed) *Baths:* 1 *Cost:* $5,500 *Avery Plans:* 14 sheets including six sheets of details dated 3/8/04

Unlike the first two homes, one suggesting southwestern influences and the other New England features, the third is not special to any environment.

A handsome home, it is another modified foursquare, nearly twice as long as it is wide. The rear kitchen-wing walls are recessed slightly on either side, so that it has an appearance of being an afterthought to the main structure. This is reinforced by the fact that the first floor of the main structure is of brick, while the entire rear wing and the upper story are shingled and stained a deep brown. The sash and trim are deep green. The house is designed for a suburban lot facing south or southeast, with a garden reached by steps from the living room on the west side.

While not as open as some later Stickley designs, the entry vestibule opens into a reception area/staircase with the living room through a large entryway to the left.

Two more bedrooms could be added to the unfinished third floor, if needed.

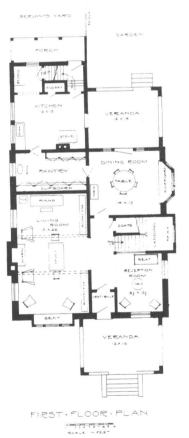

FIRST · FLOOR · PLAN

SECOND · FLOOR · PLAN

Three Craftsman Cottages

No. 3A, No. 3B, and No. 3C, November 1908

Three small cottage designs also appeared in the magazine in March 1904, along with an article about the need for small, inexpensive houses for single women. Nos. 3A, 3B, and 3C all were designed to be functional but inexpensive—"to afford a safe investment and a comfortable home to one or two persons of narrow means." Stickley was evidently getting requests for inexpensive homes, and he responded with these cottages. Numbers 3A and 3B both have three small bedrooms, even though the text says they are for two people. Number 3C has two bedrooms.

All three homes are faced with California redwood shingles on the exterior, dipped in oil to get a rich red-brown tone. The roofs, also shingled, are left unstained.

The interior of all three is finished in plain plaster tinted with watercolors, and the trim is "whitewood" finished with a dull satin-finish lacquer. The floors are hard pine. The fireplaces are done in ordinary hard-burned brick. The ceilings are only 7 1/2 feet high to reduce heating costs.

No. 3A (Series of 1904, No. IIIA) March 1904

Roof: Hip *Bedrooms:* 3 *Baths:* 1 *Cost:* under $900 *Avery Plans:* 4 sheets

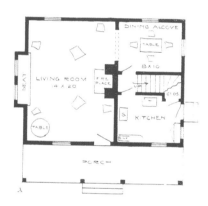

No. 3C (Series of 1904, No. IIIC) March 1904

Roof: Gable with gable dormer *Bedrooms:* 2 *Baths:* 1 *Cost:* under $900

No. 3B (Series of 1904, No. IIIB) March 1904

Roof: Hip *Bedrooms:* 2 *Baths:* 1 *Cost:* under $900

A modified one-story form of No. 3B was built by Nebraskans Frank and Bertha Coon high in the mountains in Silver City, New Mexico, in 1906.[49] It is difficult to tell if the plans for this house were produced by a local architect from a study of the original plans, or were furnished modified by the Craftsman Architectural Department. The town history, however, says the house was built by a local firm—Black and Adkins—from plans provided by mail from Gustav Stickley. The house is built of brick, and although the window arrangements are changed, it is laid out with the living and dining rooms as conceived but with only an attic above. A tiny kitchen was placed where the stairs are in the floor plan, and two matching bedrooms separated by a bathroom were placed across the rear of the house—shortening the living room. Both bedrooms have french doors opening to a rear porch.

Stickley's design (top) was a two-story home, but the Coons built a one-story version (above). The fireplace was moved to the side of the house (left) and other major changes were made.

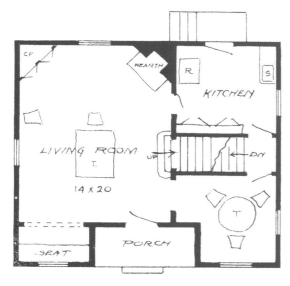

FIRST FLOOR PLAN

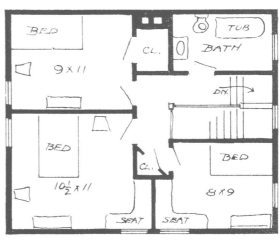

SECOND FLOOR PLAN

Stickley's floor plans (top). This 2002 photo (right) shows the room has changed little from 1906. Coon's granddaughter claims the house was furnished and decorated with Craftsman pieces. That could indicate the plans did come from Stickley. Certainly this period photo (above) from the local historic society indicates the curtains were a Stickley pattern and that the owners used his five-leg dining room table. The local history book says that the interior walls were divided into strips of natural-finished wood battens and the spaces between were covered with a burlap-like fabric.

No. 4 (Series of 1904, No. IV) April 1904

Roof: Gable with gable dormers *Bedrooms:* 4 *Baths:* 1 *Cost:* $2,000 *Avery Plans:* 7 sheets dated 3/39/04 to 3/31/04

A home with its stylistic roots in the English Arts and Crafts style, it would pass as a "Tudor" today. Fieldstone is recommended for the foundation and chimney, while the first story is constructed with deep-red bricks having wide white joints being laid in the manner known as "Flemish bond." The second story is "half timber" (cypress stained red-brown) set in roughcast plaster. The steep-pitched roof is covered with oil-soaked California redwood shingles.

The interior trim is chestnut stained brown, with rough plaster stained gray-green for the frieze above the wainscot and the ceiling stained in a lighter shade of the same color. The benches on each side of the hard red-brick fireplace are upholstered in water-green leather. The curtains are natural linen hemmed with green linen floss. The upstairs trim is Carolina pine, stained green except in the bathroom, which is finished in white enamel paint.

Irving King, a teacher at the University of Michigan, built this home (above right), and pictures of the house were featured in *The Craftsman* in December 1908 (right). The home appears to have been torn down later to make room for new apartment buildings as the university expanded. King's home had only one chimney, and that was made of brick (he said that stone work was very expensive in the area); a terrace in the front replaced the porch steps, and that was built with stone! King and his family constructed the furnishings from Craftsman ideas.

The original drawing of the inglenook area of the living room from *The Craftsman* (right), and the room as built by Irving King (center). The dining room illustration from *The Craftsman* (below right).

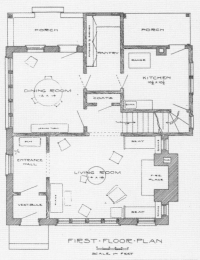

FIRST·FLOOR·PLAN
SCALE IN FEET

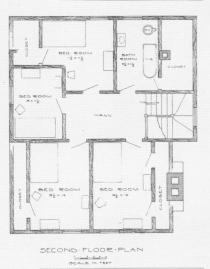

SECOND·FLOOR·PLAN
SCALE IN FEET

No. 5 (Series of 1904, No. V) May 1904

Roof: Cross gable   *Bedrooms:* 3   *Baths:* 1   *Cost:* $4,000   *Avery Plans:* 10 sheets dated 5/11/04 to 5/18/04

This house is designed for a suburban lot of 40-foot frontage, preferably on a corner. "The main purpose of the design is to produce a one-story dwelling. . . . The proportions of the building are made such as to avoid a low, rambling appearance, and the window level is placed above the eye-line of the passer-by." It is interesting to note that while this house is obviously related to the California missions being described in detail elsewhere in *The Craftsman* during this period, only this oblique reference is made in the published article: "The style of the building is regulated by the free spirit of the times, and if certain details, like the 'stepped' gables, point to well-known sources of derivation, they are introduced structurally, rather than borrowed and applied as something foreign to the general scheme." However, when the house plans were published in *Craftsman Homes* in 1909, it was called "A Craftsman House founded on the California Mission Style." Stickley had recently stayed at the Mission Inn in California, built in this style, and may also have seen similar clubhouses designed by architect Charles Lummis.

The deep recessed windows, the dark red brick of the lower section of the chimney and the red tile roof relieve the plain exterior of gray-white cement.

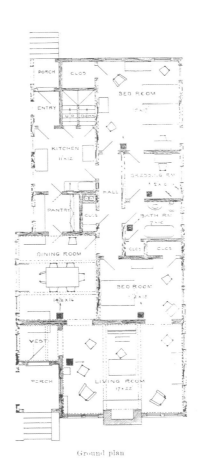

Ground plan

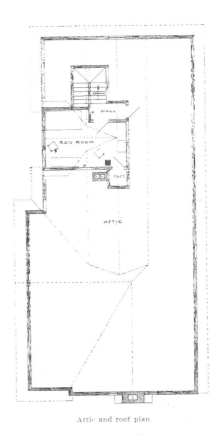

Attic and roof plan

The living room (top) and vestibule area have a low wainscot that reaches to the window sills. The walls are covered with "yellow canvas in a warm tone leading admirably to the old ivory tint of the plaster ceiling." All the woodwork on the first floor is rich brown-stained chestnut with floors in oak of the same color, while rugs in greens, yellows, blues, and reds provide relief from the wood's color. The walls of the dining room (above) are paneled with green burlap, and the plaster frieze above is tinted in a lighter tone of the same color. The ceiling is rough plaster and tinted to a pale orange. Elsewhere in the house, the bedrooms have floors of dark gray maple, with woodwork of the same material but treated in a lighter shade. The kitchen and pantry use four-foot-high wainscot of Carolina pine in a natural finish; above the wainscot, the walls and ceiling are painted in shades of green.

No. 6 (Series of 1904, No. VI) June 1904

Roof: Hip with gable dormers   *Bedrooms:* 4   *Baths:* 1   *Cost:* $3,800   *Avery Plans:* 11 sheets dated 5/25/04 to 5/27/04 and 1 sheet dated 6/30/04

Essentially a foursquare design with the second floor built out over a recessed front porch, this house was recommended for a rural setting or a lot frontage of at least 50 feet. The walls reaching the sills of the first-story windows are red brick, as are the pillars that support the second story. The wooden band spanning the pillars is mortised and tenoned at the corners. The walls above the brick are sheathed with shingles of Washington cedar, or white pine, stained a rich nut brown. The roof is cedar stained "moss-green" and the windows and trim are stained the same green. The hip roof is pierced by a number of dormers to provide light and air to the second floor. Arguably not one of the best-looking houses that Stickley designed, the house still has excellent balance and proportion and the interior space is well designed.

Harry W. Hillman, the manager of the General Electric Company's electric heating department, selected this house design (top right)—with modifications to his order made by a Boston architect—to be the world's first all-electric house. Built in 1905 (top left, photo ca. 1920, and above in 2003) as Hillman's residence in the "GE Plot," an area near the company's Schenectady, New York, plant set aside for the homes of executives of the company, the home received worldwide publicity because it ran totally on electricity. Most houses of the day had one circuit for the whole house and that was used only for lighting. If any other electric device was used, it had to be plugged into a light fixture. The Hillman house was wired with baseboard outlets and the kitchen was fully electric. Electric heaters (called "luminous radiators") were in each room; an iron, sewing machine, aluminum hot plates, a broiler for cooking, and a refrigerator were in the kitchen; and a water heater and a washing machine were installed in the basement. The house did have a separate coal-fired back-up heating system for those cold upstate New York winters.[50] The floor plans were reversed and alterations made in the original plan, including the porch façade. Cedar was used instead of brick below the windowsills and porch, but the important horizontal line design element under the windowsills was maintained.

The magazine living room (right) "is paneled in oak wainscot to the height of six and a half feet and stained a rich nut-brown and the frieze is a stencil over tan colored canvas in brown, green and blue. The ceiling is cream-tinted plaster left rough and divided by oak beams." In the dining room on the other side of the staircase, "the walls are covered with yellow Japanese grass cloth and the floor throughout is stained dark green."

The Hillman house living room plans were altered (center). In addition to the reversal of the plans, the fireplace and the chimney were relocated to the exterior wall and flanked by windows. Oak, stained dark, was used on both the wainscoting and the ceiling beams.

The Craftsman rarely showed a bedroom illustration in the house articles. The walls of this one (below right) are Japanese grass cloth to the rail, and the plaster walls and ceiling above are stained "a warm tint."

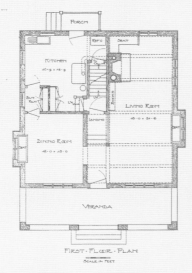

FIRST·FLOOR·PLAN
SCALE IN FEET

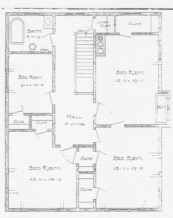

SECOND·FLOOR·PLAN
SCALE IN FEET

Craftsman House, Series of 1904, Number VIII. Plan of first floor

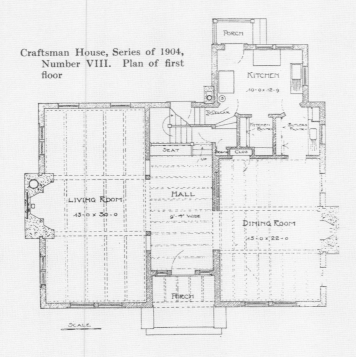

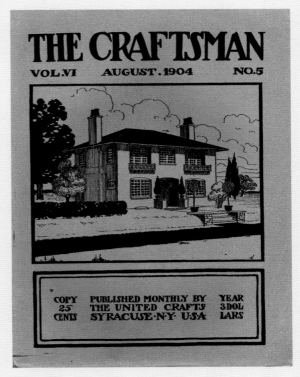

This house was considered important enough to feature it on the cover of the August 1904 *The Craftsman*.

Craftsman House, Series of 1904, Number VIII. Plan of second floor

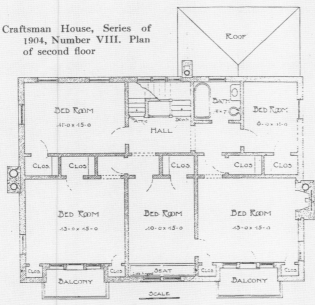

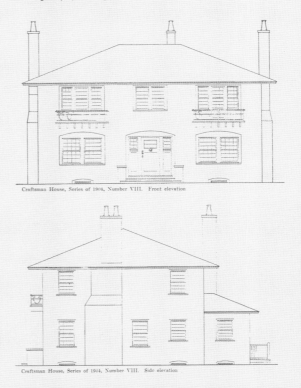

Craftsman House, Series of 1904, Number VIII. Front elevation

Craftsman House, Series of 1904, Number VIII. Side elevation

The excellent proportion and balance of the house is shown in the perspective drawing from *The Craftsman* (facing top). Two medical doctors, Dr. and Mrs. A. F. Strickler, built the home (facing above) in Sleepy Eye, Minnesota, in 1906—at a cost of $5,000, more than estimated in *The Craftsman*. It appears to be built according to the plans, except that no chimney and corresponding fireplaces were built on the right side of the house, the staircase was reversed to accommodate a lavatory on the landing to the cellar stairs, and the porch was expanded across the front of the home. The dining room size was reduced so that an office, which opened off the recessed entry, could be placed in the front of the house. The photo of the home is from a postcard, ca. 1920.

The excellent proportion and balance of the house are shown in this elevation drawing.

The wood trim in the living room (above left) is gumwood "treated with a solution of iron, by which it is given a soft green-brown color and a satin like texture." The floor is maple treated with the same solution. Canvas of a golden-ochre tint covers the walls, and the beamed ceiling has rough sand-finished plaster in the intervening spaces. The brick fireplace has a sweeping copper hood.

The Craftsman article pictured a detail of the entrance porch (above right).

The owners did not choose to install an expensive copper hood on the living room fireplace (right). The woodwork and coloring suggested in the article was carried out but in less detail.

Roof: Gable *Bedrooms:* 3 *Baths:* 1 *Cost:* $1,800 *Avery Plans:* 6 sheets (floor plans, elevation drawings, details)

This house is influenced by popular architectural designs being produced in England (as *The Craftsman* clearly states). The characteristic wide over-hanging eaves of a Craftsman Home are missing, but the sense of propor-tion—with the roof in a sweeping curve extending to cover the porch—is there. The frame of this house is covered in shingles left to weather naturally, while the roof is shingle too; it is stained a "moss-green." The remaining trim is painted creamy white.

The house's interior walls are all plaster tinted with watercolor, with Georgia pine floors except for the kitchen, pantry, and bath—these are painted and "stippled," and the floors are white maple. While wood trim is kept minimal to reduce the expense of the house, the living room trim is chestnut, finished with a light green stain. "The floor shows the same stain a tone or two darker, with the walls covered in golden brown Japanese grass cloth."

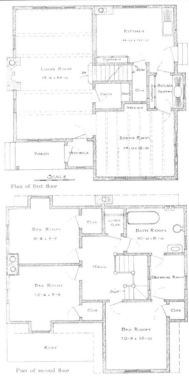

Plan of first floor

Plan of second floor

In *The Craftsman* of August 1907, Dr. Albert Soiland tells how he built this house (center left) in Los Angeles in 1905. The provided plans were used, except that a 12-foot-square kitchen "el" and servant's room was added to the right side at the rear, and a sleeping porch was placed on the addition roof. The extra windows in the attic disfigure the design, throwing off the balance achieved by Stickley. The house has not been located, and may have been an earthquake casualty. Building costs being higher than in the East, the house cost $4,000 including a small barn.

This home, of similar appearance (below left), was designed in England by architect Ralph Heaton and was pictured in *Das Englishe Haus*, published in 1910.

Roof: Cross gable   *Bedrooms:* 4 (walk-in closet)   *Baths:* 1   *Cost:* $7,200   *Avery Plans:* 8 sheets (floor plans, elevation drawings, details)

This house is influenced by the English cottage style. The first floor is faced in gray limestone and the overhanging second story is plaster over lath. There is a bowed bay window in the dining room; bay windows are not common in Stickley's designs, let alone curved ones. The proportion of the house is very well done with the light plaster on the second story hovering over the darker and smaller first story. Even the window shutters are used to balance the design.

An extensive description of the interior decoration accompanies the drawings for this house. Woodwork in the public rooms is all chestnut stained "a warm and lively gray" to blend with the gray limestone fireplace. The walls in the den are moss-green Craftsman canvas with nut-brown fumed[52] oak, and the fireplace is faced with bricks ranging in tone from deep red to light yellow. The kitchen and pantry area is finished in oak, left natural and varnished, and the floors are natural and oiled. The upper story has fireplaces in three of the four bedrooms. The two in the front bedrooms have Grueby-tile facing, while the other is finished in brick. The doors are stained as in the living room, but the woodwork is painted "old ivory." The rooms are treated in greens, yellows, and blues.

Craftsman House, Number IX., Series of 1904. Plan of first floor

Craftsman House, Number IX., Series of 1904. Plan of second floor

The dining room (left) is wainscoted in tongue-and-grove V-joint boards of gumwood stained gray. Above the 54-inch-high wainscot, the walls are plaster—tinted olive—and the ceiling between the shallow beams is tinted pale lemon green.

The sand-finished plaster in the living room (below) is stained a rich, deep red. The plaster ceiling is tinted cream and has shallow beams beside a half beam at the wall and ceiling joint. The curtains echo the ceiling color. The floors are oak, stained a deep, dark gray—to set off the vibrant colors of the suggested Donegal rugs of green, dull red, and yellow. Notice how the home is placed in its environment through the device of picturing the room with open doors—on an idyllic summer day.

No. 12 (Series of 1904, No. IXA) September 1904

Roof: Hipped with gable and shed dormers *Bedrooms:* 4 (or 3 and a den/study) *Baths:* 1 *Cost:* $1,400
Avery Plans: 3 sheets (floor plans, elevation drawings, details)

While this is a square (35 by 33 feet) house, it suggests an irregular floor plan. A series of gables and dormers that pierce the picturesque hip roof, a recessed porch, and a bay window and seat "break the box" and create a most interesting design. The rafters that support the second story also support the eaves of the roof, following the Arts and Crafts belief that the design is in the display of how the structure is built. The walls and roof are shingled, the former stained a light shade of brown and the latter left to "weather."

The plans show access from the porch to both living and dining rooms via doorways, but the perspective view shows a window instead of a door to the dining room—probably a better arrangement. This is an indication that often the plans for these homes were not finalized when they were published.

A stone fireplace dominates the beamed living room and adjacent to the room are a bedroom (or study perhaps), hall to the kitchen and bathroom, the staircase, and the dining room. The wall plaster throughout most of the ground floor "is left rough, under the float, and paneled by inch strips set against it; the plaster receiving a green stain of medium tone and the strips a somewhat darker color." The plaster in the dining room, however, is stained a "rich, warm brown." The floors are of unfinished white maple from 6 to 8 inches wide. Curtains are "linen showing at the bottom applied bands of dull red."

The three bedrooms on the second story are arranged around a hall, causing an irregular arrangement of the exterior dormers in the roof, which Stickley says is "attractive." The woodwork is pine treated with white shellac and the walls above the wide baseboards "have paper hangings in designs of gay stripes and flower motifs." The curtains should be of inexpensive muslin fabric.

The article concludes that this "cottage . . . can be made so distinctive and artistic that the luxury of cost will be forgotten in the harmony created by structural lines, concordant colors and a strict observance of proportion in all things."

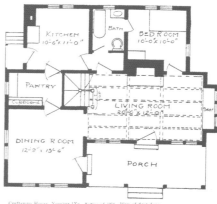

Craftsman House, Number IXa., Series of 1904. Plan of first floor.

Craftsman House, Number IXa., Series of 1904. Plan of second floor.

No. 13 (Series of 1904, No. X) October 1904

Roof: Gable *Bedrooms:* 4 (6 with servants' rooms) *Baths:* 3 1/2 *Cost:* $13,600 *Avery Plans:* 9 sheets (floor plans, elevation drawings, details)

An excellent design, this is the only Craftsman Home to get a color perspective drawing plate in the magazine, and this plate only hints, with the printing technology of the time, at the colors desired. The house is a large one, yet is designed with only four bedrooms. The master bedroom takes up one whole end of the house and includes a dressing room and private bath. There are, in addition, a den (workroom), billiard room, two servants' rooms, and an elevator! This plan is larger than any house designed in the series thus far.

Stickley proposes that the house be located on a lot no smaller than 80 by 150 feet. A white-painted pergola wraps around three sides of the house, anchors it to the land, and emphasizes the horizontal lines of the structure. At the center in front of the entrance, the pergola widens and is covered with a roof. The first story is built up with cobblestone, the rough face of the

The Craftsman uses a color plate to show this house (above right). Modified by Stickley, the home was built in 1912 (center) for S. Hazen Bond in Washington, D.C., at the highest point in the district. "Dumblane," named from Robert Tannahill's lines to "The Flower of Dumblane," faced west with views as far as the Shenandoah Mountains. Tapestry brick, advertised in *The Craftsman,* was used for the exterior sheathing of the house. The large dormer of the 1904 house design was replaced with one that matched the other shed-roof dormers. Bond had a personal friendship with Stickley, and Gustav stayed in the home when he visited Washington on business.[55] In this 2005 photo (right), it can be seen that the tile roof and wisteria-covered pergola survive, but the beautiful tapestry brick has been painted white. Sadly, the property was subdivided and houses are 50 feet from the front door of the home.

The 1904 version of the living room is shown in a color plate (top left). This is a large room—8 by 27 feet—that uses the complete end of the building and thus gets light from three sides. The ceiling is beamed. The fireplace is surrounded by 6-inch-square green Grueby tiles set flush with the wall, with a forest scene in tiles set proportionally above the hearth.[53] Flanking the fireplace are full-length windows that open to the terrace. And flanking the windows are built-in bookcases. There is a large window seat along one side of the room. The woodwork is chestnut fumed to a medium gray. The walls are colored "soft green" and the curtains are a yellow linen "figured in a pattern of rose and green." By 1912 the living room in the Bond home (top right) has evolved from the 1904 ideas into a large, but standard, Craftsman room with a tapestry brick fireplace. Bond filled his home with Craftsman furniture. In this 2005 photo (above), the home's interior survives almost intact, except for missing light fixtures sold in the 1980s and the painted fireplace.

fractured stone facing outward. The shingles that cover the second story and above are stained moss green. The wooden roof shingles are stained gray brown, as is the finished woodwork, including the window and doorframes and the front door. The chimneys are made of the same cut cobbles, carried up to a red sandstone cap, with red tile chimney pots. The windows are all of the casement type, with fixed transoms filled with leaded stained-glass designs. Stickley must have been very proud of this house, as he publishes three color plates showing the exterior, and one view each of the living room and the dining room.

Descriptions for the first-floor rooms are found with the illustrations. Except for the doors, which are chemically treated hazelwood, the woodwork on the second floor is painted an "old ivory" enamel. The master bedroom and bath again have shades of green and yellow as their primary colors. The other bath is finished in pale blue, as is one bedroom. Suggested colors for the other bedrooms are warm yellows (with green accents) and old rose, with a deep cream ceiling.

An extensive article, "Dumblane, A Southern Craftsman Home," featuring a home built by S. Hazen Bond in Washington, D.C., in 1912, was published in the February 1913 issue of *The Craftsman*. While Bond included almost every modern convenience found in the advertising pages of *The Craftsman*, including a whole-house vacuum system and the special Craftsman-designed heating fireplaces, he did not build the elevator. The bed-

room arrangements on the second floor were changed (see floor plan comparisms on page 137), the large walk-in closet of 1904 became a sleeping porch, and five bedrooms (one could be a sitting room) were created instead of four. One of the three bathrooms was also eliminated. Bond also had the garage designed by Stickley, and it included a shop where he constructed furniture for the house and also some of the metalwork and light fixtures. Bond loved the house so much that he personally had pamphlets printed describing the house and containing photos from *The Craftsman* article.

In 2003 this adaptation of the 1904 house (top) was built in Poplar Grove, Indiana. It is not as large as the original design and the interior floor plans were altered extensively. The Adams house (above), designed by Chicago architect Robert Spencer and built in Indianapolis, Indiana, may have been the inspiration for Stickley's home.[54] If Stickley did copy Spencer, he improved the design with the proportional and balanced dormers and the wraparound pergola.

Stickley also loved the design of Bond's home and had the Craftsman Architects produced a "mini-Dumblane" for readers—Craftsman House No. 153 of February 1913 (see page 451).

The dining room colors can be gleaned from the 1904 color plate in *The Craftsman* (top left). "The dining room has low panel wainscoting carried up to the top of the built-in sideboard; otherwise the room is in the same colors as the living room." In Bond's home the 1904 plan was generally carried out (above), but the three high casement windows were replaced with a stained-glass window above the sideboard (top right)—an adaptation of a Harvey Ellis design that appeared in a dining room in one of his 1903 home concepts. While there were some Craftsman lights, Bond built most of the light fixtures in his garage shop. The room, pictured in 2005, is filled with Stickley re-issue furniture.

The large brick fireplace in the hall (left) features a hammered copper hood with the motto "Each Man's Chimney Is His Golden Milestone," a hood very similar to those at Craftsman Farms.

The dining room (left) features a "marvelous fireplace with the entire chimneybreast in glass-mosaic, showing a tree motif. The motif features a flat-toned gray background with the large trees showing bright orange fruit hanging in shades of green foliage, the small trees in tones of violet surrounded with a border in yellow, tans and varying green." The walls are again tinted the ivory tone above the molding, and below to the baseboard a gray-green burlap is applied. The curtains are homespun linen with a little golden brown introduced to the hem. The "glaring light" of a chandelier is dispensed with and artificial light comes from wall sconces and candlelight at the table. In the Westchester house (below), the dining room fireplace were not built.

Roof: Gable *Bedrooms:* 4 *Baths:* 1 *Cost:* $6,000 *Avery Plans:* 5 sheets (floor plans, elevation drawings, details)

A mix of English- and Prairie School–design influences the final house offered in 1904. Perhaps the designer was familiar with Frank Lloyd Wright's Nathan house in Oak Park, Illinois. This structure required a lot frontage of at least 70 feet. There is a large entrance hall that separates the living and dining rooms. The tall window on the right side of the façade lights the staircase that is located off the hall. That window is unusual for Stickley, whose designs are normally well-balanced; the small arched cellar window below attempts, rather unsuccessfully, to restore an asymmetrical balance. The plans and perspective illustration do not quite agree, as the latter appears to show the large staircase window as a shallow bay window, yet the plans do not.

The exterior (above right) is built with red, black, and brown "clinker" bricks laid with a green—"almost black—mortar to the bottom of the second story windows." The windowsills and lintels are also brick. Above the brick the walls are roughcoat plaster tinted green and un-planed cypress timbering. Before the plaster is dry, a brush with the same green but darkened pigment is used to produce random "splotches" of darker tones on the wall surface. All exposed woodwork is treated with Cabot's No. 302, very dark moss green stain, while the roof, also of cypress shingles, is treated with Cabot's 303 moss-green stain. Two chimneys flank each end of the home built out from the walls—the one providing a shallow inglenook recess in the living room.

In the living room (center) terra-cotta shade canvas is applied to the walls, and the frieze above the door height is the same color as the old ivory-tinted roughcoat plaster ceilings. The curtains are thin corn-colored Japanese silk and blue cushions are placed in the inglenook. Note how the curved lintel and the curved sides of the benches frame and enclose the inglenook.

CRAFTSMAN HOUSE, NUMBER XII, SERIES OF 1904. PLAN OF FIRST FLOOR

CRAFTSMAN HOUSE, NUMBER XII, SERIES OF 1904. PLAN OF SECOND FLOOR

142

1905

The Craftsman Architects continued to produce one, sometimes two, and occasionally up to four homes a month target-
ing almost every economic class. The designs continued to be
eclectic and aimed at various regional areas of the nation.
A total of seventeen houses were offered in 1905.

Roof: Hipped *Bedrooms:* 3 *Baths:* 1 *Cost:* $10,800 *Avery Plans:* None

This house is strongly influenced by an early Prairie School design by Frank Lloyd Wright. His 1896–97 Isidore H. Heller house in Chicago, Illinois, is a three-story structure that also shows some of the decorative influences of Louis Sullivan. After mainly featuring suburban houses, this is Stickley's first urban house for a limited frontage lot. Despite the narrow space, the home gets plenty of light and air.

All the dressed exterior stonework is gray limestone. "Above the foundation, the exterior walls are entirely of brick; from the water table to the limestone belt just below the third story windows, [the house is] faced with dark red 'Bradford' brick (No. 00), laid in English bond and in dark mortar with narrow joints, full pointed, with which ruddy tone the door and window sills and lintels of limestone contrast agreeably in color. The wall of the third story is covered with cement, which, rough in texture and of a gray tone much lighter than the stone belt-courses above and below it, modulates between the red brick and the cornice, which is of wood, stained brown-green (Cabot's 302), as is also all other exposed woodwork of the building. The cornice is supported by modillions piercing the plaster at regular intervals, and affording a

Frank Lloyd Wright's Heller house (above), located in Chicago, may have served as an inspiration for this Craftsman Home (right). Photo from the 1911 Wasmuth Portfolio.

pleasing play of light and shadow; while the roof is designed to be covered with shingles stained like the remainder of the exterior wood work."

Throughout the first floor the woodwork is of oak—quartersawn for the principal rooms and plain oak for the kitchen area (fumed to a light tone of brown, with the walls painted in a rich shade of yellow). The floors are also oak-fumed to a rich warm brown. The hall of the second floor is also in oak. Two of the bedrooms use hazel-wood trim and the third (in the rear) is finished in gray maple. The front bedroom trim is treated with a solution of iron to a warm gray tone. "The walls are done in fawn-brown, and the ceiling is tinted to a rich cream; while the fireplace is built of dull yellow bricks, slightly deeper in tint than the ceiling." The third floor is trimmed in Carolina pine, painted white, with the doors and the floors of Georgia pine stained slightly green.

PLAN OF FIRST FLOOR

PLAN OF SECOND FLOOR

The dining room walls (above left) are "covered with blue gray burlap, stenciled in a design of royal blue, picked out with orange. The fire-place is faced in dull yellow tiles, and the ceiling is tinted to a warm cream." The window transoms are stained glass, in "a pome-granate motif in green and yellow," with dull yellow India silk curtains. In the living room (left) the walls are covered with Spanish leather in a gray-green finish. Light from the windows in the front, which also feature stained-glass transoms, reflects "upon the soft, ruddy surface of the copper hood of the chimney-piece," with its "interesting hammered design." The ceiling has a cream tint with a "slight touch of red" added. "Soft green and old-rose colors" are in the leaded-glass bookcase doors.

Roof: Gable with shed dormer *Bedrooms:* 3 *Baths:* 1 *Cost:* $2,600.00 *Avery Plans:* None

This quintessential Arts and Crafts bungalow is a suburban residence, which, "should be retired some distance from the street, and surrounded with large trees, such as might remain upon the site of an old apple orchard; since their gnarled trunks and low, spreading foliage would bring the building into harmony with the landscape." It has all the no-frills basics under a sweeping English cottage-style roof and wrapped around a central hearth.

The "first story [is] built of split field cobbles, laid in black mortar, with slightly raked-out joints; while the second story and the roof are covered with shingles, their un-planed side exposed, and stained to a moss green by the use of Cabot's 303; the same preparation being applied to the window 'trim,' the front entrance door, and all other exterior woodwork."

The descriptions of the décor of the rooms are vivid and detailed for such a simple home. In the hall and the living room a wide baseboard is used, with paper hangings in old yellow approaching a terra-cotta quality; the frieze being slightly darker than the side walls and showing a stenciled design in brick red, gray, and dark blue, while the ceiling is tinted to a light cream shade. The living room fireplace is built of "arch brick," and flanked at the right by a seat, which is fitted to the corner and follows the side of the room to the hall entrance. Above the seat, a wide band of gray-green leather is fixed to the wall with copper-headed nails, and the same

John and Mary Cone built this design (top) in a suburb of Hartford, Connecticut, shortly after it was published. Cone was an executive for Aetna Insurance Company, and the house may have been one of several that were built by the company for their executives. Its sylvan setting on a large lot is exactly what Stickley called for and it was built very close to the original plans. The first-floor exterior stonework was replaced with wood shingles (above). The solarium may be original or added at a later time. The house as built is slightly larger than the Craftsman plan as each room is about one foot larger in each dimension.

tone of green is repeated in the canvas covering the cushions, which are embroidered in an appliqué design of russet, terra-cotta, and rich blue. The same colors are once more shown in the rug, green heightened by a band of terra-cotta appearing in the portieres of canvas, and a cream tint in the plain lace net window curtains.

In the dining room a "pleasing color-effect is assured by the warm green wainscoting, with very wide stiles and narrow panels, which is carried around the room to the height of the mantel. The frieze shows a background like the body of the wall, stenciled in light yellow, terra cotta and black, while the green is repeated in the cushions and pillows of the window seat. The fireplace also differs from that of the living room—in this instance showing 'arch bricks' of varying shades below, and a plastered front above the shell, which is made of heavy board." In the second story, the trim is "whitewood."

The bedrooms are each treated differently: the principal room is treated in yellows and greens: "the walls and frieze in light shades of yellow; the rug in deep yellow and spring verdure shades; while cream-white appears in the ceiling and in the window curtains of point d'esprit lace." The rear bedroom has walls in rich iris blue. The ceiling should be tinted to a light cream, and an iris design, in blues and greens, used in the covering of the window seat. The small bedroom is of sea blue and green tones: "a deep turquoise shade appearing in the design of the Japanese matting, with other carefully graded effects in the wall paper and the cotton crepe covering of the cushions accompanying the wicker furniture." The woodwork is painted white. The bath is also treated in white and blue, the latter in "the Delft shades. The walls are covered with 'Sanitas' of a simple tile design, with which the rug agrees in pattern and color. The floor used throughout the second story is comb grained pine, while the kitchen floor is laid in Georgia pine, stained to a light green."

The fireplace mantels in the living and dining rooms match the ones published in the illustrations in *The Craftsman*, but they were switched! Perhaps it was simply an error by

the construction workers. Stickley's concept (above left) was followed in the Cone house living room (above right)—note the reversed V-shaped wood trim above the portal.

Roof: Cross Hip *Bedrooms:* 3 *Baths:* 1 *Cost:* $2,000 *Avery Plans:* None

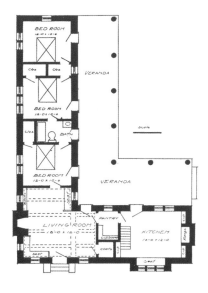

Here Stickley offers an inexpensive getaway home—a theme he returns to over the years. This "house in the wood" finds later expression in the structures planned for his Craftsman Farms. It is a nice house with an interesting L-shaped plan that is probably derived from the "ranch" homes in the Southwest. "This is a structure of fieldstones set at random, and, with their weather stains and accretions, offering pleasing variations of color." It is provided with wide verandas arranged to front a lake and to have a southern and western exposure The eastern bedroom wing "extends into the wooded portion of the land, where the trees provide protection and coolness," while the western wing is in a clearing, hopefully with lake views.

Spruce shingles, "dipped in oil, and laid wide to the weather," cover the roof. The entrance steps and veranda floor are of split cobbles laid in cement, while the columns are tree trunks, left with some short limbs "in order to afford conveniences for the suspension of fishing tackle and other implements."

Inside, the living room ceiling is traversed by a great beam, with smaller ones upon either side and running at right angles to it, "all rough hewn, and having one side flat, on which to rest the ceiling boards, and their ends squared, so as to provide good joints."

The living room woodwork, including the open bookcases and movable furniture, is cypress stained a gray-brown. The kitchen is a large room for both cooking and serving meals when the open-air dining room in the niche portion of the veranda cannot be used. The attic may be used for storage or additional sleeping rooms. In the bedroom wing, the walls are plastered and may be papered or tinted with watercolor.

It is interesting to note that the elevation drawings, including the side elevation (above), show eyebrow windows in the roof, while the perspective drawing (top) does not.

No. 19 (Series of 1905, No. IIIA) March 1905

Roof: Gable with a gable dormer *Bedrooms:* 3 *Baths:* 1 *Cost:* $900 *Avery Plans:* 2 sheets (floor plans, elevation drawings, details)

The first of four inexpensive homes featured as full-page all-in-one plates in the magazine, this house is a Cape style with a sweeping roof that looks like a bungalow—an inviting, practical and simple home. The foundation of this house is built of rubble; the walls are shingled and stained to a moss green (Stickley calls for Cabot's 303 stain), "a practical manner of building assuring economical heating; since the shingles, when laid over building paper, offer a thick protection against cold and draughts." All the exterior woodwork—shingles, and door and window-casings are "given a single color with the view of producing a monotone effect."

The wood trim and floors are stained a warm brown, "the walls being covered with either paper, paint, or tinted plaster, and the 'trim' being of cypress for the first, and poplar for the second story."

THE LIVING ROOM

No. 20 (Series of 1905, No. IIIB) March 1905

Roof: Gable with a shed dormer   *Bedrooms:* 3   *Baths:* 1   *Cost:* $1,000.   *Avery Plans:* None

In this second inexpensive house, the foundation is also of rubble stone, and the exterior walls are "faced with shingles stained to a gray-green; thus offering an agreeable background for the grass-green door and window casings.

"The entry gives access to both living room and kitchen, the former of which is made attractive by an ample arch brick fireplace, at the left of which there is an ingle seat piled high with pillows. The side opposite the fireplace is occupied by a window-seat flanked with bookcases; the windows above the seat being mullioned, glazed with square panes, and hung with cream-white curtains. A wainscot of V-jointed boards of uneven width, with a simple flat heading and base, is carried around the room on a level with the mantelshelf and the tops of the bookcases. The wood trim and the floors are stained to a warm brown; the walls are tinted or papered in gray-green, and topped by a paper frieze in green, golden yellow and cream; the ceiling is a deep shade of the latter color; and the floor is covered with green grass-matting, or a plain Ingrain rug." The kitchen extends the entire depth of the house and also is planned for use as a dining room, "after the manner of the old-time Dutch kitchens."

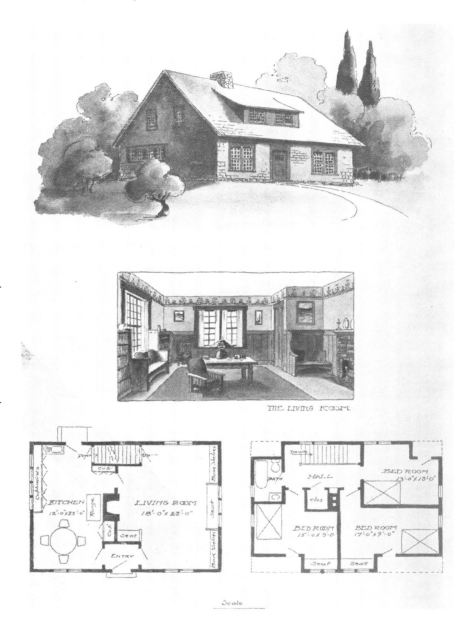

THE LIVING ROOM

No. 21 (Series of 1905, No. IV) April 1905

Roof: Gable *Bedrooms:* 4 *Baths:* 1 *Cost:* $5,000 *Avery Plans:* 6 sheets (floor plans, elevation drawings, details)

Designed to fit on a corner lot, this substantial and roomy suburban house is built of shingles over a brick first story. It is a sophisticated building that looks deceptively simple. Again, Stickley's sense of proportion shines through with an asymmetrical design that looks at first glance to be symmetrical. The second-floor overhanging box bay window balances with the first floor side bay window nicely, and the banding created by the use of different materials on each story keeps the profile of the house low, capped with the simple gable roof. It should be noted that the second story cantilevers slightly over the first, allowing shadows to provide interesting effects, as well as slightly increasing the size of the rooms on the second floor.

The first story is "of arch brick in red color varying from deep red to almost black. The medium dark bricks having the peculiar bluish tones brought out by their being slightly burned—while the hard burned ones are soft black. The shingles of both the second story and roof are of cypress—as is also all the exterior woodwork. All is stained a dark gray. Cypress when treated in this way has, in certain lights, a silver sheen, while in other lights it is a soft, dark gray and almost black, and is only improved by the weather."

At the left of the hall is the living room; its size accentuated by two large beams spanning its width, and by the inglenook, having a fireplace with seats and bookcases on either side. The dining room features a sideboard recessed into the bay window. The kitchen opens upon the veranda "where there is ample room for outdoor dining.

"The second floor hall is well lighted and has a long seat backed by the stair balustrade . . . making a very comfortable lounging place. The woodwork and walls are the same as in the hall below. The bedrooms are all done in cream white enameled woodwork, with walls tinted or papered, the colors varying with the exposure."

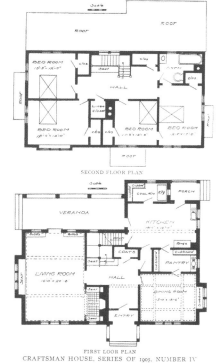

SECOND FLOOR PLAN

FIRST LOOR PLAN
CRAFTSMAN HOUSE, SERIES OF 1905, NUMBER IV

Roof: Hip with shed dormers   *Bedrooms:* 2   *Baths:* 1   *1906 Cost:* $1,000   *Avery Plans:* 2 sheets (floor plans, elevation drawings, details)

This home, with Number 23, continues the series of inexpensive cottages offered in March 1905. Stickley adds: "Originally designed as Cottage Homes for the Workman, [they] are equally suited for summer homes in the country, or at the shore. Each of the four designs is in itself a careful study to combine the essentials of a modest and home-like dwelling, with grace of outline and attractive interior arrangement, and each, if properly constructed, would be a comfortable home for a small family, a place to live in and be happy under one's own roof, with a door yard and garden, and the inviting companionship of the soil, for the children of the family, instead of the brick walls and asphalt pavement of the crowded city."

This Voysey-influenced, picturesque little "Hansel and Gretel" cottage "is of plaster, with a shingled roof; having a wide overhanging and rather striking entrance porch, whose strongly bracketed roof affords protection for the terrace. This is laid on metal lath nailed to furring, which is put on over the sheathing. Enough color pigment should be added to the plaster walls to tone it a soft shade of écru, although by leaving it the natural gray color a slight saving could be made in the cost. While still wet the finishing coat of plaster is roughened with a broom, which makes an interesting surface. The roof shingles are stained a rich brown color, as is all of the exposed woodwork, with the exception of the front

THE KITCHEN

THE LIVING ROOM

A CRAFTSMAN COTTAGE

door, which is stained grass green. The chimney, which is built of brick, is treated with a coat of plaster."

In the living room a simple wainscot of V-jointed boards is carried around the room and forms a back for the built-in seats. "The fireplace is of arch brick and here we introduce a feature which is one of the best inventions of the day, that of the Jackson Grate, which is to all appearances a grate of the ordinary type—but which has connected with it hot air pipes which carry heat to the bathroom and bedrooms above." (This idea intrigued Stickley enough that in later years he marketed his own "Craftsman Fireplace.") The

woodwork throughout the first floor is of cypress stained dark gray. "The walls of the kitchen are painted in a medium tone of buff, or yellow ochre softened with a little burnt sienna, and the ceiling deep cream. In the living room a scheme of green is carried out. The walls are papered a rich moss green and the ceiling and frieze tinted a deep cream. Rag rugs for the floor are of plain green with dashes of yellow and brick red."

The wood trim of the second floor is of poplar stained soft green. The walls are papered in simply designed wallpapers, or tinted and left plain. The bath has its walls painted a deep cream tint.

About 1906, in a somewhat modified form, 16-year-old architect Leonard Willeke took this house design and built it (his first house) for his sister near Cincinnati, Ohio. Indications of the aniline green stain in the woodwork still survive. This house is proportionally a bit higher than Stickley's concept.

Roof: Hipped   *Bedrooms:* 3   *Baths:* 1   *Cost:* $1,000   *Avery Plans:* None

If Number 22 is cute and comfortable looking, Number 23 is boxy and plain—a square box with a porch added. It is not really a cottage, but a very small foursquare designed to occupy a narrow lot. The exterior is sheathed in cypress boards, the cracks covered with narrow battens. A stain is applied over the exterior, which gives a "dark gray effect with reflected tones of silver, suggesting the weathered effect occasionally seen on pieces of unfinished wood . . . exposed to the sun and rain."

The foundation of the house is of field rubble, and the chimney of red brick, all of which are "designed to blend with Nature's surroundings." The window sashes are all painted white and are mullioned with small panes in the upper sash and large ones below. The fireplace of red arch brick is fitted with the "Jackson Grate," which heats two rooms on the second floor.

Throughout the first story the wood trim is of Carolina pine stained a warm brown color. The kitchen walls and ceiling are painted and the living room can be papered or the plaster tinted.

On the second floor the largest sleeping room and the bathroom receive heat from the living room fireplace. The wood trim throughout the second story is of poplar painted white. "This gives the general effect of white enamel which always lends itself to tasteful treatments for sleeping rooms."

THE KITCHEN

THE LIVING ROOM

A CRAFTSMAN COTTAGE

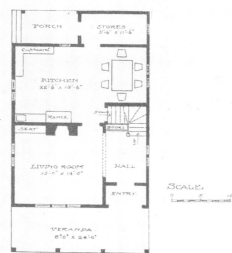

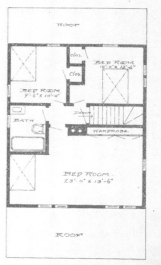

Roof: Gable with shed dormers *Bedrooms:* 4 *Baths:* 1 *Cost:* $2,300 *Avery Plans:* 5 sheets (floor plans, elevations, details, and section through house)

Its wide sweeping roof cleverly gives this full two-story house a single-story look, and the proportional bands of windows add to the design. This house may have been influenced by some of the homes being built in the Arts and Crafts community of Rose Valley, Pennsylvania, by Will Price. It has been planned that its "exposure and arrangement will 'let the sunshine in'; to leave no space reserved for the habitual gloom of the old fashioned country parlor. Spacious and inviting in all its appointments, it is intended for a home in the country, to live in and to enjoy, and to let Nature play her part in lending cheer and health and comfort to all within its walls."

The house is built with a wooden frame "plastered with cement, 'rough cast,' which is unimpaired by extremes of temperature and is interesting in texture and color, the latter varying from dead white to creamy yellow. The roof is of spruce shingles, with their natural reddish color intensified by a Venetian red stain, and the exterior wood work is stained a rich olive green, toning almost into yellow."

The foundations and chimneys should be of split field rubble. "At the entrance is a small terrace laid up of field stone and cement, the sides of

The plans at Avery Library show a version of the house different than the house published in *The Craftsman* and later in *Craftsman Homes*. Instead of three dormers in the front, the house has one long dormer. There is no known explanation for this discrepancy.

FRONT ELEVATION.

CRAFTSMAN

The Harry Acly home (page 155 and this page) in Pittsfield , Massachusetts, was built about 1916 from this plan. Acly was employed by the General Electric Company. His home followed the plans provided, except that the center dormer was enlarged to match the other dormers (wisely—the house has better balance and symmetry), the kitchen was placed in the large storeroom area and a separate dining room was located in the area where the plans called for the kitchen. Some of the woodwork and built-in furniture was not installed—or may have since been removed, as the early photos show that casement windows were originally installed in the rear of the living room and these have been replaced by full double-hung windows. The second-floor hall seat area was turned into a second bathroom. Acly and his wife lived in their home about forty years before retiring.

In the rear of the Acly home (above), where the ground slopes away, an internal garage (rare in Craftsman Homes) was built in the basement area. The rear porch was screened in this early photo, and was later enclosed completely.

The Craftsman says: "At the rear of the house [right] is a veranda intended for use both summer and winter, as it is enclosed on three sides by the walls of the house and so . . . may be entirely glassed in across the front—making a sun parlor to attract all the warmth and light of a winter day."

which are raised so as to hold wooden boxes planted with scarlet geraniums. A large climbing rose should shelter one side, and the other should be covered by the luxuriant growth of a bitter-sweet vine, whose brilliant berries yield delight long after the frosts have come and its leaves have fallen. The importance of these accessories is seen the moment the front door is opened, for the broad hall to which it gives entrance leads straight through the house to the veranda, and the first glimpse is of a vista of sky, vines and trees. Even in winter, when branches are bare and the sky is gray, this arcade effect loses nothing of the exhilarating feeling it gives of light, freedom and open space. The sensation of warmth and color is felt in the hall itself, for the walls are done in yellow brown, not too dark in tone, with a frieze of old rose in which there are suggestions of yellow." The ceiling is in deep cream, and all the woodwork is of chestnut finished with a grayish-brown stain.

"The floors of both hall and living room are of oak boards of uneven width, laid with plain butt joints (not tongued and grooved), and the rugs should be of gray-green with plenty of warm red and brown for color accent. At the windows should be straight hanging sash curtains of cream color, hemstitched or fagoted with faded rose."

At the left of the hall is the large combination kitchen and dining room. "The walls of the kitchen are wainscoted about four-and-a-half feet high, and above this the walls are covered with cream colored 'Sanitas' in

a simple tile pattern. The ceiling is treated with a coat of paint lighter in tone than the wall. The woodwork is all of brown ash, finished with a light green stain, which allows the warm tones of the wood to show through. The floor is of maple, tongued and grooved. The windows are double hung, over which are hung thin white curtains of dotted mull."

The upper hall is treated in the same way as the big hall below. At the end of the hall is the bath, "done in white enamel as to woodwork, with walls wainscoted to the height of four-and-a-half feet, and buff 'Sanitas' above." The woodwork of the bedrooms is all in poplar. "Assuming that

the front exposure of the house is east, the color scheme might be carried out as follows: The northeast room in brown woodwork, rose-tinted or papered walls, cream ceiling, rose and green rugs. The northwest room in gray woodwork, tan walls, white ceiling and rugs introducing browns, tans and greens. The two south rooms having the warm exposure can be in cooler colors; the woodwork in green stain, and for the front room a scheme of old blues. The back one may be in soft gray-greens with cream ceilings. The floors throughout are of comb-grain pine."

FIRST FLOOR PLANS

In the living room (above) as conceived by Stickley "the ceiling . . . is beamed with gray-finished chestnut. The plaster has a natural gray sand finish. The fireplace is formed of field rubble in tones of brown, red and gray. The wall panels are stenciled with a simple tree motif done in strong green, brown and creamy yellow" to which a hint of red has been added.

The two early exterior photos (see pages 155–156) show casement windows to the left of the Acly fireplace just like the illustration in *The Craftsman*. Those windows have since been replaced by larger double-hung windows, and if there was wainscoting and built-in bookcases, they have been removed. The Avery Library plans show a tile fireplace surround. Acly's fireplace follows the concept pictured in the magazine (right).

A view of the Acly center hall and staircase looking into the living room beyond (facing above left). The built-in china cabinet in the Acly's dining room still features hand-hammered copper hardware (facing above right), and if not a product of the Craftsman Workshops, the hardware is copied after his work. *The Craftsman* article illustrated the original concept of a combined kitchen and dining room (facing below).

Roof: Cross gable *Bedrooms:* 7 *Baths:* 3 1/2 *Cost:* $12,000 *Avery Plans:* 8 sheets (floor plans, elevations, exterior sections, details)

This is one of Stickley's best large house designs. "We feel that we have come a step nearer to those ideals for which *The Craftsman* stands." This house must have been appreciated and built somewhere, but no example has been found. "Its construction is a simple balloon frame, sheathed and steel-lathed and then covered with cement plaster of the natural color, or slightly darkened. The exposed wood-work of the frame, stained dark green, contrasts" with the dark red color of the roof shingles.

The cement terrace is covered with a pergola. "The shadows of the recess [and] the flicker of sunlight through the vines, will afford chang-ing pictures of suggestive beauty." The pergola columns are stained green, and the split field rubble used for the foundation of the terrace should be laid up in black mortar, slightly raked out. "Balconies with their wrought iron railings; the generously over-hanging eaves, frankly exposing the structural work; the broad dormer window; and the three chimneys of split rubble crowned with red chim-ney pots" are highlights of the design. The windows are all double-hung sash. The kitchen woodwork is hard pine colored a light green.

"The woodwork of the hall and corridor on both stories is of white quartered oak, colored greenish brown, and the walls are tinted a deep cream. The servant's room is finished in hard pine, colored to a nut-brown."

Stickley wrote about the house above: "One of the most attractive features of this house is at the rear. It consists of a court, or patio, enclosed on three sides, with a generous pergola, which will be just the thing to allure the family to a meal out-of-doors. We Americans have not yet given ourselves the joy of as much out-door life as we might easily have, were we so minded. When out-door life can be added to our staid American customs, without exposing us to the gaze of the outside world, or adding extra labor to the servants of the household, it is a novelty highly to be desired. The court is built of split rubble with solid cement floor."

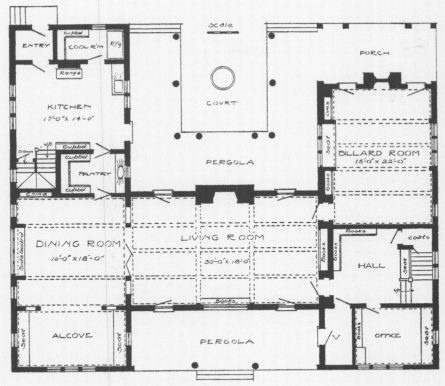

CRAFTSMAN HOUSE. SERIES OF 1905. NUMBER VI. FIRST FLOOR PLANS

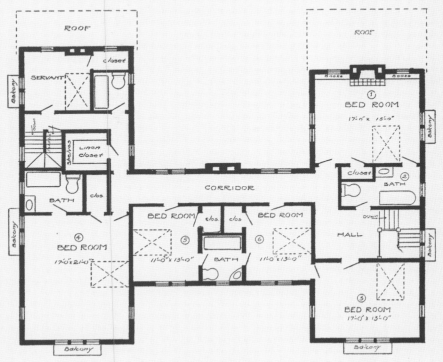

CRAFTSMAN HOUSE. SERIES OF 1905. NUMBER VI. SECOND FLOOR PLANS

Stickley's published floor plan provided reference numbers for each room. The bedroom (1) woodwork is of ivory enamel, with the rest of the walls "tinted a pale gray green with a pattern frieze arrangement of leaf forms and berries in tones of golden yellows, deeper greens and a touch of heliotrope above. The floor and doors are of hard comb grained pine, colored this same green." The ceiling is of cream. Pale yellow rag rugs are on the floor. The window curtains are of "white Swiss." The fireplace is faced with deep green, mat-finish Grueby tiles. The bathroom (2), as are all the bathrooms, is floored and wainscoted with white tiling. The woodwork and doors are the same as in the bedroom.

The woodwork of bedroom (3) is also of ivory enamel, "with a silvery blue tint for the walls. The curtains are of figured linen, with cream ground and a poppy motif in pink and greens similar to the one used in the billiard room." The ceiling is white; the doors and floor of this room are of hard comb grained pine, colored "delicate greenish gray."

Bedroom (4) has doors and trim of poplar, colored "a grayish tint with the color of the wood showing through. The walls are covered with quaint figured paper, white ground with a scattered flower pattern in faded yellows and gray greens. The ceiling is white, brought down to form a dado. The curtains are of sheer linen lawn, hemstitched in yellow. The floor is covered with Japanese matting in silver green." The wood trim and doors of the other bedrooms (5 & 6) are of hard pine colored a golden-gray. The walls are papered in a two-toned paper—"a shadowy yellow background with pattern in a somewhat deeper tone." The window curtains are of "homespun with quaint cross-stitched pattern in yellow and sage green." The matting is of natural un-dyed grass.

Stickley lavished a color plate (above) on the living room of this special home. The plate is an excellent example of Stickley's interior color palette. The room is symmetrical in all its appointments. A large redbrick fireplace with hand-wrought copper hood occupies the center, flanked on either side with large doors that access the terrace. These doors are directly in line with windows on the opposite side of the room. Allowing cross-ventilation in moderate weather. The high wainscot of oak in the living room is colored to a greenish brown. The wall tone is a soft gray tan, suggested by the lighter markings of the wood, with a stencil pattern introducing rich russets, clear greens, and a hint of old blue and orange. The rug is a gray green, repeating the hint of green in the woodwork. The ceiling is rough un-tinted plaster (whoever drew the color plate did not read the description! Bad editorial coordination— probably the plate was hand colored without reference to the accompanying article).

Bedroom No. 1 (right) is pictured with a cozy chair pulled up to the fireplace. The text says this room's trim is painted ivory, but the illustration implies a dark stain or paint.

The woodwork of the largest bedroom (above), like all the upstairs woodwork, is of poplar, and in this room it is finished in white enamel. The doors are stained a dark green, "but thinly, so as to allow the natural wood effect to show as much as possible, and the floor is stained green to match the doors." The panels above the wainscot are of Japanese grass cloth in "light, cool green, verging almost upon an old-gold in tone." The frieze is cream-hued and the ceiling white. "The curtains are of white homespun, with double appliquéd hem in soft old blue. The rug is of gray rag, with white warp and stripes of old blue to match the draperies."

When Feldman sold the house with all its furnishings, the wife of the new owner hated the Stickley furniture and had it all sold or given away in Mexico. The dining room pieces, including the built-ins, were retained, but wood-carvers were brought in from across the border to carve designs on the furniture. While the movable furniture has since disappeared, the built-ins remain. The sideboard now has ornate carving wrapped around the Stickley hardware (left).

Roof: Gable with shed dormers *Bedrooms:* 5 *Baths:* 1 *Cost:* $5,200 *Avery Plans:* 7 sheets (floor plans, elevation drawings, details)

This house relies on a saltbox shape, the asymmetry of the porch on the right, the added living space on the left, and proportionally placed shed dormers to carry the design, which has an Adirondack flavor. A banded building, it has a stone first level and a shingled upper story. Stickley said, "In outward appearance [this house] is a cottage, built on simple lines, with the ample spread of roof and the low eaves which always give the impression of comfort and homeliness. Absolutely unornamented, its beauty lies wholly in the symmetry of the design and in the materials employed in the construction. In interior arrangement, it has all the room and the convenience of a large house, for the rooms are so planned that, both as to the apportionment of space in each one separately and in the directness of communication between them, there is not one meaningless barrier or one foot of unused space." The house is a variation on the No. 24 exterior design but has a more sweeping front roof to cover a large porch.

The woodwork, used through the first floor and in the upper hall, is of chestnut left looking natural, "slightly grayed, and the walls are tinted a cool gray-green, the gray tone predominating sufficiently to give it a silvery cast." All the floors of the lower story are of oak, gray-finished like the chestnut but in a slightly darker tone. The study has ample space for bookcases— the furnishings of this room are all in tones of brown, relieved with little

In Stickley's concept drawing (top) the lower story, including the pillars and steps of the veranda, "is of vary-colored split rubble stone, laid with dark cement, well raked out. The veranda is floored with cement, and in winter the addition of a temporary sill would make it easy to enclose the whole porch with glass. The entrance door is of oak, with small panes of glass of a slightly yellow tone in the upper part. The upper half story and the roof are of shingles, stained moss green, and the window sashes are stained a medium tone of brick red, giving an accent to the varying colors of the rubble used in the lower story as well as a contrast to the solid mossy green above. The chimney is of brick, topped with red tiles."

An example of No. 28 was built by Stickley-devotee Carlos Recker in Indiana (above). Its unique historical and architectural significance was forgotten and diluted through misinformed "improvements," such as the lime green aluminum siding seen in this 2001 photo.

Recently the current owners discovered an original Arts & Crafts stencil (above) beneath three layers of wallpaper and a layer of paint, and found box beams hidden by a drop ceiling.

Carlos Recker and his wife Anne Butler built this home (above) in the Indianapolis suburb of Irvington in 1908. The home may have been built not only as his residence but as a place to showcase Stickley's wares, as Recker was a successful Indianapolis interior designer and also part owner of Sander and Recker Furniture, which was Indianapolis' authorized dealer for Craftsman furniture. In January 1909, the *Indianapolis Star* published an article titled "How Others Built." It states that the Recker house was the first purely Craftsman house built in Indianapolis and notes "the plans were drawn by Gustav Stickley." The article also mentions that "Mr. Stickley provided the plans, and so keen was his interest in the work that he kept himself informed of the progress of the building operations." This early color photograph (above), probably from the 1940s, shows the original color scheme still in place: a moss-green stain applied to the upper story above a brown stain on the first story, which was clapboard instead of stone. The wood shingle roof shows a variation toward brown of the second-story green stain.

touches of green and corn color. The kitchen trim is of cypress stained green. The small kitchen porch is "so arranged that it can be enclosed in winter to provide for the keeping cool of vegetables, etc., without ice."

A "split level" effect is achieved by building a little room over the low ceiling of the downstairs study, opening off the landing midway up the stairs and consequently on a level of its own just between the rear two bedrooms. This space could be used as a small library, writing room, or children's room. "A rug in greens and deep blues, and window curtains of pale shades of pink and yellow, would form a charming color scheme in connection with the chestnut woodwork, which is the same as in the lower story."

Upstairs, all the woodwork is finished in ivory-white enamel, with doors of southern pine and floors of comb-grained pine, all stained light green. The walls of the largest bedroom (at the rear of the house on the right side) "should be tinted a pale golden yellow, and the ceiling white. The curtains should be made of white dimity. The bedroom in front of the room just described has wallpaper with white background and flowered patterns in Dresden yellows and greens. The curtains are of cream point d'esprit. The center bedroom in the front of the house is the same size. The walls in the center room might be papered in a very pale silver green tint. Rag rugs in pale green and a little gray blue cover the floor. The other front bedroom has walls in tan, with the ceiling in cream white to match the woodwork. The frieze in this room should be of very pale delft blue, with a flower pattern. The rag rug might be in pale delft blue and ivory. At the rear of the house, to the left, is the servant's bedroom. This might be papered in blue and white, with the bedstead in white enamel and the furniture in green-stained or natural oak."

"The chief feature of the living room is the open fireplace, hooded with hammered brass. The mantel-breast is of green Della Robbia tiles, mat glaze. Recessed on either side is a comfortable, cushioned seat, behind which the chestnut wainscoting runs up to a casement window of leaded antique glass in clear greens and yellows. One especially charming feature of these twin recesses is seen in the tiny ceilings, which are directly above the casement, low enough to lend that indescribable sense of coziness felt in any low-ceiled alcove, and to leave unbroken the broad line of the frieze above. This frieze should be either stenciled or painted in a conventional flower motif. The walls above the wainscot should be either tinted or covered with burlap in a rich moss green. The ceiling would be best in a deep cream tint. The window seats would harmonize admirably if upholstered in russet leather or canvas. The rug would naturally be in russet and greens, the russet of a golden hue rather than red." A comparison with one of Stickley's rare color illustrations picture the fireplace tiles to be yellow or gold/brown (left), and not as described.

No. 29 (Series of 1905, No. IX) September 1905

Roof: Gable *Bedrooms:* 4/5 *Baths:* 1 *Cost:* $6,500 *Avery Plans:* None

This house is a sort of everyman's house, the kind that Stickley was trying to get the average middle-class person to build. It is symmetrical and very straightforward. Stickley romantically says the house "depends for its charm almost entirely upon the beauty of its structural features, and upon the wise selection of the colors employed." The lower story and the chimneys at each end of the house are built with split rubble. The second story is covered "with shingles of white cedar, which may be given a weathered effect by a soft gray stain, which, as it fades, will become very rich in color value, taking on a tone of silvery gray which has a peculiar iridescence in the changing lights. The roof, shingled in cypress wood, is stained a moss green, while the window frames and casings repeat this same color in a deeper shade." The window sash throughout the house, and the four front columns, are painted white.

"One feature of the first floor arrangement is that not only the entrance hall, but the living room and dining room open directly upon the piazza, giving an air of informality that is delightful." Oak, fumed to a

Stickley's design pictured in *The Craftsman* (above) is a handsome home. Two homes that are related to this design have been located: the G. C. Kinsman house in Decatur, Illinois (center), pictured in this 1906 photo from *The Craftsman,* and the C. F. A Phair home in Presque Isle, Maine (right), shown in a 1987 photo. Note that both built homes have reduced the number of windows on the second story. Each of these houses differed from the original.

gray brown, forms the trim throughout the first floor, except for the
kitchen, where pine has been substituted. The floor is also oak but somewhat darker in tone. For the wall tint,
a dull yellow is suggested, but the
frieze space and the ceiling are both
in sand finished and un-tinted gray
plaster. "For the floor covering a rug
in russets, greens and soft yellows will
lend a needed contrast, the same
touches of color appearing in the
casement draperies of soft challis."

The Craftsman describes the living room (above):
"Dividing the ceiling space into three parts are two
transverse beams, and between these beams at the
front are three triple windows, balanced on the opposite side of the room by a bay window with three casement windows and a seat. The walls around the room
are divided into narrow panels reaching from the baseboard to the window tops, except where the fireplace
and bookcases are grouped. These bookcases run flush
with the face of the tiling of the fireplace and on a line
uniform with the mantel. Because of its rich markings,
chestnut has been selected as the trim, in color a trifle
lighter than the gray brown of the floor tone. A fresh
silvery green" is chosen as the wall tint. The ceiling
and frieze are of sand finished plaster and un-tinted,
though at well-spaced distances along the frieze line,
a stencil pattern "in deep greens, soft yellows and just
a hint of coral pink," gives some color. The window
draperies are a soft Japanese crepe with a flower motif.
"The tiles of the mantel are in the soft, cool greens of
good pottery and the rug should carry out this same
color in its border. For upholstery a canvas similar in
tint to the wall tone would be our choice, and a cush-
ion or two in pomegranate or old yellow would bring
in another touch of foliage and field tones."

Kinsman eliminated the ceiling beams and much of the
woodwork, and built a brick fireplace, in his redesign
of the living room (center).

In the commissioned plans for the Phair home, the den
(right) replaced the living room, and was finished in a
rustic look with a large fieldstone fireplace. Most of the
woodwork was pine throughout the home.

The hall illustration from *The Craftsman* (above) was the influence for the Phair house entrance hall (left), which captures the spirit of the original design. The woodwork was not originally painted.

The G. C. Kinsman House, Decatur, Illinois, 1906

The G. C. Kinsman house in Decatur, Illinois, was changed quite a bit and adapted to the styles prevalent in the area. *The Craftsman* quotes the article from the local paper soon after it was constructed in 1906: "At once the most praised and most abused house in Decatur is that of G. C. Kinsman. . . . There are those who have said that he ought to be prosecuted for building a barn like that on the best residence street in the city. There are others who pronounce it the most beautiful house . . . it is a matter of gratification . . . that many who come to censure stay to praise."

Surely its reputation as a radical house design was quickly forgotten, for within a few years three Prairie School homes, two designed by Frank Lloyd Wright, were constructed within a few blocks of the Kinsman residence. Today these three houses survive and are recognized as important architectural monuments. The Kinsman residence exterior has survived, but the interior was gutted and the home turned into several apartments.

C. F. A. Phair Commission, Presque Isle, Maine, 1906

The C. F. A Phair home was a special commission for the president of the local lumber company and was built sometime in 1906. The house that Phair asked the Craftsman Architects to design appears to be derived from Craftsman Home No. 29 of 1905 but is altered to be a new design. The living room was turned into a large study/den and the dining room became the living room. The rear of the house was expanded to include a dining room and kitchen and yet the house still looks longer than it is deep. A large porch was added behind the "den." The front porch was retained, but the recessed area with three entrances was eliminated. The front windows on either side of the porch were extended in bays with an interior window seat.

The existing plans in the former owners possession are signed as produced at the office of the Craftsman Architects at 29 West 34th Street in New York City, which indicates the house could not have been designed much before December 1905 when Stickley relocated to New York City. In all probability the house was one of the first commissions to be finished in the new office and was constructed in the spring of 1906. The home served as a home and law office for many years and still exists today as a restaurant, with a large new kitchen built to the rear.

No. 30 (Series of 1905, No. X) October 1905

Roof: Gable with shed dormers *Bedrooms:* 5 *Baths:* 1 *Cost:* $3,000 *Avery Plans:* 7 sheets (floor plans, elevation drawings, details)
A set of blueprints from the linen drawings is in the collection of The Craftsman Farms Foundation, Parsippany, New Jersey.

An example of the type of "ranch" house being built in the Southwest—Stickley must have seen similar designs on his trip to the West in 1904—He calls this home "a simple and inexpensive house, well adapted to the suburbs or the country." The rugged western ethos is translated for the suburbs. "The house is to be built entirely of shingles, upon a foundation of field rubble. The wall shingles should be of cedar, oiled and left to weather into soft silvery-gray tones, and the roof and exterior trim should be stained a mossy green. The red brick chimneys give a note of contrasting color."

There is a lot going on in this house design—it is not as simple as it looks—and Stickley points out the details: "Character is lent to the shingled walls by square corner posts and uprights, with [rare for Stickley] curved brackets at the top to support the eaves. The windows appear generally in groups of three, and the window-frames and sash are stained to the same green as the uprights. The broad overhang of the roof projects three-feet six-inches beyond the walls. The three dormer windows, which light the upper chambers at the front of the house, also add to its exterior attractiveness. One especially interesting structural feature is given by the slight projection of the upper story over the lower at the ends of the house. This takes up about half of the breadth of the eaves, and, where it overhangs the square bay at the end of the living

The illustration in *The Craftsman* (top) makes this house look like a very small cottage—it is not! Edward C. and Daisy Dutcher Hammond built their version of No. 30 in Auburndale, Massachusetts, in 1909 (above). The house straddles a slope so that the basement at the one end is fully exposed and the front of the home faces the side of the lot. The other end faces the street and has french doors that were to open onto a porch, which was never built. A pergola was built, which helps make the side of the house appear to be the front. The drive crosses in front of the home down the slope to a garage in the basement area. It is an interesting example of how the owner/builder of a Stickley house could make changes. From blueprints in the current owner's possession, it appears that Hammond traced or copied the blueprints from Stickley, included his modifications, and then listed himself as the architect. Changes were made in the window arrangements, and the master bedroom, kitchen, and porch off the dining room were all enlarged.

room, the grace and strength of the lines is especially worthy of note." All of this surrounds a deep recessed front porch that, while it takes away space from the interior of the house, allows the owner to partake of the outdoors in almost any type of weather.

The kitchen "is finished in the same chestnut woodwork as the rest of the lower floor, with walls painted a pale straw-color. The upper hall shows the same woodwork and color scheme as the lower, and the windows on the landing are curtained with gray homespun linen like the hall and den. In all the bedrooms the woodwork is finished in white, and the floors throughout are of hard comb-grained pine stained a very soft moss green. The windows upstairs are all curtained with white muslin."

The Craftsman describes the hall and staircase arrangements (above): "Over the entrances to the stairway and coat-closet opposite the front door should be hung heavy canvas curtains of dull brownish green, not unlike the color of old pine-needles, embroidered and appliquéd with bright golden browns and soft yellows. The window curtains in both hall and den should be of gray homespun linen, simply hemstitched. The ceiling of the hall is divided by two broad beams."

Hammond chose to place a door to the closet at right (center), and added two homemade, and over-large, lighting fixtures. Most of the home's light fixtures were dual gas/electric, and Hammond hand-made some of the fixtures in the Stickley style. The hall wallpaper pictured birch trees with accents in blues, greens, and orange. The bell also dates from Hammond's ownership.

Hammond built his home four years after it was published. The 1905 emphasis in spindles had begun to fade and Hammond used the more symmetrical broad slats but with the traditional Stickley newel posts in his staircase (right). The front door can be seen at the center. It is interesting to note that the hall illustration (top) shows the staircase on the left, but the floor plans (facing) show it on the right!

Edward C. Hammond, who built a version of this home, is supposed to have built the first four-wheel drive car in the basement. His wife, Daisy Dutcher Hammond, graduated from Wellesley with a degree in horticulture. She was given the choice of a maid or a gardener—she hired the gardener. The lot was assembled from four parcels and the 3/4-acre site is unusual for Auburndale. A large side garden is planted in the English style.

In the den published in *The Craftsman* (above), a thick beam goes around the walls at the ceiling. Just below, "in place of a frieze, is a simple design stenciled upon the golden brown paper in pale tans and deep browns, relieved by just a touch of old blue. On either side of the entrance is ample space for a bookcase."

The den or office is down three steps from the rest of the first floor and under the large staircase (left). Hammond opted for more closet space in the den, and did not follow Stickley's instructions for the beam around the wall at ceiling height, choosing a thin strip of wood, perhaps because the ceiling in this "split level" room is not as high as the rest of the house.

FIRST FLOOR PLAN.

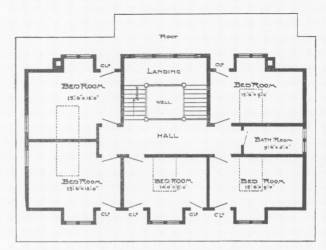

SECOND FLOOR PLAN.

The living room takes up the entire width of one side of the home. In the magazine illustration (facing below) there is a bay window along the one wall, which holds a deep seat, "adding visual interest to both the interior and the exterior of the house. The three windows above the seat are stationary, but a casement at each end permits a free circulation of air. The fireplace is faced with hard-burned brick. The walls should be covered with cartridge paper in the same tone of brownish green that appears in the portières of the hall, thus establishing the color link between the two rooms. The frieze and ceiling should be of the rough gray plaster, to which is given just a hint of tan, and the woodwork is of the same greenish-brown chestnut as in the hall." Window curtains are of bright orange, either silk or "of some soft, thin wool material."

The Hammond living room (facing above) was built with double-hung windows replacing the built-in bookcases, and a beautiful Grueby-tile fireplace. Beams were added to the ceiling, and wainscoting topped with a plate rail was installed. French windows on either side of the built-in seat opened onto the unfinished porch. Hammond owned a lumberyard and used only the best woods for the house. The original wallpaper in the living room above the wainscot was similar to the Grueby landscape tiles on the fireplace.

The home features a spectacular Grueby-tile fireplace surround (left), with a set of six rare scenic tiles inset below the mantel.

The end of the living room opposite the fireplace has room for an Arts and Crafts–style piano (below). "The large spaces on the side of the [living] room toward the hall give ample room for a piano and for additional book-cases if desired." Seen beyond the living room through the archway is the entrance hall, and the dining room in the rear.

In the published dining room drawing (left), *The Craftsman* says that "the wall panels are covered in dull blue, and the plaster of frieze and ceiling is tinted a deep cream. Brown tones are introduced in the wood-work, and greens in the furniture, which should be of oak stained a soft green. The light from the triple win-dow in front is softened by curtains of some thin, light material, in tan color, relieved by a figure giving a touch of old rose and green. At the back of the room is built an ample cupboard for china, opening on both sides so as to give equally convenient access from dining room and kitchen."

In the Auburndale house (above), doors that open onto an elevated dining porch replaced the double-hung win-dows. The built-in china cabinet and the kitchen door exchanged places, and ceiling beams were added. More alterations were done to the kitchen in the '90s but the house has had only two owners and is quite original except for changed wallpaper and two added bathrooms.

Roof: Gable with shed dormers *Bedrooms:* 3 *Baths:* 1 *Cost:* $2,200 *Avery Plans:* 7 sheets (floor plans, elevation drawings, details)

This is a charming small house—almost looking like a gingerbread house from "Hansel and Gretel." Atypical of the broad, wide roofs with projecting purlins of most Craftsman Homes, it could easily be an English country house. Despite the departures, the typical Craftsman proportion and balance is present. The creative grouping of the windows adds to the visual appeal of the cottage.

"In order to give the most effective setting to the sweeping lines and warm coloring of the house, it should occupy a lot large enough to permit surrounding of trees and shrubbery." The roof of brown shingles covers the second story, providing a contrast with the lower floor's cream-colored tinted cement finish. The foundation of the house is of rough fieldstone. The cement walls of the lower story are built on metal lath. The porches, copings, and steps are also of cement, tinted like the walls. The roof and gables are of red cedar shingles dipped in oil—"a treatment which gives them a rich tone of brown. All the exterior wood trim—the cornice, window casings, doors and ceilings of the porches—is of cypress stained to a soft, mossy green. The chimney, placed rather low in the steep slope of the roof, is of hard-burned red brick, surmounted by chimney-pots of light terra cotta, a color combination that harmonizes admirably with the brown of the shingles."

Interesting structural features

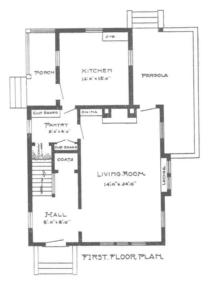

FIRST FLOOR PLAN

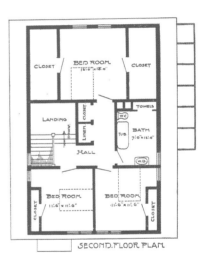

SECOND FLOOR PLAN

abound in this house. "It is distinguished by the unusually long line of the roof, with its steep slope, low eaves, and the bold spring outward of the roof-line at the overhang. This outward spring is repeated with charming effect in the little roofs of the dormers, and in the hood over the small entrance porch. This hood is also of shingles, and is supported by heavy brackets of the moss-green cypress, strongly curved outward. The brown-shingled gables project slightly over the cement walls of the lower story, carrying the sheltered effect all around the house."

Roof: Hip with gable dormers   *Bedrooms:* 4   *Baths:* 3   *Cost:* $15,000   *Avery Plans:* 12 sheets (floor plans, elevation drawings, details)

"The previous five models given of *The Craftsman* houses have ranged in cost from $2,000 to $6,000, and have been designed to demonstrate the possibility of having ample space, convenience and beauty in a home quite within moderate means. This is a much larger house and is a nobly proportioned building in the form of a cross, which is brought into rectangular shape by the addition of verandas and pergolas at the four corners, and is especially suited for a large corner lot giving plenty of garden room."

This author and his architectural consultants, normally in general agreement, disagree about the merits of this house. The author agrees with Stickley that this is a "nobly proportioned" building. All the Stickley hallmarks of balance and proportion—a roof balanced in size to the structure, and the banding and grouping of windows—produce a pleasing house. Some of the author's consultants feel that Stickley should have continued to create the smaller, more tightly organized, homes he had been extolling. This big house, they say, strays from the Craftsman ideal and could have been produced by any "run-of-the-mill" architect of the period. Admittedly, the juxtaposition of the brick central section with the half-timbered and stucco upper stories in the wings is awkward and perhaps the house would have been more effective all in brick. Stickley was trying to appeal to people across the economic spectrum, and he knew he

The perspective drawing does not do this home justice—the right side certainly is badly drawn. The elevation drawing gives a better idea of the proportions of the house. "The central part of the house is built of hard-burned red brick laid in black mortar. The same material is used for the lower story of the wings, the upper story being half-timbered and of rough gray plaster. The half-timbers are of redwood, rough finish, as it comes from the saw, and simply oiled and left to weather. The roof and the gable ends of the central part of the house are shingled with redwood shingles treated in the same way, as the color effect so gained is a delightful tone of rich, warm brown, with just a slight over-tint of gray-brown. The cold gray of the plaster is very effective in connection with the rich coloring of the timbers, and it is harmonized with the reds and browns of the main portion of the house by making the copings of verandas and pergolas, and the window and door lintels, all of gray sandstone. Accent is given to the entire scheme of color by having the columns of the verandas and the construction of the pergolas painted white."

needed to offer more for his well-heeled clients. His furniture, after all, was not cheap!

"The interesting structural effect of the exterior is aided by the arrangement of the many windows. These are usually in groups of three, but in the front elevation of the main part of the house, a row of five windows is shown in both lower and upper stories, giving an admirable division of the broad wall space. Another important structural addition is that of the two massive brick

chimneys built outside the walls at the back of the house, where they break the gray expanse of the two wings, giving almost the effect of brick towers from an exterior viewpoint, and affording very large fireplaces within.

"The living room, dining room and library may be considered both separately and as one. Practically, it is one very large room, for the broad openings and free vistas convey no sense of separation, yet the divisions are so marked as to allow decided

"The main feature of interest in the living room is the big, inviting fireplace nook [top]. Square, heavy oaken posts and beams frame in deep recess, one great charm in the construction being the short straight beams that run diagonally across the corners giving a sturdier and more rugged effect of solidity and strength than is apparent in the low arch so popular in English interiors. Massive, high-backed oaken settles are built in on either side of the recess, and the nook is ceiled with oak paneling. The mantel breast covers the whole of the wall surface at the back of the space enclosed, giving a broad expanse of dark-red brick. The fireplace opening is capped with a lintel of red sandstone that blends with the color of the hard-burned brick, and a shallow recess in the mantel-breast above has a shelf and lintel of the same stone." This beautiful inglenook features the inverted-V sandstone lintel from his Syracuse home that shows in his designs from time-to-time, and blends a little Baillie Scott with the spindles of Frank Lloyd Wright."

"In the dining room the prominent structural feature is the large sideboard [above] with projecting china cupboards. Above these cupboards the space to the top of the window casing is lined with tiles showing a soft luster of surface finish and beautiful color effects. The same kind of tiles line the space at the back of the sideboard, and the upper part of the recess is filled with three windows of hammered antique glass, heavily leaded. These windows should be rich in color."

variety in the harmonious whole of the color scheme, and the rooms are so arranged in the floor plan that only a part of any one can be seen from any point in either of the others. To quote an eminent English architect of the new school, the plan gives that pleasant sense of mystery, which piques the interest by the fact that there is always something 'round the corner.' The connecting link that brings this group of rooms into one well-planned whole is the woodwork. This is of quarter-sawed white oak, slightly fumed with ammonia and stained gray-brown with a subtle undertone of green, a color that is subdued and restful without being somber. A high, paneled wainscot occupies the greater portion of the walls in all three rooms. Where the construction permits, the wall is cut away above this wainscot and posts are used. The floors throughout are of oak fumed and stained to a darker shade of the color seen in the woodwork.

"The colors in the living room are yellow in its dull autumn tones, and rich olive green, accent being lent by the dark brick-red of the fireplace. The walls, from the top of high wainscot of greenish brown oak to the ceiling, are tinted or papered in a soft yellow, and the ceiling is of a very light tint just tinged with green. The ripe yellow wall color is seen also in the soft, light window hangings of silk or mohair. The rugs are 'hooked,' and introduce brick and yellow tones with soft olive green.

"The walls of the dining room are done in soft gray-brown, with gray-green tones showing not only in the woodwork, but also in the tiles, rugs and leather cushions of the chairs. The glass doors are curtained with soft, light material of a golden yellow hue, as are also the two casements. The ceiling shows the same light tint as in the living room. The wall space in the Library, above the wainscot that runs around the room, is covered with moss-green Craftsman canvas. The frieze and ceiling are tinted like the ceilings of the other rooms."

Upstairs, "both hall and study repeat the woodwork and color scheme of the living room. The upper walls, which are tinted a warm yellow, show a small spot pattern in stencil. Opening from this study is a small bedroom of irregular shape, designed especially for a boy's room, where the walls are a pomegranate red, with frieze and ceiling of deep cream. The woodwork of all the upstairs rooms in the front part of the house is done in old ivory enamel. The oak floors are finished in soft moss-green in all the bedrooms and the doors are all in the brown finish that prevails throughout the lower story and in the hall."

"The large room in the right wing has a private bath decorated to harmonize with the bedroom. This room is large and irregular in shape. The walls are done in a soft yellow shade that verges on tan-color, and the ceiling has a very light tint with just a suggestion of gray-blue. The fireplace at the rear of the room is faced with square tiles, brick-red in color, and has a hood of hammered copper, fastened in place with big brass nails. The window curtains show a deep cream tone, and the bed-cover, dresser-scarf, etc., match them in color and material. The rugs are of woven rags in tans and browns, with the heavy stripes in dark blue."

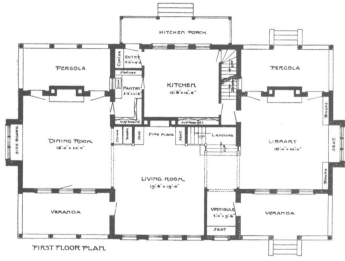

FIRST FLOOR PLAN

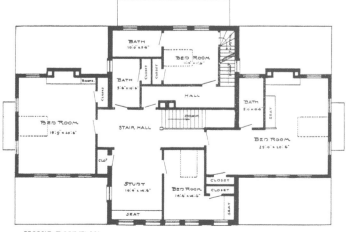

SECOND FLOOR PLAN

of the color chosen over the natural tint of the wood, giving more the effect, in this case, of a naturally mossy-green tone of wood than of applied color. The thin stain merely brings the wood itself into harmonious relation with any preferred color scheme. The walls are either tinted or papered a soft yellow verging on brown, suggesting the color that is known as Byzantine gold. The frieze has a ground of tan-color, with the figure in soft greens and pinkish yellow tones like those seen in a yellow peach. A touch of deep red is given by the fireplace, which is built of red brick. . . . Bits of yellow in the small decorative accessories would add life and sparkle to the prevailing quiet tones, and the scarfs for table and sideboard might be of yellow linen. The window curtains should be of plain unbleached material, either linen or cotton, and should hang in straight simple folds . . . and the rugs

should be of rags in raft brown tones, with bands of green and possibly a touch of gray-blue.

"The walls and ceiling of [the] kitchen are painted a soft corn-color, and the woodwork is of hard pine finished in light brown. There is no wainscot, only a baseboard, and the oil paint on the walls is easily kept bright and clean."

The second-story woodwork is pine, and the bedroom is stained "a delicate" silver gray. In the large bedroom the walls are tinted or covered with a plain paper "in a light shade of green with the ceiling and frieze of cream-color." The frieze has either wallpaper or a stencil, "where touches of strong yellow would appear, and a brighter tone of green than that of the walls." Window hangings of "simple, crisp white muslin" is suggested. "The small bedroom might be treated in pinks, using the salmon shades." The walls could

be papered with "a figure in old rose with just a touch of green on a pinkish-white ground. The floor could be covered with a grass matting rug, with small foot-rugs of cream and salmon-pink in front of the bed and dresser." The bed cover, bureau scarf, and window curtains "should be of pure white muslin either plain or dotted. The walls and ceiling of the bath-room might be in creamy-white, and the window curtain of some inexpensive material with a white or very light ground and blue figures."

The dining room as Stickley planned it (far left), and as the Robbins built it (left). From the photo it appears the home was built with interior changes that made it more "rustic" in appearance. The ceiling appears to be exposed wooden beams supporting the second-story subfloor.

In the Stickley concept (right), the wainscot that runs all around the room is 4 feet high, "and the head casing of the windows and doors is carried in an unbroken line along the walls to form the frieze, which is further accentuated by another band of wood at the ceiling angle." The fireplace (far right) in the Robbins home was of rustic fieldstone and not the urbane one pictured in *The Craftsman*.

Roof: Cross-hipped with shed dormer *Bedrooms:* 4 *Baths:* 1 *Cost:* $3,500 *Avery Plans:* 4 sheets (floor plans, elevations, cross section, details)

Pictured sitting on the edge of a lake, this compact true bungalow is published as a summer residence, or "camp." Stickley, and perhaps his market, was fascinated with the idea of the vacation "getaway" house, and offered a number of them (No. 18 of 1905 is another successful example) in *The Craftsman*. The recessed porch void provides a visual interest, breaking the box-like structure, as well as providing access to the outdoors in all weather. These early homes point the way toward the cottages designed later for Craftsman Farms.

The article on this home is a primer on the Arts and Crafts philosophy: ". . . the best form of a summer home is a bungalow . . . a house reduced to its simplest form, where life may be carried on with freedom and comfort and the least amount of effort." It harmonizes with its surroundings, because "its low, broad proportions and absolute lack of ornamentation" make it seem "to sink into and blend with any landscape." It may be built of any local material so it is never expensive. It is beautiful because it is planned and built to meet simple needs in the simplest way, and it is individual for the

The front of the bungalow shows a deeply recessed porch (top right). The low, widely overhanging roof, its expanse broken by the group of dormers in front and the extension at the back, "gives a settled, sheltered look to the building, and this is emphasized even more by the deeply recessed porch in front." In what is becoming a hallmark of most Stickley homes, "the ends of the beams [purlins], squared off at the eaves, also give a hint of the construction . . . ." The rear view (above) shows the cleverly arranged kitchen separated from the main part of the house by an outdoor dining room. Certainly with the risk of fire, and miles from any fire department, this is a prudent design.

"Another interesting structural feature is seen in the extension of the heavy square lintel of the front door [top left] into a massive beam that runs from end to end of the recess. The same square, massive effect is seen in the door posts, to which the beam is bolted with large spikes, and in the window casings, which are so thick that the casements are recessed rather deeply from the outside by reason of the construction. The door of heavy oaken planks . . . is entirely in keeping with the primitive, sturdy seeming of the whole building . . . ." The door in the article's elevation drawing, however, shows a twelve-light-window standard Craftsman door.

same reason, as the needs of no two families are alike.

He waxes poetic on the selection of color. The exterior is cedar shingle, with the foundation and chimney of rough gray stone. The stone should be available locally, but the wood would vary with the locality; for instance, in California it would be redwood. The color would also vary with the locality. Where the surroundings include gray cliffs and boulders, simply oiling the cedar shingles and leaving them to weather into a soft, silvery gray could achieve kinship with the landscape. It should be built among green trees or on a green grassy slope, and the roof could be stained to a "soft wood brown, and the walls a mossy green."

In the living room, all the interior woodwork is of pine "stained a soft, warm green, the plaster walls in sand finish and left in the natural gray, and the chimney of rough stone with a good many red tones among the gray. The floor of the inglenook would be tiled with rough, hard burned tiles of a dark red color. The rugs on floor and balcony would be rag, with a body color of medium dark gray and wide stripes of brick red and navy blue. The . . . sleeping rooms are plastered, walls and ceiling. The plaster is sand finished, and can either be tinted . . . or left in the natural gray." The ceilings should be left in the natural color.

No cellar is provided, "but the walls have a footing below the frost line and space for ventilation under the floor to prevent dampness."

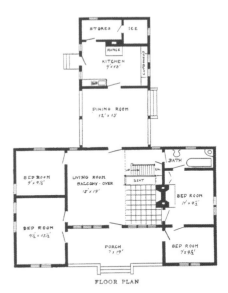

FLOOR PLAN

The living room (above) "occupies the whole center of the house, and it is one of the best examples yet of the Craftsman idea of the decorative value of the actual construction of a building. Every feature has its part to fill in the decorative scheme of the whole, and there is not a feature that is not actually necessary to the structure. The only ceiling is the inner side of the roof, supported by heavy beams that actually belong there . . . the whole room is of wood, save for the rough gray plaster of the walls and the stone of the fireplace. A balcony runs across one side, serving the double purpose of recessing the fireplace into a comfortable and inviting inglenook, and of affording a small retreat, which may be used as a . . . lounging place. The rail of solid boards looks from below like a wide frieze, and one or two gay Indian rugs hung over it add a touch of barbaric color. The floor of the balcony provides a low, beamed ceiling to the inglenook. . . . The same heavy post and beam construction that gives such interest to the exterior of the house also appears here, ruling the sturdy, rugged character of the whole room."

Roof: Gable *Bedrooms:* 3 *Baths:* 1 *Cost:* $4,200 *Avery Plans:* None

This house is one of a number of designs in 1906, 1907, and 1908 where Stickley tries to work out the long rectangle-type house design. It "is the kind of a home that a plain, honest man would like his children to grow up in and remember all their lives as 'home,' for children reared in such surroundings should develop into strong, sincere men and women as naturally and inevitably as plants thrive in good soil." This house has construction that "is frankly revealed in all its salient features. With its sturdy proportions and its few and simple lines, the whole building seems to belong to the soil from which it rises. The foundation of split field rubble is sunk so low in the ground that the floor of the porch is but a few inches above the grassy slope of the terrace, giving that sense of closeness to the earth that is one of the great charms in all primitive dwellings. Rough cast cement is the material used for the house itself. The rugged effect of this is greatly enhanced by the surface treatment, as gravel is used to give a roughness of texture that could not otherwise be obtained in plaster. The last coat of plaster should be darkened with a little lampblack to give it a gray tone, and stippled with a coarse, stiff broom. While the plaster is wet, gravel varying in size from a pea to a walnut should be thrown against it. Some of the gravel will fall off, but enough will remain sticking into the plaster to give the walls a most interesting surface. In this

FIRST FLOOR PLAN.

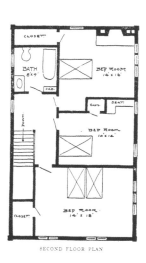

SECOND FLOOR PLAN

house, a mossy-green pigment is stippled on over the final coat of plaster and gravel. This acts rather like the stain on wood in casting a tone over the surface through which the natural color may be seen."

All the exterior woodwork is of cypress, "darkened with a brown stain through which the natural character of the wood is apparent in all its variations of tint and grain, and the roof is of thick, rough cypress shingles treated the same way. Plain to severity, this house owes all the beauty it possesses to the materials of which it is built, to the massive simplicity of its construction and proportion, . . . and in the proportion and grouping of the windows." The large, solid wooden posts at the corners of the building are repeated across the front to correspond with each pillar, and the lengthwise beam sunk in the wall at the top of window and door casings ties the whole structure together. The floor and steps are of cement colored a dark brick-red and marked off in blocks like tiles. This note of color is repeated in the red brick chimney."

The idea of showing the real structure of the building is carried out in the interior as well. "The posts and beams in the large irregular room that takes up almost the whole of the lower story are there for decorative effect, but the effect is decorative because it is the real structure. Although the exquisite finish of the woodwork takes from it any suggestion of crudeness, it is absolutely

primitive in the simplicity of its frank appearance of usefulness. The room is complete in itself before a single article of furniture is put into it.

"The woodwork throughout the lower story is of chestnut stained a rich dark brown, and the floors are of quartered oak in a rather darker shade, laid with wide boards. The [plaster] walls are finished in a neutral tint, not too light and tending toward a green tone. The frieze and ceilings throughout the lower story are left in the natural gray sand-finished plaster.

"The rugs [should be] mainly green in tone with some touches of tan and pomegranate red. Warmth and atmosphere will be given to a room in these cool, shady colors if the windows are curtained with corn-colored silk or cotton crepe—any

material thin enough to flood the room with yellowish light."

On the second floor the bathroom is positioned directly above the kitchen, for economy in the plumbing connections. "Also, the rear bedroom has the luxury of a fireplace, which comes above that in the ingle nook. If the upper fireplace be done in dull brick-red tiles, an effective color treatment for the room would be a scheme in pomegranate reds and yellows. The woodwork throughout the upper story is of poplar, stained to a dull green, and the floors are of hard comb-grained pine, done in brown. The center bedroom would be attractive with corn yellow walls and cream ceiling, with crisp white muslin curtains at the windows. . . . The front bedroom . . . is in dull blues and soft yellows . . . ."

"The lavish use of woodwork in the living/dining room [above] makes the chief beauty of the room. The broad plain panels show to full advantage the charm of chestnut, which, when properly sandpapered, lacquered, and waxed, takes on a surface like satin. The play of changing tones of brown and green gives a never-ending fascination to the wood when thus treated, so that in itself it becomes the most beautiful decoration in the room."

The fireplace (above), located in an inglenook alcove to the rear of the dining room, "is of hard-burned red brick with a heavy plank shelf and a tiled hearth."

Roof: Gable with gable dormer *Bedrooms:* 4 *Baths:* 1 *1906 Cost:* $6,500 *Avery Plans:* 7 sheets (floor plans, elevations, cross section, details)

· FIRST FLOOR PLAN·

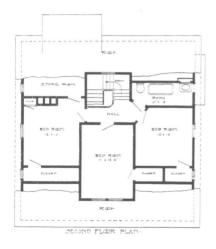

· SECOND FLOOR PLAN·

For the first time, clapboards are used on a Craftsman Home. Stickley did not like clapboards because the small, thin, smoothly planed boards generally available gave "a flimsy, unsubstantial effect to the structure." In this building, Stickley specified that the clapboards be of cedar or cypress, unusually broad and thick, and "stained either brown or green and planed or left with the rough surface, giving to the walls a sturdy appearance of permanence." Structural uprights that remind of half-timbering delineate the horizontal clapboards, but the effect is somewhat bizarre. "The structure of the house is plainly revealed by the comer posts and exterior beams and uprights. When the boards are planed, this framework should be planed also, and painted in a light cream so that the structural features are strongly accented." If un-planed, the timbers should be left rough, and stained "a tone of green or darker brown."

The structural features are planned to add to the apparent width of the house, by means of the prominent horizontal lines of the beams. This device is especially apparent in the grouping of the three windows that light the gable. They are rather far apart, but they are pulled together by the beams, so as to form a symmetrical group rather than to give the impression of three separate windows. The same effect is "preserved by the massive beam that extends the entire width of the house, not only

defining the height of the lower story, but serving as a strong connecting line for the window and door framings, which all spring from the foundation to the height of this beam." The foundation is of split field rubble.

The lower floor has a layout suggesting a center hall plan, and the dining room can be closed off by the use of pocket doors (rare in Craftsman Homes). Heavy woodwork with wood wainscoting is eschewed

in this house, yielding to plaster, wallpaper, and grass cloth.

The structural features on the exterior of the house are used in the framing of the windows and in the division of the wall spaces by means of beams and uprights in the interior. The living room has no frieze, but a corner beam divides the ceiling from the walls, and a broad fumed and brown-stained chestnut "wainscot rail runs all around the room at the height of the mantel-shelf."

No. 38 (Series of 1906, No. VI) July 1906

Roof: Gable *Bedrooms:* 3 *Baths:* 1 *Cost:* $9,500 *Avery Plans:* None

Stickley tries another rectangular house design, although larger than No. 36 and not as clean a design. The swooping brick arches of the porch are not in harmony with the rest of the design. Note too that the large purlins that usually support the roof eaves have been replaced by triangular brackets, a device that Stickley does use, but rarely. "Low, broad and roomy, this Craftsman house is especially calculated to crown a hill-top or terrace, as its . . . wide, low-pitched roof and severely straight lines seem to demand the dignity of a commanding position."

The foundation is of split field-stone, and the first story is of hard-burned "clinker" brick, both laid in black cement mortar. The second story and gables are of rough gray plaster with massive timber construction, the timbers of cypress stained to a medium tone of gray-green. The roof is of thick white-cedar shingles, dipped in oil and left to weather. "The oil merely gives a deeper tone to the natural color of the wood, taking off the raw look of the shingles while they are new."

The windows, which appear in groups of two and three at the front of the house, are double-hung, with small, square panes in the upper sash. The recessed porch across the front is floored with square tiles of red clay laid in black cement, and its back walls are of gray cement plaster. "The brick walls of the lower story show in front only between the arches that

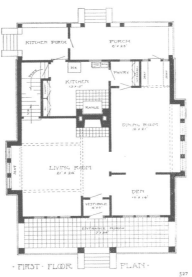

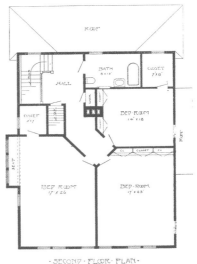

surmount the low, broad openings from the porch, and in the parapet that surrounds it on the three sides. Another porch is at the rear of the house, and is divided by a partition into a kitchen porch and an outdoor dining room.

The kitchen and pantry at the back are, of course, entirely separated, but nothing interferes with the sense of spaciousness that marks the front of

the house because, despite the structural divisions between the living room, dining room, den, and vestibule it is all really one room. The staircase, instead of being in the middle of the space, is placed in a corner at the rear of the living room, running up over the kitchen and by its position effecting the utmost saving of clear space at the front of the house on both lower and upper stories."

Roof: Gable *Bedrooms:* 3 *Baths:* 1 *Cost:* $7,000 *Avery Plans:* 6 sheets (floor plans, elevations, cross section, details)

This house (top) was built in slightly modified form in Danville, Kentucky, about 1911 by William S. Lawwill (above). A double window and added dormers (these may have been added after the house was built) provide more light to the attic rooms. The porch pillars are square and made of local stone. The interior arrangements were also modified slightly.

Without the porches, this house is 36-feet square, so it is basically a foursquare plan—yet the drawing makes the house look like the earlier rectangular homes Nos. 36 and 38. No bay windows, recesses, or projections are seen, the design depending entirely upon the proportions and the treatment of mass and spacing. "There is a well-balanced arrangement of the lower [story] and absolute symmetry marks the design of the upper story and the roof." The material used for the façade walls is cement plaster on metal lath. The cement is left in its natural gray color, and the roof is of white cedar shingles left to weather to a similar tone of silvery gray. Color accent, as well as emphasis of form, is given by the wood trim, which is of chestnut stained to a soft brown, "yet showing the strong markings of the grain. As in most of *The Craftsman* houses, the short, sturdy round wood columns of the porch are painted pure white and they give much greater strength and durability, as well as a better structural effect than square columns built up of boards." The foundation of the house, and a portion of the chimney, is of rough ashlar, split and fitted together.

"As there are no partitions in the main rooms of the lower story, the space is all treated alike as to woodwork and color scheme." The woodwork is of chestnut stained to a soft tone of greenish brown. "The wall space above the wainscot is treated in a dull gold color, and in this instance is covered with canvas, although equal effect may be obtained with plain paper of the same color, or with a coat of paint, stippled to a dull, velvety finish, on the plaster. The use of this color gives a rich subdued effect that seems to fill the room with reflected sunshine." The ceilings are tinted a cool greenish white.

The rugs on the floors of both living and dining rooms "are in tones of brown, golden yellow and green, and the window curtains are of a light,

In Stickley's concept (above), "a heavy beam runs all around the living room at the ceiling, and elsewhere beams are used only when absolutely necessary to mark divisions or to emphasize structural effects. . . . A six-foot paneled wainscot extends all around the walls, and projects into the room wherever the suggestion of a division is needed. The fireplace extends to the ceiling and is very broad. The mantel-breast and hearth are both of red brick, laid in black cement, those of the mantel-breast laid cross-bond, and the hearth bricks flat, with the broad side up. The fireplace opening is low and wide, capped with red sandstone. A decorative bit above is the panel formed of three large landscape tiles in tones of golden yellow, moss green and brown, with a touch of vivid dark blue in the poster-like river that runs through the landscape."

The Craftsman-style fireplace, however, was replaced by one of a colonial style (center)—under examination the woodwork around the fireplace appears to all be original, but removal of the paint may reveal that the fireplace surround was added in later years. The post-and-panel divider between the staircase/entry and the living room was not built; instead a door was installed into the kitchen, thus the staircase is not as open as in Stickley's design, but the woodwork style is still Craftsman.

While the downstairs woodwork was painted in later years, the upstairs (left) survived intact. Lawwill added a fireplace to the existing chimney in this upstairs sitting room/hall.

Another interior modification (above) was the elimination of the post-and-panel arrangement dividing the living and dining rooms. A wall replaced that, and a bookcase was added on one side. The built-in sideboard was never built.

In Stickley's concept drawing (right), a large square beam marks the division between the living room and dining room—"a division that is further emphasized by the posts placed about three feet from the wall, with paneling the height of the wainscot, and open spaces above." In the dining room a sideboard occupies the entire rear end of the dining room. The wall above the sideboard and below the row of casement windows, extending across the whole end of the room, is "tiled with square, matt-finished tiles of dull gray-green."

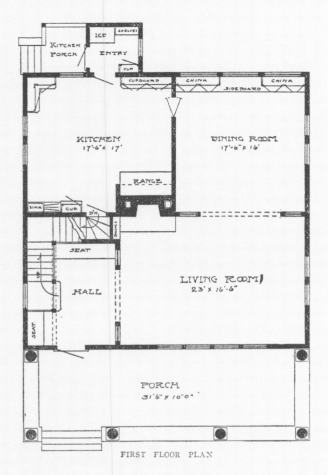

FIRST FLOOR PLAN

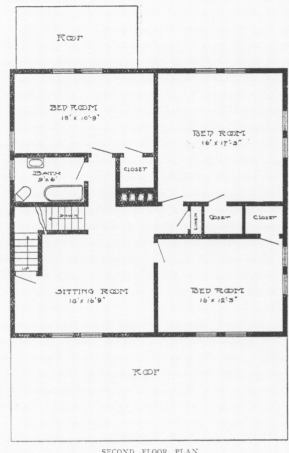

SECOND FLOOR PLAN

creamy crepe material, with figures in golden yellow, apple-green and pomegranate. As no pantry is provided, the kitchen is larger than usual. All the woodwork is of chestnut, stained brown and given two coats of lacquer so that it may easily be cleaned."

On the second floor, the stairs open directly into a large room instead of the customary upper hall. This room is designed as an upstairs sitting area. "The woodwork is of chestnut like that of the lower story, but instead of the wainscot there is only a baseboard. The wall is papered with plain ingrain paper of a rich mossy green, with frieze and ceiling

of greenish white. All the bedrooms are finished in white wood, enameled to a warm ivory tone. The doors are of chestnut, stained light brown, and the floors are of hard comb-grain pine, stained brown to match the doors." One bedroom "has walls of old rose, either paper or tinted plaster, with ceiling and frieze of a warm cream-color, and the plain picture molding of ivory enamel like the rest of the woodwork. The curtains in this room are of white muslin, and the bed cover and other fabric accessories are of pure white with touches of embroidery and appliqué in old rose and green. Another [bed]room has the walls paneled with Japanese

grass cloth of a soft yellow tone with the silvery shimmer that characterizes this material. The ceiling and frieze are greenish white. The fabrics are of natural unbleached linen with a conventional design embroidered in gray-blue. The third [bed]room has the walls papered with a two-toned stripe in soft browns. The frieze shows one of the woodland landscape designs, and the ceiling is in deep cream. The curtains, bedcovers, etc., are of gray homespun, and the rug shows tones of green and brown. In the attic the available space beneath the roof is utilized partly for a storeroom and partly for a maid's bedroom."

No. 40 (Series of 1906, No. VIII) September 1906

Roof: Hipped *Bedrooms:* 4 *Baths:* 1 *Cost:* $10,000 *Avery Plans:* 9 sheets (floor plans, elevations, cross section, and details)

This unique house is related to vernacular styles from the Caribbean or Gulf Coast Louisiana and bayou houses, with the big hipped roof and the front verandas. The towers are also highly unusual for a Stickley design. He says this house "should be a decided change from the forms hitherto used, and yet should not depart in any way from the simplicity and directness of construction and arrangement that form the fundamental principles of all the Craftsman house plans."

This is not a large house, yet it has the feeling of dignity and spaciousness that usually belongs only to a large building. This is mainly due to the square tower-like construction at each front corner and to the double verandas, both ample in size and deeply recessed, that occupy the whole width of the house between the towers. Of these, one is the entrance-porch, and the other an outdoor sleeping-room. This is Stickley's first use of the idea of the sleeping porch—"an idea that is essentially in harmony with all our theories of life. We have outdoor living-rooms and dining-rooms to bring the life of the home as much as possible into the outer air, and we believe that in the near future the porch that may be used as an outdoor sleeping-room, will be a part of every house that is built with special reference to health and freedom of living." (Stickley's own Syracuse home had a sleeping porch in the rear, but this is

A version of No. 40 was built along the Mississippi River (above) in 1913 for lumber baron George Leavenworth. According to local lore, when the house was being built, it was considered such a modern curiosity that people rode the Sunday afternoon trolley from the nearby town to the then-suburban site to view the construction of this unique structure. After the house was completed, Mrs. Leavenworth, a former teacher from Michigan, opened a Montessori kindergarten in the third floor (attic) of the house. In the 1920s author William Faulkner visited the home several times.

There were many changes from the drawn plans (top). Two extra dormers were placed on the roof to light the attic. Square columns instead of round ones support the front porches and roof. The house is aligned so that the towers are not east/west as planned, but north/south. The floor plans were considerably altered. Beyond the possible removal of some built-in furniture in the 1920s, the home has survived almost intact over the years and now houses an Arts and Crafts collection of antique pieces and reissued Stickley furniture.

In *The Craftsman's* concept drawing (above), the fireplace, located in the center of the house, is in the corner of the living room, with the dining room beyond. But Leavenworth extended the living room across the front of the house and moved the staircase to the other side of the living room (top). The living room appears to have rust red tinted plaster walls. While the original plan does not call for them, benches were added to either side of the living room fireplace to create an inglenook.

the first use of the concept in a Craftsman design.)

The home is of cement and half-timber construction with a tiled roof and a foundation of local fieldstone. The foundation is continued up to form the parapets that surround the recessed porches on the lower story. The walls are of cement plaster on metal lath, "the plaster being given the rough 'gravel finish' and colored in varying tones of green. To do this is a very simple matter, and the result is a surface most interesting both in texture and color. The plaster is first colored by the use of about six or seven per cent of green ultramarine, and while it is still fairly soft the gravel is spattered over it by means of a shingle. The gravel should be of a size that

will pass through a screen with a half-inch mesh and be retained on a quarter-inch mesh screen. After the gravel is on, a rather thick green paint should be stippled on with a very stiff brush or the end of a broom, taking care to make the application rather irregular and not too thick."

All the exterior wood trim is of cypress, stained to a darker tone of the same green as the walls. "In this house the exterior woodwork is decorative in its lines and in the division of wall spaces, and yet obviously an essential part of the structure. The horizontal beams serve to bind together the lines of the whole framework, and the uprights are simply corner-posts and continuations of the window-frames. The roof is of dull

Stickley's concept drawing (above) shows the "den" room on the first floor of one of the "towers," and Leavenworth carried out the ideas (above right)—even the built-in bench seat—closely, while adding high wainscoting. The woodwork, partly "blue tupelo" (gumwood)—which was supposedly treated in mud from the river—and six-foot-high cottonwood wainscoting, is used liberally on the first floor. This still has its waxed finish, and the remains of the green undertone that Stickley called for (what was probably an aniline green stain). The windows on the ground floor are very tall and admit a great deal of light into the house. The relocated dining room (facing) is a design gem. The details of the interior of the Leavenworth home, and the date of its construction, could lead one to speculate that the revisions to this house were carried out, at least in part, from alterations to the original plans provided by the Craftsman Architects.

red tiles. The thick round pillars, painted white with just a suggestion of green, lend a sharp accent that emphasizes the whole." The house is arranged so that one chimney, with four flues, serves for all the rooms. The entrance door is at the left end of the porch, "which by this device is made to seem less like a mere entrance and more like a pleasant gathering-place where outdoor life may go on." A screen of vines may hide the whole porch. The dining-porch at the back of the house, under a vine-covered pergola, opens into both the dining room and an entry that leads to the kitchen. The construction of the pergola is the same as that of the porches, with round white pillars and square beams colored green. The upper porch at the front of the house is exactly like the lower in size and construction, and is planned so it may be screened or glassed for an outdoor bedroom in all but the coldest winter weather.

With the towers included, the entire frontage of the house is 50 feet and it is 40 feet deep. The interior has the usual open arrangement of the Craftsman house, with the variation given by the tower nooks. One of these forms the entrance from the front door to the living room. "To understand the charm of this it will be necessary to compare the entrance as shown on the floor plan of the first story with the illustration of the tower nook in the dining-room. The construction is exactly the same, with the exception of the crossed ceiling beams, but the entrance is rather more screened from the room by the running out of the partition to the center of the nook. In the opposite nook, which is used as a den, the partition is all cut away, leaving only the beam construction overhead to mark the angle made by the corner of the dining-room."

The woodwork of the whole of the first floor is brown fumed oak, but of a "light, luminous tone in which there is a subtle undertone of green. The walls up to the plate-rail are covered with Japanese grass cloth in one of the almost indescribable hues that come in this beautiful fabric. It is a very soft, woody shade of pale silvery brown, which might be compared to sunburned straw if it showed a golden and reddish tone, instead of a silvery luster over a hint of olive green. The ceiling is of deep ivory, in which appears the merest suggestion of green. The plaster is left in the rough sand finish and is painted with oil paint. The last coat is of white lead mixed with turpentine and colored with a very slight touch of yellow ochre and the merest trace of green. The frieze as shown here is plain, and the same color as the ceiling, but if a richer and more striking color-scheme is desired, nothing could be better than one of the English landscape friezes in rich, dim, autumnal tones that show soft, pale brown, deep olives, and a few traces of dull red. A plain frieze that would give a pleasant color variation would be of grass-cloth in a tone of dull leaf-green, rather pale and silvery.

"The mantel-breast and hearth is of large square tiles, matt finish and of a dull tone of brownish yellow. It is bound at the corners with strips of copper, and the fireplace-hood is also of hammered copper. The floors throughout are of fumed oak, with rather wide boards. The windows are entrained in a thin material of golden yellow, giving an effect of sunlight in the rooms. The stairs are at the back of the living room, and run up to a broad landing lighted by casement windows." Both stairs and upper hall are treated the same in woodwork and wall-surface as the lower rooms. All the floors on the second story are also of fumed oak, and the doors are also of oak on the hall side. However, the woodwork in all the bedrooms "is of ivory-white enamel. The east tower bedroom walls are divided into narrow panels by strips of the white woodwork, making a wainscot that extends to the height of the cap-moldings of the doors. These panels are covered with Japanese grass cloth of a rich reddish-yellow hue like the sunny side of a peach. The ceiling and frieze are of the palest possible peach tint. The west tower bedroom is cooler

This view of the living room looks toward the den in one of the towers. The edge of the fireplace inglenook bench can just be seen on the right. The Leavenworth design makes this room very long and narrow but larger than the original plan.

in color effect. The walls are painted with a dull velvety finish, in sea-green—just the color that shows on the under side of a wave that is about to break into foam. The ceiling is a very pale tint of the same color."

The small bedroom between these tower rooms is designed for occasional use or for a child's room. The casement windows are set high so as not to give a view of the porch. The walls are finished in a soft, pale tea color. The servant's room is in the attic and is lighted by the dormer window that appears at the back of the house. The remainder of the attic is devoted to storage room and is lighted and ventilated by the slat windows in the towers.

SIDE ELEVATION

FRONT ELEVATION

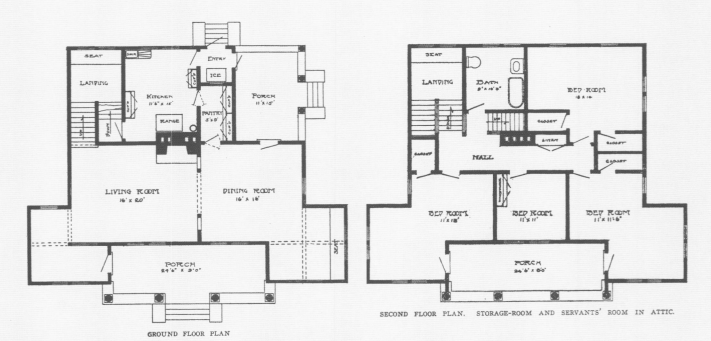

GROUND FLOOR PLAN

SECOND FLOOR PLAN. STORAGE-ROOM AND SERVANTS' ROOM IN ATTIC.

Comparing the original plans (above) to the Leavenworth home plans (below), the tower entrance foyer is to the right instead of the left. The tower nook extension of the dining room became an office/music room/den because the living room extends the full width of the front of the home, and the dining room is placed where the stairs and kitchen were planned. The enclosed porch in the plans was eliminated and while an entrance was maintained, the doorway enters straight into a small room (used by the family as a library) with a fireplace and a servant's stairway to the upper floors. This library/hall area has doors leading to every other room on the main floor. The kitchen was moved to the right rear of the house. Four bedrooms and a sitting room as well as two bathrooms open off the hall. While the changes seem to be for the better on the first floor, the large hall on the second floor means that the bedrooms are smaller in size.

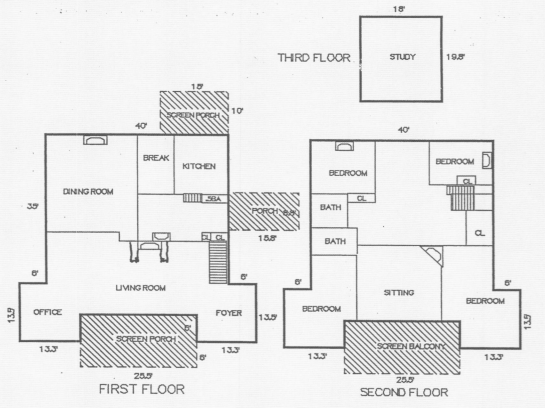

FIRST FLOOR

SECOND FLOOR

No. 41 (Series of 1906, No. IX) October 1906

Roof: Hipped with shed dormers *Bedrooms:* 4 *Baths:* 1
Avery Plans: 4 sheets (floor plans, elevations, cross section, details)

This is one of Stickley's weaker designs. It is offered for the kind of long narrow lot that many people were purchasing in the expanding suburbs, so in a practical sense it is a well laid out plan. But it is visually unexciting—if not arguably ugly. The crenelated box bay—the "elevator shaft"-looking tower midway between the front and rear—awkwardly divides the structure, and the half-timbered sections do not blend with the shingled sections—a mixed metaphor of visual elements.

Yet Stickley tries to justify this "ugly duckling": "*The Craftsman* house published this month differs only in certain individual features from others we have designed in much the same style. It is built of plaster and shingles, and its plan is plain to any one who will study the floor plans and elevations. The lines of the house are severely plain, and yet the building has a homely, substantial friendliness that is most attractive. The structural features are so planned that, while they harmonize absolutely with the general severity of outline, they yet relieve it from any monotony and give to the house just the touches that go to make up its individual character."

Stickley's handsome interior design triumphs over the ungainly exterior.

Roof: Mansard with gable dormers *Bedrooms:* 4 *Baths:* 1 *Cost:* $3,750
Avery Plans: 5 sheets (floor plans, elevations, cross section, details)

Another awkward looking house, it has poorly balanced elements—the dormers are too small for the size of the roof and add nothing to the look of the building, and the small gables on the side of the structure do not help the already poor proportions. The mansard roof looks back to the previous century, and inserting half timbering in the dormers just adds to the problem. The better draftsmen in the office must have been on vacation this month.

Designed for a small family, the home is comparatively inexpensive. It is vaguely similar in appearance to Craftsman House No. 6 of June 1904, although the floor plan is quite different. One way to get one's money's worth in building at moderate cost "is to use shingles throughout," so this is a shingled house. Stickley tries to justify the design with some salesmanship: "Although the house is almost a perfect square, it has many features that serve to break the flat surfaces of the walls. In front, the vestibule projects beyond the wall of the house, and slightly beyond the two bays, which form a shallower projection on either side. Two dormers appear in the upper part of the front, and a small gable at either side. In the upper part of these dormers and gables there is a glimpse of plaster and half-timber construction, all the more interesting for being rather unexpected in the shingled wall.

"The rooms, being all open, should be treated as one large room

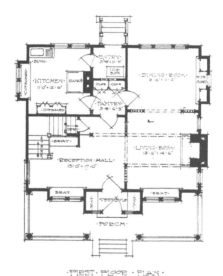

· FIRST · FLOOR · PLAN ·

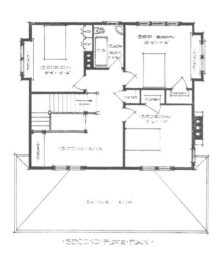

· SECOND · FLOOR · PLAN ·

so far as the woodwork and color scheme goes, and the necessary diversity can easily be gained by the rugs, pillows and small belongings."

No. 43 (Series of 1906, No. XI) December 1906

Roof: Cross gable with shed over rear porch *Bedrooms:* 4 *Baths:* 1 *Cost:* $5,500
Avery Plans: 4 sheets (floor plans, elevations, cross section, details)

This house is a more successful design than the previous two. It is rendered in a different and more artistic hand, so the designer was probably different. English in influence, the plan type looks back to the previous century, utilizing a modification of some common Victorian house plans. In trying to come up with homes that will interest people, the designers seem to revert every-so-often to tried-and-true house plans, probably hoping to reach a more conservative element of *The Craftsman* readership.

While the home is designed to be built of cement plaster on a frame of expanded steel lath, it could be constructed from hollow cement blocks, "showing that there is a growing demand for the use of hollow cement walls in dwellings, on account of the resistance to heat and cold." Stickley believes "in the suitability of cement construction to the straight and simple lines of the Craftsman houses. Stickley recommends a 'pebble-dash' finish, which gives an interesting roughness of texture to the walls, and takes very kindly to color. The color itself must be determined by the location of the house and the prevailing tones of the landscape. In a country like Southern California, for instance, with its tawny, sun-soaked coloring, nothing could be so good as a light buff or biscuit color, which is obtained by adding four pounds of dry yellow ochre to one hundred pounds of Portland cement mortar containing two parts of sand to one of cement. This is the prevailing tone of the plastered adobe houses in the Mission style of architecture so much used in that country. In the North and East [this color] is not so harmonious as the greens and grays. A very attractive shade of dull light green is obtained by using half-a-pound of yellow ochre to one hundred pounds of cement mortar, and the addition of lamp-black in varying quantities gives satisfactory tones of gray. The pebble finish is obtained by spattering pebbles ranging in size from a pea to a marble against the mortar before it is dry, and then stippling on a pigment to bring the pebbles into harmony with the color of the house. This stippling should be done with a stiff broom, using a soft brown tone for the biscuit-colored mortar, and a darker green for the light green groundwork. On a gray mortar, the pebbles might be allowed to remain in their natural colors. The visible part of the foundation as shown is of very hard and rough red brick. A quarry-faced broken-joint ashlar or some darker stone would [also] be very effective with either gray or green cement. If it seems best to build the foundation of concrete the visible part of it should be faced with red brick to give the definite effect of a foundation as separate from the walls of the house.

"The exterior timber-work would best be left un-planed, and should be stained to a soft gray-brown tone like old oak. The use made of timbers in the gables and under the slope of the roof does away with any appearance of monotony in the plain plastered walls. The balustrades of the porches should be of the same color and planed smooth. The brick chimney is plastered like the walls. With a brick foundation, the roof should be of dark-red square-edged shingle tiles."

Inside, "all the woodwork on the lower floor is of oak, stained to a luminous gray-brown tone in which there is a subtle suggestion of green. This color effect is easily gained, as it only needs one coat of one of the Craftsman stains applied to the natural wood after it is sandpapered perfectly smooth, and then one coat of a specially prepared liquid wax, rubbed down with a piece of coarse cloth or burlap." The woodwork in this house plays an especially important part, as the entry hall, living room, and dining room are all wainscoted. This wainscoting is paneled in different designs, and comes complete, ready to put up, at so much a running foot from the lumberyard. Stickley is looking for ways to reduce the high cost of his extensive woodwork by suggesting this method instead of carpenter constructed and fitted woodwork.

"In this instance the wainscot used is five feet in height. The upper walls and ceilings of all these rooms are also treated alike.

"As shown here, the woodwork covers so much of the walls and is so warm and luminous in color that the upper walls would best be very quiet and simple. For a year or two after the house is built, nothing could be better than the natural gray of the sand-finished plaster for both walls and ceilings. If more color seems desirable after the house has been furnished and lived in for a time, the

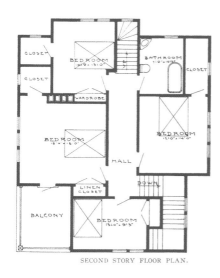

FIRST STORY FLOOR PLAN.

SECOND STORY FLOOR PLAN.

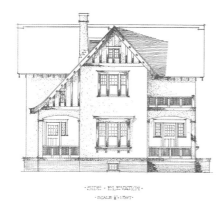

· FRONT · ELEVATION ·
· SCALE ⅛" · 1 FOOT ·

· SIDE · ELEVATION ·
· SCALE ⅛" · 1 FOOT ·

ceilings can be given a smooth finish and a tone of ivory with a slight tint of green, and the walls left rough and colored a dull pale yellow that also has in it a suggestion of green. This coloring would preserve a harmony of tone with the woodwork and yet give a warmer and sunnier atmosphere in the room than the gray."

Stickley recommends furnishing the rooms "with cushions in dull green or dark brown and portieres of moss green. Brighter bits of color could be given by the window curtains, smaller cushions and pillows, table scarves and other minor accessories, and among these should be an

occasional touch of terra cotta or brick red . . . ."

This is a house of porches. A square porch at the front serves as an entrance, and above this is a balcony that may be used as a sleeping porch. "At the back of the house there is a kitchen porch, and a square dining-porch that opens from both pantry and dining room." This porch can be glassed in for colder weather. "As these porches link the interior of the house with out of doors, they should give a suggestion of the interior treatment as well as that used on the outside of the house."

1907

As in 1906, fewer homes are offered to readers. This probably was because Stickley's interests were turning elsewhere— toward the expansion of his furniture business and the establishment of his offices in New York City, and his interest in acquiring property in New Jersey for what would become Craftsman Farms. Numbers 44 (January) and 45 (February) are awkward looking homes, but Numbers 50 (April), 51 (May) and 52 (October) are among his better designs. Of the ten homes published in 1907, nine are published by May and the remaining one in October. In February, Stickley offers three homes he describes as "cottages." They are substantial homes, bigger than the illustrations make them look. The following month he again offers three buildings—this time a series of log cabins. Responding to reader request, all of these structures attempt to offer homes that are inexpensive—at least not as costly as the homes Stickley had been offering.

No. 44 (Series of 1907, No. 1) January 1907

Roof: Cross hipped   *Bedrooms:* 3 (and sleeping porch)   *Baths:* 1   *Cost:* $6,000   *Avery Plans:* None

Stickley responds to reader requests for a home made of fireproof material with this uncomfortable looking structure. The perspective drawing may be part of the problem, because it makes the house look very small and not very deep, while the floor plans and elevations make it look bigger. In any case it is not a handsome exterior design, but the interior illustrations indicate a much more exciting living space. Stickley offers a house that can be built of either concrete or hollow tile block. *The Craftsman* claims "the structural interest of the design and the use of color will negate the effect of coldness or barrenness that is often associated with these materials." What Stickley does here is take something he is used to working in (i.e., wood) and converts the wood beams and timbers into concrete ones.

In this illustration (above), the hammered copper hood of the fireplace is framed by a band of wrought iron while ideas taken from Stickley's line of spindle furniture are shown as room dividers and in the staircase, as he integrates his furniture with his interior designs. He also continues to integrate the concept of living outdoors within his home designs. This porch (above) could easily be an interior room with the quality of its fittings, but it is also designed to be part of the exterior surroundings of the house.

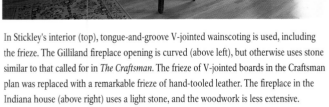

In Stickley's interior (top), tongue-and-groove V-jointed wainscoting is used, including the frieze. The Gilliland fireplace opening is curved (above left), but otherwise uses stone similar to that called for in *The Craftsman*. The frieze of V-jointed boards in the Craftsman plan was replaced with a remarkable frieze of hand-tooled leather. The fireplace in the Indiana house (above right) uses a light stone, and the woodwork is less extensive.

The living room of the Gilliland house (top) closely follows the concept (above) in *The Craftsman*. Beyond the post-and-case divider (the bookcases face the living room, while china cases face the dining room) is the dining room. While Stickley carries the ceiling all the way to the roof peak and added support trusses, Lawrence put the trusses higher and finished the ceiling around them. A view of the high-ceilinged living room (above left) from the balcony above in the Gilliland residence shows the double row of windows that allow plenty of light to flood the area.

No. 52 October 1907

Roof: Gable *Bedrooms:* 2 (each section) *Baths:* 1 (each section) *Avery Plans:* None

Stickley only designed two multifamily homes. His focus was on suburban and country houses, but he did try to design residences that could be built on city lots. This one—another long rectilinear design that could blend with other homes in a neighborhood, was specifically created for a subscriber "who owned a lot in Brooklyn thirty feet wide by one hundred feet deep, [and] desired to build within this space a Craftsman house [that] would accommodate two families who desired to live independently of one another as they would in separate houses. The house has been built and is now occupied, and the owner has kindly given us permission to reproduce the plans and two perspective drawings, to serve as a possible suggestion for other city houses which must meet the same conditions." So somewhere in Brooklyn, like a needle in a haystack, a Stickley-designed home may still survive, waiting to be discovered. "The house is of half-timber construction, with plastered walls, a shingled roof and an outside chimney of brick laid in Flemish bond. The cellar walls are of concrete faced with split field stone over the grade line." Only the front porch, the vestibule, and the rear entry can be used in common by both families. "There is no connection between the two apartments." The bedrooms at the rear of the house have porches, "which are glassed in for the winter and screened in summer to serve as outdoor sleeping rooms."

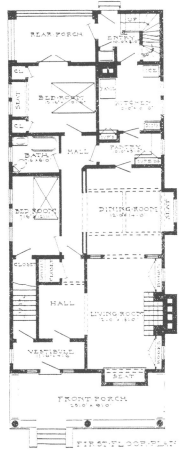

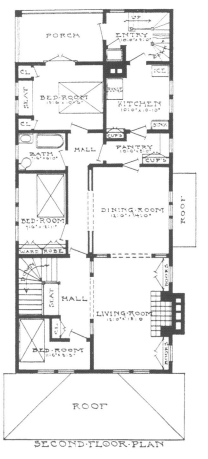

Archer H. Barber Commission 1907, North Adams, Massachusetts

Roof: Hipped with shed dormers *Bedrooms:* 6 *Baths:* 2 *Avery Plans:* None

Stickley says that, under his agreement with Barber, he can publish this house, but he cannot offer working drawings to the Home Builders Club, as it is a special commission. Barber, who was the president of the Barber Leather Company, built this home in North Adams, Massachusetts, where he raised two daughters, and died in 1950. This is one of Stickley's earliest commissions. And it shows how much Stickley was willing to work with the owner of the home to create something the client desired. Stickley appears to be talking out of both sides of his mouth when he says that deviating from Craftsman principles is itself a Craftsman principle. "The house was built for Mr. Archer H. Barber about a year ago. As the owner himself said in a recent letter to *The Craftsman*, 'The house is very livable and is meant to live in all over all the time.' Also, one of the fundamental principles that rule the designing of the Craftsman houses is evidenced at every turn here; that is the modification of every arrangement to the individual taste of the owner and the requirements of himself and his family. So, in the very fact that it shows some departure from the strict Craftsman scheme of arrangement, it is therefore all the more in accordance with the real Craftsman idea of home building."

The home is built on a hillside so that in the rear the basement is aboveground and gets plenty of light. One

The Archer H. Barber home (top) is pictured in the November 1908 issue of *The Craftsman*. The house, in this 1988 photo (above), has changed little over the years. The rear of the Barber home (right), with sweeping porches on both the basement and first-floor levels, commanded a twenty-mile view of the Berkshire Hills.

of the features is a "Dutch Room" that contains a billiard table and opens out onto a porch from which one may walk directly out onto the hillside. "The lower walls, porch parapets, the columns of the arcade and the chimneys are built of solid limestone laid in broken joint ashlar. The . . . stone itself is precisely the same formation as is seen in the outcropping rocks of the hills all around. The upper part of the house is of half-timber construction with panels of rough plaster corresponding in tone to the stone of the lower walls." All the beams, porch pillars, window frames, and other exterior woodwork are of cypress. The roof is made of cypress shingles.

"The interior woodwork is unusually fine, and the different woods are so combined as to give the interest of a strong contrast that yet does not violate the rules of harmony. The living room and dining room are done in solid mahogany. Oak is used for the third floor, the kitchen, pantries, back hallway and servants' hall on the first floor, and for the Dutch room and all the other basement rooms. The reception room and main staircase as well as the sleeping rooms on the second floor are all done in whitewood enameled to an ivory white." The doors are all mahogany, except for oak in the servants' part of the house and chestnut in the Dutch room.

Japanese grass cloth is used to cover the walls of the hall, reception room, and living room, and the prevailing colors are dull blue and straw yellow, blue predominating in the rugs, hangings, and furniture of the living room, and yellow in those of the hall and reception room. In the dining room the wall covering is green Japanese burlap, and the rugs and hangings correspond. The bedrooms are all papered in delicate tones, and the servants' portion of the house is painted with enameled paint.

The billiard room, "done in Dutch style," was located under the porch in the basement and featured Stickley's drugget rugs.

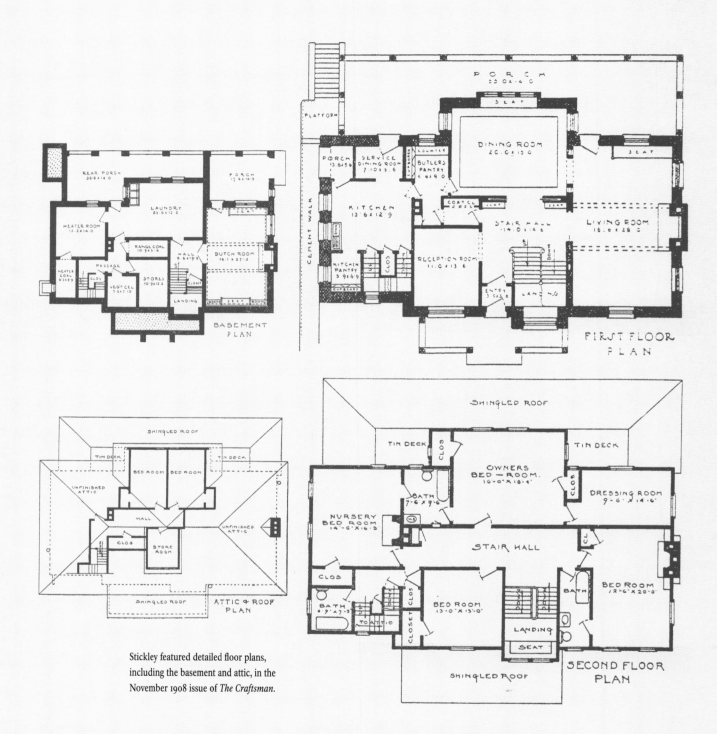

BASEMENT
PLAN

FIRST FLOOR
PLAN

ATTIC & ROOF
PLAN

SECOND FLOOR
PLAN

Stickley featured detailed floor plans,
including the basement and attic, in the
November 1908 issue of *The Craftsman*.

1908

With his interests devoted to developing Craftsman Farms and establishing his Home Building Company, Stickley's architects produce only five homes for the magazine. But there are numerous articles on the work of other architects, and long and detailed studies of the buildings being developed or proposed for Craftsman Farms. No. 56, published in September, is one of his finest homes. He also is well on the way to establishing a "style," with all the homes having a common "look." In November, Stickley announces he is again making house plans available to readers on a monthly basis, after a break of eleven months.

Three Craftsman Cottages
No. 53 (Bungalow No. I), No. 54 (Bungalow No. II), No. 55 (Bungalow No. III) November 1908

In the November 1908 issue of *The Craftsman*, three little cottages are featured, all planned for Stickley's Craftsman Farms. Stickley envisioned a boys' school as well as a working farm, and housing would be needed. He points out to readers that while these cottages would not make an ideal home, they could be put to use as vacation and "get-away" cabins. They are built from the native materials found on the site as much as practical. "The porches on all three of the cottages, and the open-air dining room in No. [53], are floored with red cement. Although there will be a number of different woods used in the construction of the cottages, two of the group shown here will be built of cypress, not stained or treated in any way, but left to weather as it will. All the roofs save one are shingled, the surroundings determining the color. The . . . cottages will probably have roofs of dull red, repeating the note of color seen in the tiled roof of the large residence near by." (Stickley is referring to his planned home, which was never built. The planned clubhouse, later converted to his residence when it was built, had a green tile roof added about 1913.) These cottages, if they were ever constructed at Craftsman Farms, no longer exist.

No. 53 (Bungalow No. I) November 1908

Roof: Gable *Bedrooms:* 2 *Baths:* 1 *Avery Plans:* 3 sheets (floor plans, section and elevation drawings, detail drawings)

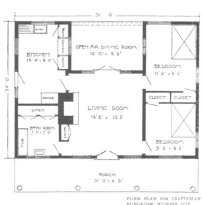

FLOOR PLAN FOR CRAFTSMAN
BUNGALOW NUMBER ONE.

"In the first bungalow the walls are sheathed with boards eight or ten inches wide and seven-eighths of an inch thick. These are to be laid like clapboards, but, owing to the thickness of the boards, it will be necessary to put a little triangular strip between each board and the joist to which it is nailed, as the wood would be liable to warp or split if the clapboards were nailed to the joist without any support between. One thing should be remembered [if the wood is untreated], the nail heads that are exposed should be slightly countersunk and puttied, or the rust from the nail will streak the wood.

"The fireplaces will all be built of selected split field stone, and will have large metal hoods like that shown in the detail of the living room. There is a reason for the use of these hoods, beyond the customary arguments that they are decorative and that they make the fire draw well, for each one conceals the simple apparatus, which will heat the whole house. In the drawing mentioned it will be noticed that a broad band of metal goes all around the fireplace opening. This band, or rather frame, is four inches wide and is made to fit into the opening exactly. The hood is riveted to the frame and the whole thing may be taken out at any time when it is necessary to clean or repair the hot-water heater behind."

No. 54 (Bungalow No. II) November 1908

Roof: Gable   *Bedrooms:* 2   *Baths:* 1   *Avery Plans:* None

FLOOR PLAN FOR CRAFTSMAN
BUNGALOW NUMBER TWO.

"The walls of the second bungalow [No. 54] are covered with cypress shingles, split or rived instead of sawn. These shingles cost twice as much as the others, but . . . they are so much more beautiful in effect. The sawn shingle is apt to get a dingy, weather-beaten look under the action of sun and wind, but the rived shingle has [a] smooth natural surface [that] takes on a beautiful color quality under the action of the weather. The shingles to be used for this particular bungalow are seven inches wide by twenty-four inches long and will be laid seven and one-half inches to the weather."

No. 55 (Bungalow No. III) November 1908

Roof: Hipped   *Bedrooms:* 2   *Baths:* 1   *Avery Plans:* 3 sheets (floor plans, elevation drawings, detail drawings)

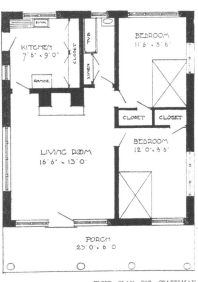

FLOOR PLAN FOR CRAFTSMAN
BUNGALOW NUMBER THREE.

No. 56 September 1908

Roof: Gable with shed dormers   *Bedrooms:* 5 (including maid's room, plus a nursery, billiard room, and sleeping porch)   *Baths:* 2   *Avery Plans:* None

This home is probably one of the first projects by Stickley's home building company. It is a spectacular home, putting an Arts and Crafts interpretation on a classic Georgian house design. The author feels it is one of his finest creations, but some of his consultants are not as enthusiastic. The home certainly embodies Stickley's best Arts and Crafts detailing, from the use of materials like the exceptionally thick siding, to the quartersawn oak woodwork, to the Grueby-tiled fireplaces, to the built-in furniture—and all within a structure exhibiting his fine sense of proportion.

"The dwelling illustrated here is a Craftsman house that is now being built at Colonial Heights, New York. Although it is not yet completed we are, through the courtesy of the owner, publishing the plans and perspectives for the reason that they may contain some suggestion to our other readers. We have found that the suggestive value of pictures and descriptions of Craftsman houses that are built to suit individual tastes and needs is greater than that of the purely theoretical plans which we published a year or two ago.

"The lower story and the chimneys are of fieldstone laid up in dark cement with wide joints. A heavy beam, running entirely around the house, rests upon the stone walls of the lower story, and forms a base for the upper stories, which are of frame construction covered with shingles. This beam not only adds greatly to the strength of the building but is one of the most interesting structural features of the exterior, giving

Stickley's concept drawing (top) is matched almost perfectly by the home built by Stickley's firm in Colonial Heights, New York, for an unknown client (above). The house is pictured after the removal of aluminum siding to reveal the original shingles. A home was built by Dr. Arthur A. Finch in Astoria, Oregon, ca. 1912–14 from the same plans (facing), but did not follow them exactly. The house was later converted into a two-family dwelling and the front porch removed. Two front doors were created in the conversion. The current owners are restoring it as a single-family home.

as it does a definite horizontal line that separates the upper and lower walls, which differ so widely in character, and affords an apparent as well as an actual, resting place for the upper structure. The upper walls are covered with shingles stained to a cool gray brown tone, and the shingles of the roof are moss green. Any effect of monotony in the color is removed by the white porch pillars and window frames."

The house features the hallmark Stickley open floor plan on the downstairs and ample size bedrooms on the second floor, and a billiard room and extra bedroom/servant quarters, plus a nursery, which could make a large bedroom, on the third floor. There is also a sleeping/sun porch.

More research needs to be done to find out who first built and occupied this home. In 1990 the aluminum siding that had been placed on the house was removed, revealing most of the shingle siding intact. In addition, a room built on top of the rear porch pergola was removed, restoring the home to its former glory.

Astoria, Or.

Dr. Finch and his wife, Gertrude McConnell Finch, ordered the plans and started construction on a site overlooking the Columbia River—where it enters the Pacific Ocean—in Astoria, Oregon, in 1912 and finished building (above) in 1914. The entire façade was done in wood shingles, and three dormer windows were installed instead of the four called for in the plans. The front porch was elongated across the front of the house to take advantage of the spectacular view, the pillars supporting the second-story porch were extended to the top of the railing and other minor changes were made. This early photo (left) is from a postcard made soon after the house was built.

Stickley offered a rare rear view of the home in the article in *The Craftsman* (below left). The Colonial Heights version (below right) has an upper porch instead of a pergola—the extra shed-roof dormer may be a later addition.

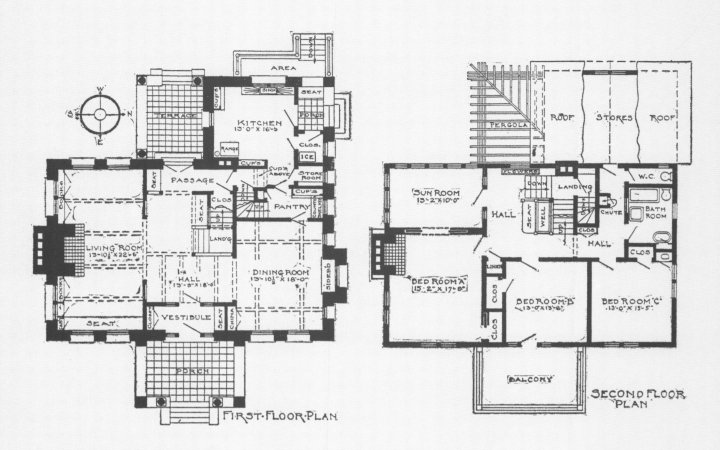

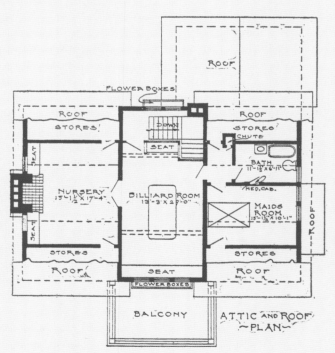

244

The porch as Stickley envisioned it (above) was duplicated in the porch for the
Colonial Heights home (right).

The living room of the Colonial Heights
home (left) is visually defined by post-
and-panel dividers and beams at right
angles to those defining the hall and
entrance door to the left.

In the interior of the Colonial Heights home, Stickley's concept (top right) was followed carefully. "The ceilings of hall, living room and dining room are beamed, and all the rooms are paneled high with quartered oak stained to a soft grayish brown tone, so that the friendly effect given by the liberal use of wood is felt as soon as one enters the house." The dining room (top left) has a built-in sideboard and china cabinet, including Stickley hardware. The hall and staircase (above) link the living and dining rooms in an open floor plan. The parquet floor is not original.

This was an exceptional Stickley design. Unfortunately, when the second owner passed away in the late 1980s the bank auctioned the house to a developer who razed the home, which was in incredible condition, and subdivided the property to build two ugly concrete boxes.

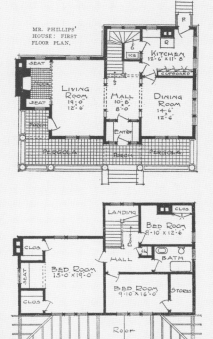

MR. PHILLIPS' HOUSE: FIRST FLOOR PLAN.

SECOND FLOOR PLAN.

A detailed drawing in the magazine's advertising section (above left) showed the front porch and pergola.

"The interior is equally typical, showing as it does the recessed fireplace nook that serves at once to make the living room larger and to provide a sheltered nook where the warmth and home comfort of the whole place seem to center." The inglenook was pictured in *The Craftsman* as a concept (center), and later is the as-built inglenook (left). The period photo shows that the house interior closely matched the plans, but that Stickley's hardware and lighting fixtures were not used—despite his company building the house!

Unknown Client Commission, New Jersey, ca. 1908

Roof: Gable with small raised roof dormer in front   *Bedrooms:* 4   *Baths:* 1   *Avery Plans:* None

Built on a lake in northwestern New Jersey, this is a special and unique home commissioned from Stickley and probably supervised by the Craftsman Home Building Company. It may even predate that company, as there are structural elements that indicate an earlier date—it looks very much like some of the designs of the 1906–7 period, and the newel and porch posts are cut in exactly the same manner as in the Phair house of 1906. So the assignment of 1908 is a best-guess estimate. The owner must have been very involved in the design because there is one feature not seen in other Stickley designs. The house has two five-sided towers built into each corner of the side of the home facing the lake.

The house has two sides that could appear as the "front." The entrance is through a portico on the side that faces the street, but by floor plan this is the back of the home (above). The real "front" of the house (top), with its two facetted "towers," faces the lake, and has three porches.

Two views of the large living room with its massive field-stone fireplace. The Stickley furniture and the mounted birds and animal heads date from just after the construction of the house.

The dining room, with its floor-to-ceiling wall paneling, extends into one of the "towers," and the Stickley sideboard occupies the space under the yellow-glassed high window (right). The built-in corner cabinet (above left) in the dining room—as well as the sideboard—appears to have been built in Stickley's Eastwood, New York, factory. The large Grueby-tiled fireplace (above right) in the dining room flanks the door to the kitchen.

This house is sited on the steeply sloping shore of a large lake and, like the Archer Barber home of 1907, the basement is fully exposed in the rear. Between the two "towers," porches are arranged on each of three stories, giving excellent views of the lake from each level of the house.

Above the fieldstone first story, the upper levels were probably sided with shakes but are now sheathed in aluminum siding. There also appear to have been later alterations to the roof's original overhang.

The front door is of unusual height—8 1/2 feet—and it opens into the rear of the house. To the right is the door to the kitchen and to the left is the living room, which runs from front to back. In the center is the staircase and off the front of the living room and in front of the kitchen is the dining room. There is a large sideboard and a corner china closet, and while built for these specific locations, they are not "built-in," as they are full pieces of furniture designed in the Craftsman workshops in Eastwood, New York. The house was originally furnished in Craftsman pieces, some of which have stayed with the house.

The woodwork appears to be chestnut on the main floor and gum-wood on the bedroom level, and all of it is finished in the warm medium brown that is used on the upper floor at Craftsman Farms.

The staircase (top) features heavy square spindles as a divider, similar to houses like the 1909 Taylor house in Summit, New Jersey. The large bench seat is typical of earlier homes.

One of the bedrooms (above) features a Grueby-tile fireplace. The wood is gumwood. The trim and doors on the second floor are of gumwood, in about the same color stain as the second floor of the Log House at Craftsman Farms. While the door hardware and sconces are not Stickley products, the doors, with the soft yellow hammered glass lights, are found in most high-quality Stickley homes.

The staircase (above) is centrally located, with a hall on the second floor allowing access to four bedrooms and a small "den" or sewing room.

The "settle post" newel posts throughout the house are all the same, as is this porch railing post (above right) on the second-story balcony.

The kitchen (right) still has many of its period cupboards, left, and it has been tastefully updated with cabinets made in similar wood and style, and a new stove.

1909

This is the breakout year for Stickley as he produces twenty-four houses for the magazine while designing at least seven special commissions. The designs range from small mansions to vacation cabins. He produces a number of compelling houses, using simple, clean designs where the visual interest is created by the mixing of construction materials as well as carefully placed porches and pergolas—always exhibiting his sense of proportion and balance. He also tries to expand the technology used in house construction. All this is in a framework of standard house types: the long rectangular two-story, the story-and-a-half low-roofed bungalow, and various modifications of the square plan of the traditional four-square presented as suburban residences, or farmhouses, or cabins.

No. 58 January 1909

Roof: Gable *Bedrooms:* 4 *Baths:* 1 *Avery Plans:* 4 sheets dated 3/20/09 (floor plans, sectional drawings, elevations, details).

This home "updates" an earlier successful design to Stickley's current thinking, as it appears to be a modification of No. 36 (Series of 1906, No. IV) of May 1906. The house has severe lines and a simple form but a real sense of proportion and balance. It is a simple and practical home. "The house is modeled very closely after a design which we published some time ago and which proved to be one of the most popular of the Craftsman house plans. Modifications and improvements, however, have been suggested by people who have built this house, so we have considered it best to incorporate these various suggestions into a new set of plans, which we publish herewith for the benefit of the Home Builders' Club. The house as shown here has plastered or stuccoed walls and a foundation of fieldstone, . . . [and as to color] some surroundings might demand a warm tone of cream or biscuit color verging on the buff, with a roof of dull red; or a dull green pigment brushed over the rough surface and then wiped off so that the effect is that of irregular lights and shades instead of smooth solid color, might be more attractive where a cool color scheme is permissible. In this case the shingles of the roof would better be oiled and left to weather to a natural brown tone.

"The front porch is very simple in design and is almost on a level with the ground. If it should be decided to use shingles or clapboards instead of plaster for the walls, the square pillars of split field stone would naturally be

Marshall F. Wilkinson, the owner of a large laundry service company near Reading, Pennsylvania, built the home in 1910 with some minor modifications. The butler's pantry was eliminated and the dining room made larger, and the trim around the door and window casings differs slightly from the normal Craftsman design. Natural chestnut is used throughout the house, although some of the upstairs rooms have been painted. In the rear, the summer kitchen was built, with a sleeping porch above it.

replaced by heavy round pillars of wood, either left in the color of the other exterior woodwork or painted white. In a plastered house the beams, window frames, etc., would be best in a wood brown tone; but if the walls are shingled or clapboarded, the woodwork would naturally harmonize in tone, care being taken to have it dark enough to give the needed accent to the color scheme of the house. The outside kitchen at the back is recommended only in the event of the house being built in the country, because in town it would hardly be needed. In a farmhouse such an outside kitchen is most convenient, as it affords an outdoor place for such work as washing and ironing, canning, preserving and other tasks [that] are much less wearisome if done in the open air. The position of the chimney at the back of the house makes it possible for a stove to be placed upon this porch for the uses mentioned. The porch might also be glassed in for winter use, because an outside kitchen is almost as desirable in winter as in summer."

In the interior, as always, the main feature is the fireplace, but in this house there are two, one in the living room and one in an alcove to the rear of the dining room.

Large bookcases flank the stone fireplace of the Wilkinson home living room (above left), just as pictured in *The Craftsman* (left). The fireplace had a hot water tank installed, with a spigot projecting out of the brickwork on the side. "The chimneypiece is built of field stone laid up in black cement and runs clear to the ceiling, preserving its massive square form to the top. A bookcase is built in on either side and above each one of these are two small double-hung windows. The tops of the bookcases serve admirably as shelves for plants."

The Wilkinson home has a three-light Stickley fixture in the nook, which is reminiscent of the nook idea in Stickley's Syracuse home (top left). "Beyond the dining room again is a nook, the end of which is completely filled by a large fireplace which uses the same flue as the kitchen range and the stove in the outside kitchen. The seat in this nook is not built in, but a broad bench or settle would be very comfortable."

The entrance foyer fits beside the staircase in a corner of the living room (top right).

The dining room (above right) has a "servant's" rear staircase on the right, and visible through the post-and-panel divider is the living room, with the front staircase and foyer to the left.

A detail of the newel post on the main staircase (above left) shows a less dramatic taper to the tops than in some Stickley homes.

Hicks House in 1989, before the owners attempted to restore the exterior.

FIRST FLOOR PLAN

SECOND FLOOR PLAN

Roof: Cross gable *Bedrooms:* 4 (plus a billiard room) *Baths:* 2 *Avery Plans:* None

This is another fine house design—it is clean, elegant, and bold, yet at the same time restrained—relying solely on the mass of the house, the arrangement of the window voids and recesses, and the massive overhanging roof for its success. Its inspiration comes from England and Voysey.

Stickley says a client ordered this home, and thus it was probably built by the Craftsman Home Building Company somewhere in the New York metropolitan area. It is interesting that he sometimes was able to negotiate releasing the plans designed for clients to others in the "Home Builders' Club," but there were cases where he noted he could not.

"The walls [of the home] are constructed of vitrified terra cotta blocks [commonly called 'hollow tile block'], the plastering being laid directly on the blocks both outside and inside. The foundation and parapet of the little terrace are of field stone laid up in black cement. We like especially the design of the entrance, which is placed at the corner of the house where the living room projects beyond the reception hall; the corner thus left is filled by the terrace, which is left open to the sky. Above the entrance door the wall runs up straight to the second story, where it terminates in a shallow balcony. Provision is made here for a flower box, as the severity of the wall seems to demand the relief in color and line afforded by a cluster of plants and drooping vines. The roof, which has a

"High wainscots are used throughout the reception hall, living room and dining room. . . . The woodwork in all these rooms is of course the same and the choice and treatment of it gives the keynote to the whole decorative scheme. As we have planned it here, the wainscot is all made of fairly wide boards V-jointed—a device that is much less troublesome and expensive than paneling and in a character is quite as effective. We would recommend that the wainscoting be made of one of the darker and stronger woods, such as oak, chestnut or cypress; or it may be made of Southern pine treated with sulphuric acid. . . . This treatment darkens the surface of the wood and brings out the grain by charring—much after the Japanese method of treatment—and excellent effects are obtained upon pine or cypress. Oak and chestnut do not lend themselves so readily to this treatment, as the color quality of these woods is better brought out by fuming, or brushing over with strong ammonia."

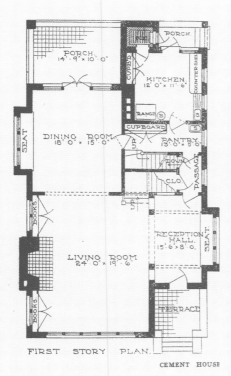

FIRST STORY PLAN.

CEMENT HOUSE

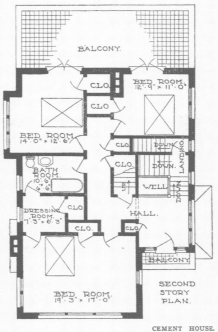

SECOND STORY PLAN.

CEMENT HOUSE.

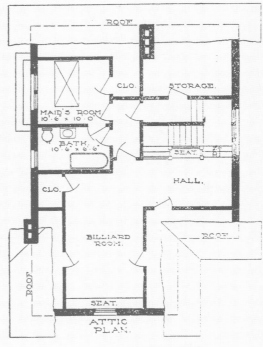

ATTIC PLAN.

CEMENT HOUSE.

wide over-hang, is covered with rough heavy slates supported on strong beams and girders which are frankly revealed. . . . The charm of these slates is that they are rough surfaced and uneven at the edges, looking more like slabs of split stone than like the small neat lozenges we have been accustomed to associating with the name of slate. They are laid rather small and thin at the ridge pole, increasing in size and weight as they go down until at the eaves they are large, broad, massive looking slabs as well suited to cement construction as tiles.

"The tile roof [Stickley is probably referring to a hollow tile block laid up under the roofing material, not roof tile] over the bay window and in the reception hall is also covered with slates and serves to break the straight, severe line of the wall. All the windows are casements and their grouping forms one of the distinctly decorative features of the construction."

Roof: Gable with shed dormer   *Bedrooms:* 2   *Baths:* 1   *Avery Plans:* None

Increasingly, Stickley makes use of the sweeping gable roof extending to cover the porch. Here he creates a charming little cottage. He says it is a farmhouse, and that "as we are building it especially for Mr. Chester A. Lerocker, at Bogota, New Jersey, its plans are not open for general use." (Stickley probably did not stick to this, as this house is featured in *More Craftsman Homes.*) The small town of Bogota lies just to the west of the Palisades cliffs along the Hudson River near New York City. While still considered country, it was being developed by 1900 and farms were disappearing. It is highly unlikely that this house would have been built in Bogota—at least for its stated purpose. A search of town records revealed that Lerocker did live in Bogota during that period in an Arts and Crafts bungalow that still exists, but not one designed by Stickley. Since there are a number of cases of Craftsman homes being built by parents as wedding gifts, it is probable that the house was built—Stickley says "we are building"—but it is likely that, if it still exists, it is located elsewhere.

This is confirmed by what Stickley says next: "This house is one that imperatively demands the environment either of the open country or of a village where there is sufficient space to give plenty of grass and trees as its immediate surroundings. The walls are sheathed with rived cypress shingles, chemically darkened to a brown weathered tint. The foundation is of field stone sunk low into a site that has not been too carefully leveled off.

"The broad roof, [which] extends sufficient to shelter the porch, [has a second floor dormer] with its group of casements which give light to both bedrooms and the sewing room on the second floor. The windows in the rest of the house are in groups of three with a double-hung window in the center and a casement of the same height on either side."

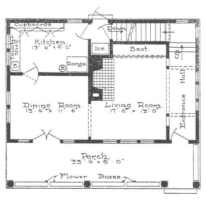

First Floor Plan.
FARMHOUSE.

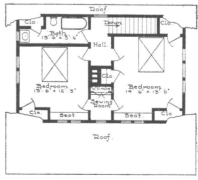

Second Floor Plan.
FARMHOUSE.

No. 62 March 1909

Roof: Cross gable *Bedrooms:* 4 *Baths:* 3 1/2 *Avery Plans:* 7 sheets (floor plans, sectional drawings, elevations, details)

Stickley states that this house is designed for a location in the southern part of the United States. Its chief features are a connection with the outdoors through broad terraces, porches, pergolas, a large outdoor fireplace, a sleeping porch, and a large front balcony. The design is certainly influenced by the work of Charles and Henry Greene and the large California "bungalows" that Stickley regularly published in *The Craftsman*. It is odd that the two exterior views in *The Craftsman* do not show the front of the home.

Another feature that is different from the typical Craftsman Home is the way the roof eaves are supported. Normally they would be solid beams extending outward horizontally—called purlins—but here they are knee braces. These triangular-shaped braces are large oversized supports that make a statement visually. While few Craftsman Homes have them, several commission homes do, including the H. M. Martin house (1909) and the J. C. Bolger home (1912), as well as House No. 199 (1915). Perhaps this house was designed for a western client and exists, but the only example that has been located is in the mountains of New York State.

"[T]he walls of the lower story are to be built of cement or of stucco on metal lath. The upper walls are shingled. The roof is of red tile and the foundation and parapets are of fieldstone. The material used, however, is entirely optional and can be varied

In the illustration published in *The Craftsman* (top) the right side of the house is detailed. The front porch is to the left and the pergola wraps around to the rear. William and Katheryn Merwin fell in love with these plans but ignored Stickley's sound advice as to a suitable location when building it (above) high in the Catskill Mountains in New York State between 1909 and 1911. A good part of the year snow piles up against the porch doors, which are designed to be open to the air and sun—and when it melts, water gets under the best of weather seals, causing rot and water damage. Bats get in under the open ventilating grids in the attic. This house was modified from the plans in a number of ways. The vertical boards called for in the plans were used on the sides of the house, but they were not cut in a sawtooth design. The large trusses under the eaves at the roof peak were not installed. While wood shingles do side the second story, yellow brick and fieldstone instead of stucco are used to sheath the first story. The published floor plans were reversed.

according to the taste of the owner or the requirements of the locality, as the building would look quite as well if constructed entirely of cement or of brick. If a wooden house is preferred, the walls could be either shingled or sheathed with clapboards, while the roof is equally well adapted to tiles, slates, or shingles. The first of the perspective drawings shows the side of the house instead of the front, as by taking this view it is possible to include both porch and court and also to show the balcony and sleeping room on the upper story. A broad terrace runs across the front of the house and continues around the side, where it forms a porch, which is meant to be used as an outdoor living room."

Stickley offers a second exterior illustration (above). "The second drawing gives a view of the whole house as seen from the rear, the viewpoint being from a corner diagonally opposite." This illustration shows that the house is designed for outside living with the extensive piazza and pergola. In the Merwin dwelling (top), the extensive pergolas were never built, removing a sense of balance and proportion—and taking away the visual drama of the design.

Stickley offers no drawings of the interior of his house, but once the interior of the Merwin home is seen, the desire to build it can be understood. The term *spectacular* is an understatement. The broad curved stair treads (above) are not a normal Craftsman design and may have been a Merwin concept. The scalloped handrail also is not a typical Craftsman feature.

The entrance to the den is through a door opening off the large hall at the foot of the staircase (above left).

At the top of the staircase (center), the upper story rooms are accessed from a wonderful inner open "court" wrapped around the staircase.

The living room (left) has a built-in alcove seat as planned, right, but the inglenook around the fireplace was never built.

The Merwin house floor plans, in addition to being a mirror image of these plans, also made some modifications. The hall and staircase area was enlarged and the lavatory relocated, the den wall being pushed back flush with the porch exterior wall, making the den narrower but creating a large hall and staircase. The french doors from the hall to the porch were replaced by a built-in seat, and the door from the living room directly to the porch was not installed. The rear hall off the dining room was not built, and the built-in sideboard was moved to the long interior wall. The fireplace inglenook was never built, nor was the outdoor fireplace.

The sleeping porch was made into a fifth bedroom, and the staircase opening enlarged, creating a two-story "court" in the center of the house.

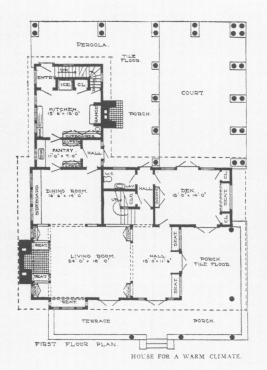

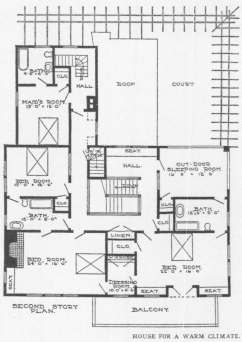

HOUSE FOR A WARM CLIMATE.

The living room (above) is separated from the dining room, on the right, and the hall and staircase at the rear, on the left, by post-and-panel dividers.

The front door features Craftsman hardware (left). The house still has a number of original Stickley lanterns and hardware fixtures.

In June 1913, Laura Rinkle Johnson offered a rare first-person article about the experience of building a Craftsman Home. Her husband William was a local banker. "When looking for a design from which to build a home we naturally turned to the back numbers of *The Craftsman* magazine, and there found a plan that strongly appealed to us, and which, with some alterations, has proved to be a most livable home. . . . The house seems well suited in shape and proportions to the location we chose for it. It nestles down under the sweeping branches of the trees as though it were as much an integral part of the landscape as the sheltering boughs above!

"The exterior trim is cypress, and the rafters and exposed purlins are of yellow pine. The windows throughout the house are casements, opening out, and the sash are painted white. The exterior doors are of oak. The sweeping roof in front forms the covering of the porch, being supported by four posts each 16 inches square.

"There is a large fireplace, built of split fieldstone, gray in color. The floors of the inglenook, as well as the vestibule, are of Welsh quarries, in two shades of red, which we find give just the right touch of color. The living and dining rooms are paneled in chestnut, the former to the height of 5 feet 10 inches and the dining room (and entrance hall) to the height of 7 feet. The finish is soft and dull in effect. This result was obtained by fuming slightly with ammonia, then shellacking, sandpapering, waxing and polishing, until a soft warm shade of brown was attained. In these rooms, above the wainscoting we used a green art canvas for wall decoration.

The large inglenook is a centerpiece of the interior design. The Johnson house reversed the floor plan published in *The Craftsman* so the bench appears on the left in the original illustration (top) and on the right in this 1993 photo of the inglenook (above). The Johnsons lived in this house for 39 years, from 1913 to 1952.

This gives an excellent contrast with the brown of the woodwork and the gray of the fireplace stones. The chestnut ceiling and beams were waxed before the fuming was done. For this reason the ammonia had no effect on them, the result being a lighter shade than that of the wainscoting. The floors, both upstairs and down, are of maple, first treated with an iron-rust stain, then shellacked with orange shellac, sand-papered, waxed and polished. The finished floors are of a dark velvety brown color, most effective.

"We have found storm windows and weather strips entirely unnecessary. We have also learned from experience and observation that the only practicable form of casement and French windows are those opening outward: they are proof against wind and rain, since the harder the wind blows, the more securely the windows fit. The curtains in these rooms are very simple and . . . the material we have chosen is English wool casement cloth, a warm tan in color.

"The upper floor . . . rooms are necessarily rather small, but we find that they answer our purpose admirably. The plaster is rough-finished and is painted yellow in the north room, pink in the west, tan in the east. while the south chamber has walls and ceiling of a soft gray, with a bluish tinge. The woodwork is cypress, shellacked and waxed.

"From early spring until late in the autumn we occupy the sleeping porch, which is fitted with a doubled bed and one single bed. The view from this porch is very unusual, extending for miles in three directions."

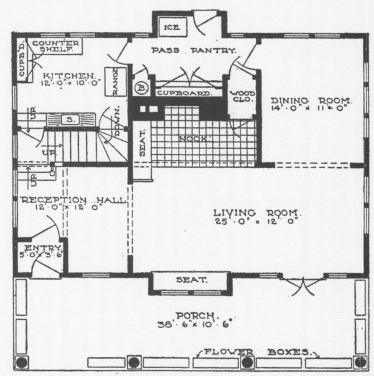

FIRST STORY PLAN

A CRAFTSMAN FARMHOUSE.

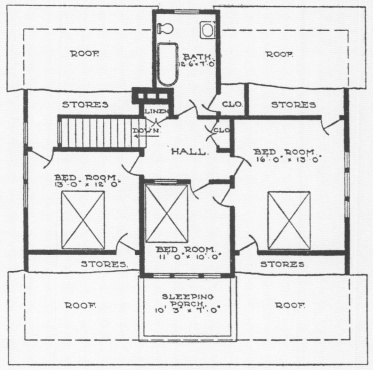

SECOND STORY PLAN.

A CRAFTSMAN FARMHOUSE.

Corwin Linson Commission, Atlantic Highlands, New Jersey, April 1909

Roof: Hipped with cut corner gable dormers   *Bedrooms:* 5   *Baths:* 3   *Avery Plans:* None

Another elongated house with a sophisticated and elegant design, the Corwin Linson commission in Atlantic Highlands, New Jersey, is an illustration of how preliminary plans could get changed before the actual construction. Between the publishing of the drawings as a Craftsman Home Building Company advertisement in April 1909 and the construction that summer, it was decided to rotate the house 90 degrees so that the long part of the home faced the top of the slope and the plans were reversed so that the front and side of the illustration became the rear and side. The rear of the house now faced the view of the Atlantic Ocean off to the northeast.

Linson was a New York City artist who traveled every summer, so he wanted the home to be designed not only for his own use, "but also to the usual requirements of the tenant who wants to rent a handsome and roomy house for the summer season. It is with this in view that the house is to be made practically

The Linson home was pictured in *The Craftsman* before it was built (above). When actually constructed it was rotated 180 degrees and the plans reversed (center). The view published in the magazine (right) sat on the edge of the slope of the hill, with views of the ocean. In addition, a porch with a shed roof was built on what was now the side of the house (to the left of the structure in the center photo), to provide a sheltered approach to the inset porch and entrance door, now in the rear of the home (at right in the lower photo). A large sweeping deck now wraps around the house and the sleeping porch is enclosed (above the expanded entrance porch on the right of the bottom photo).

indestructible, the concrete construction with hollow walls guarding against fire and the furnishing and interior woodwork being of the most substantial character."

The foundation up to the first floor is fieldstone found on the site. "The upper walls are of concrete, built according to the latest improved method, which is currently known as 'Ham's Method,' because it was invented by William Deane Ham of Knoxville, Tennessee. This form of concrete construction is interesting enough to merit some description because it not only gives two solid walls which are practically monoliths tied together at intervals of fifteen inches, both vertically and horizontally, with iron or copper ties, but also because it does away with the costly and cumbersome wooden molds which are growing more and more expensive as the price of lumber increases and which are useless after the walls are built. No one denies the desirability of air spacing in either block or monolithic construction, for the fact that the hollow wall insures coolness in summer, warmth in winter and dryness in all seasons has long been established. The only question at any time has been as to the best, most economical and most practical method of building hollow concrete walls, and the use of steel molds, which is the distinguishing feature of this method, seems to have solved it. The molds are made interchangeable so that they may be used upon building after building, and another marked advantage is that any desired finish, from the perfectly smooth surface to the roughest pebble-dash, may easily be obtained by this method.

"The severity of the large plain wall spaces in this house is made less evident by the grouping of the many windows, which are all casement with small square panes. This is one of the houses where exterior decoration would be a mistake as its distinction rests chiefly upon this very severity. The decorative structural features are all inside, where the interior trim is unusually interesting, both in color and form. The ceilings are beamed and the walls wainscoted with yellow pine, which is used throughout the house for the interior woodwork. This pine is treated by the sulphuric acid method we have several times described in these pages."

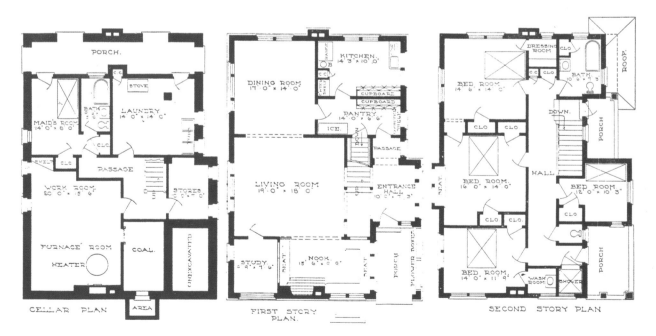

These plans were reversed when the home was built. The first floor study room was never built.

The entrance hall and staircase (above) are opposite the entry foyer.

The Craftsman illustration shows the fireplace surrounded by built-in benches set next to a private study hidden behind a doorway (above left).

When Linson built the home, the plans were reversed, the benches were eliminated, and the study never built (left). The french doors on the right lead to the entrance foyer and staircase.

The dining room (below) has a full-length sideboard and cabinets on one wall. The ceiling beams are the joists for the second story.

No. 64 April 1909

Roof: Gable   *Bedrooms:* 5   *Baths:* 1   *Avery Plans:* 6 sheets

This is a handsome house, and is another variation of the long, deep house plan. The exterior is related to the earlier No. 60 house. Again, with the exception of the shallow gable roof, it owes a lot to the influence of Voysey. It has all the hallmarks of Stickley designs—irregular window groups balanced, with voids and projections breaking up a severe block-like rectangle. The house exudes both strength and safety. "We have had so many demands for houses of concrete construction without timbers that we have shown it here in that way. As it stands here, it is a house that would lend itself very kindly to vine covered walls, as these would tend to soften the severity of the lines and wall spaces. The roof of this house is unusually flat, and is meant to be covered with a kind of roofing which we have found particularly durable and satisfactory. This is a composition roofing [probably 'Ruberoid'-brand roofing material used on the log house at Craftsman Farms] that is one-eighth of an inch thick and comes in rolls—like matting. It is laid in strips from the ridge pole down to the eaves and cemented together where it joins. Over each seam is laid a wooden strip or batten five or six inches wide, and the roof at the eaves is wrapped over to form a roll, softening the line into a rounded effect not unlike that of a thatched roof. Such a roof, if properly put on, should last for twenty-five of thirty years without repair."

CONCRETE HOUSE: FIRST FLOOR PLAN.

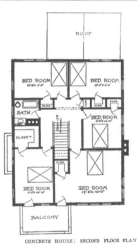

CONCRETE HOUSE: SECOND FLOOR PLAN.

No. 65 April 1909

Roof: Gable with gable dormers   *Bedrooms:* 3 (plus maid's room and billiard room)   *Baths:* 2   *Avery Plans:* 5 sheets

This adaptation of a chalet-type house is an attractive stone and cement bungalow that uses a mixture of materials cleverly. "The use of split field stone for the walls of the lower story and the square pillars of the porch would be so effective that it would be a pity not to use it in a part of the country where stone is easy to get. In such a house the gables would better be of plaster with the half-timber construction, as shown here. This kind of house lends itself admirably to the use of heavy timbers, such as appear all around the walls at the top of the first story, especially as timbers are used with such good effect in the exposed rafters and girders, which support the widely overhanging roof. We wish to call special attention to the construction just over the recess in the middle of the porch, where a beam twelve inches square rests on top of the two beams of equal dimensions, which appear at the sides. This raises the line twelve inches just over the recess in which are placed the French doors leading into the living room and the windows on either side, so that by this device we not only obtain a highly decorative structural effect, but admit more light to the living room. Just above is the sleeping porch, also recessed for a part of its depth and protected by a heavy wooden balustrade. This porch affords ample room for two beds, one at either end."

Perhaps used to dealing with clients who altered his plans, Stickley bends over backwards to tell the reader what should be obvious: "The floor plan

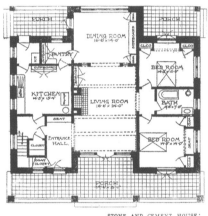

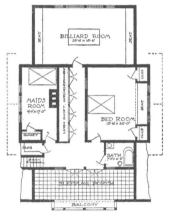

STONE AND CEMENT HOUSE: FIRST FLOOR PLAN.

explains the arrangement of the interior, which in many respects could be altered to suit the convenience of the owner. For example, the fireplace in the living room could easily be recessed, forming an attractive fireplace nook. In that case, the range in the kitchen would face the other way. The kitchen itself could be thrown all into one, omitting the small pantry and store room. Built-in cupboards could easily supply the place of the pantry, and the kitchen porch could be enclosed for an outside kitchen and

cool room. Also, instead of the built-in sideboard and china closets which extend all across one side of the dining room, an arrangement could be made by which a door would open from the dining room upon the porch at the back, which could then be used as an outdoor dining room or sunroom, instead of a sleeping porch opening from one of the lower bedrooms. Upstairs the billiard room could be used for a bedroom, if needed, or it could even be partitioned across the center to form two rooms."

F. S. Peer Commission, Ithaca, New York, April 1909

Roof: Gable with shed dormers   *Bedrooms:* 6 (with sewing room plus a sleeping porch)   *Baths:* 2 1/2   *Avery Plans:* None

The F. S. Peer house is another example of how plans were changed from concept to construction, including the location—Stickley placed the home in Utica, when the location was actually in Ithaca, New York. The house was designed to look "English" through the use of half-timber construction, perhaps because Mr. Peer came from England.[57] Although the floor plan is different, there is a certain similarity in appearance to the design of Craftsman Home No. 10 in 1904.

By the time the house was built, it had lost the third story, the gable side dormers, as well as several rooms and the tin-roof porches. The new design, with the shed dormers, does look more like a typical Craftsman Home.

The F. S. Peer home as pictured in the April 1909 issue of *The Craftsman* (above). By the time the home was constructed, the third floor was removed, the pergola in the center was expanded across most of the house, and the covered tin-roofed porches eliminated. The conservatory, or "hot house," was built.

The house really has two fronts. The conceptual published view is of what became the rear yard. The front, or formal, side of the house (center) looks similar and was published in *The Craftsman*.

The main difference between the two sides is that the back, or garden side (right), has a pergola which wraps around it. More of the house can be seen in winter when the wisteria on the pergola is not in bloom.

SECOND FLOOR PLAN.

FIRST FLOOR PLAN.

The house has a center hall with entrances from either side (top). The plans called for a beamed ceiling. The living room (above), pictured in *The Craftsman*, was supposed to have a beamed ceiling, but Peer chose to cover the rafters with a plaster ceiling.

No. 66 May 1909

Roof: Gable   *Bedrooms:* 3   *Baths:* 1   *Avery Plans:* None

Stickley continues to explore the long two-story gable roof design again, mixing his materials well and providing a small home with well-balanced proportions. No. 66 is a cement (lower-story) and shingle (upper-story) home that would fit a narrow city lot nicely. "The lower story of the house is of cement on a low foundation of split field stone. The pillars and all the woodwork are of cypress, which must be either chemically treated or painted to withstand the action of the weather. The second story is covered with hand-split shingles seven inches by twenty-four, left to take on the beautiful gray driftwood color that time gives to them.

"We wish to call attention to the suggestion of a pergola at the rear of the house. This is merely a three-foot projection on a porch running under the second story, and is built of the exposed timbers of the house supported by pillars. It not only adds to the attractiveness of that corner as seen from the street, but, covered with vines, would give a lovely outlook for the dining room windows, and, since a door connects it with the kitchen, may be itself used as a dining room in warm weather. All the exposed windows on the second story are hooded to protect them from driving storms. It is an attractive feature in the construction, especially in connection with the window group—a long French casement flanked on either side by a double-hung window— looking out upon the balcony."

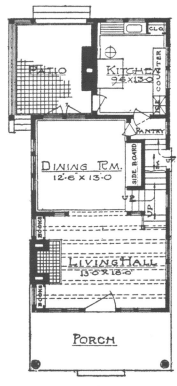
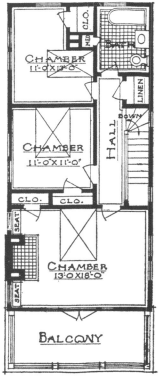

CEMENT AND SHINGLE HOUSE:
FIRST AND SECOND FLOOR PLANS.

288

No. 67 May 1909

Roof: Cross gable   *Bedrooms:* 6 (plus attic)   *Baths:* 2   *Avery Plans:* None

Another variation on the long rectangular house, this exterior is almost Arts and Crafts perfection. Stickley takes the exterior of No. 52 and simplifies it, removing the clutter and cutting the use of various materials to the bare bone. He also enlarges the side gable to help the design. Looking at the illustration one would think that this is a large home, but it is only 19 feet wide. This house is built of cement on a split fieldstone foundation. If built in a neighborhood of older houses, it is suggested that "the natural color of the cement be deepened to a granite gray" so the house will not stand out in contrast.

"*The Craftsman* inclines to the use of casement windows. The small square panes are always attractive in a room and spaces are left beneath casement windows for built-in seats, handsome paneling, or, as in this case, book shelves; things which go to make a room interesting in itself, independent of the furnishings."

Despite the narrow width, a maid's room with bath is provided on the main floor and the attic is big enough to add extra bedrooms "or a billiard room."

The living room features a large tapestry brick fireplace, and the dining room, to the rear left, "is wainscoted with V-jointed boards and is separated only by narrow partitions from the living room." Less successful is the frieze. Instead of the usual board defining the frieze at the window tops, thin wooden strips link the window and doorframes below the tops of the frames.

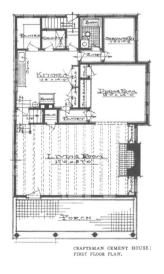

CRAFTSMAN CEMENT HOUSE:
FIRST FLOOR PLAN.

CRAFTSMAN CEMENT HOUSE:
SECOND FLOOR PLAN.

Dr. Mary E. Richards Commission, Garden City, New York, May 1909

Roof: Hipped   *Bedrooms:* 4 (the office could be used as a fifth)   *Baths:* 2   *Avery Plans:* None

The Craftsman Home Building Company built this pleasant house, modeled after the English country cottage style, in Garden City, New York, for a Dr. Mary E. Richards. It is similar to buildings constructed by English architects Barry Parker and Raymond Unwin about this period. An advertisement in the May 1909 issue of *The Craftsman* tells readers about the house before it was constructed, and it appears to have been built according to the plans.

The lower-story exterior is cement on metal lath. The upper story cantilevers out slightly on each side of the house, dramatically supported by the exposed second-floor joists. Additional visual interest is provided by the half-timbering. The hipped roof perfectly caps the design. The exterior wood is all cypress, treated with sulphuric acid, and the cement surface is left rough and tinted "to tone with the delightful browns of the woodwork."

Almost all of the Home Building Company homes are designed with a center hall layout, despite Stickley's stated desire to eliminate it. It seems that most of his clients liked that feature. Richards needed an office and the hall made sense—the open post-and-panel division between the hall and the living room does create a feeling of spaciousness. The interior of the home has been painted and the room arrangements modified over the years.

FIRST FLOOR PLAN.

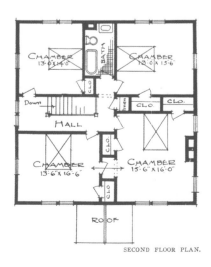

SECOND FLOOR PLAN.

No. 68 June 1909

Roof: Gable   *Bedrooms:* 3   *Baths:* 1 1/2   *Avery Plans:* None

This brick house is a formal-looking structure with its balanced lines and the sidewalls carried up into a parapet above the roof—it uses the vernacular of some houses from the Federal period. The pergola and porch roof inject the Craftsman style into the house. The view is of the rear of the house, showing its connection to the garden. There is no porch or pergola over the front entrance. No illustration of the front of the home was published.

Stickley suggests the wood be "the soft, deep brown . . . chemically treated cypress" and the roof be slate. "The walls of [each] wing, thrown out at either side, are also carried up beyond its roof, where they form the parapet of a little balcony." At the second-story level there is "a projecting cornice, which, extending about the whole house, marks the belt course."

"One of the most interesting features is the front entrance, which is shown in the . . . floor plan. One enters the house through a vestibule, the floor of which is on a level with the ground. Within, opposite the entrance door, three steps go up to the living room. Owing to this difference in floor levels, the stairs that lead from the living room to the second story can run up over the vestibule, and thus space is economized. The construction of this door is especially interesting. It is made of three wide thick planks—V-jointed, with three small square lights in the top. The wide strap-hinges that extend almost the entire width of the door are of hand-wrought metal."

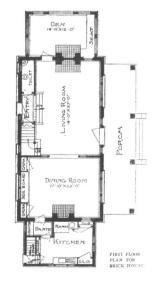

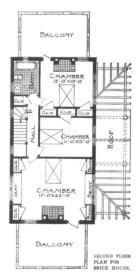

Roof: Gable   *Bedrooms:* 3 (plus small sewing room and sleeping porch)   *Baths:* 1   *Cost:* $3,000   *Avery Plans:* None

The technique (not a line drawing, but watercolor?) for the drawing of this home is different from most of those published during 1909. The house also is different, as the traditional large overhanging roof is missing. Perhaps a freelance architect drew the house—hired for a short time at a busy shop. It is a handsome house and a larger roof might not have improved the design. Stickley acknowledges the difference but does not explain it: "The chimneys are a continuous wall from base to top, the roof having almost no projection over the ends of the house. It is built entirely of rough stone, except for the necessary timbers, window and door frames, which are cypress. The roof might be painted a dull red. . . . All the timbers are left exposed, making a rugged finish consistent with the rough exterior of stone.

"The chimneypiece [in the living room] suggests the exterior of the house because it is of the same material, and thus brings the whole into closer relation. There is a great deal of woodwork in this room and throughout the lower story; as the house was planned, this wood is of elm stained to a soft brown. Elm is a very desirable finishing wood because of the variety of the graining. It has the long wavelike vein of cypress and, beside that, a short, close, rippling figure that covers the rest of the surface. Thus it is suited to places where small areas of wood are required, as well as to expanses that need a heavy

The illustration in *The Craftsman* shows a house without the characteristic wide eaves (top). Royal H. and Louise S. Morrow built this house (above) almost as planned near Brevard, North Carolina, in 1915. However, they raised the second-floor dormer all the way across the front of the home, changing the window configuration in the process. They also made some interior changes by altering the living and dining rooms and the staircase wall. Royal was a civil engineer who worked with the U.S. Forest Service on the design of many projects, including the Blue Ridge Parkway, and Louise had studied art in Europe. This was their second house of Craftsman design, having previously built a version of No. 96. The stone to build the house was salvaged from the ruins of the Hume Hotel, which had burned during the Civil War.

Local librarian Catherine Reichbacht built a version of No. 69 using stucco instead of stone (facing above) in Elmhurst, Illinois, a suburb of Chicago. The upstairs plans were reversed. This incarnation shows some influence of the Prairie School in its realization. This photo was made shortly after construction was finished. The house now has an attached garage, but has recently had the interior restored. A period photo (facing above) shows that the home has changed little since it was built, although there is now an attached garage (facing below).

and striking grain to give them character. The inglenook is wainscoted with V-jointed boards. At the joints of the boards that mask the end of the seat, keys of wood are inlaid, giving an extra firmness to the joint."

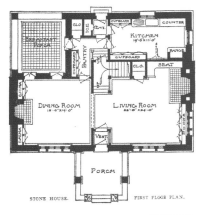

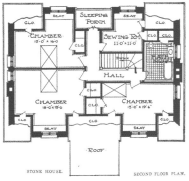

The bench, bookcase, and fireplace in a corner of the planned living room (above right).

The living room fireplace in the Morrow home (center right) is made of huge blocks of stone.

The living room became the dining room in the Morrow house (right), and the planned fireplace and inglenook (above right) were never built. The interior is rough plaster with dark-stained pine trim.

View of the upstairs hallway in the Morrow home (above). The two doors lead to the bedrooms.

The rear dining porch (center) can be accessed through the living room or the pantry.

Royal and Louise Morrow sit on the rear porch in the 1930s (left). The Morrows owned the house for the rest of their lives, and their grandson still lives there.

Roof: Gable *Bedrooms:* 4 (plus sewing room and servant's rooms) *Baths:* 1 1/2 *Avery Plans:* None

The Craftsman Architects pay homage to the brothers Charles Sumner Greene and Henry Mather Greene, the California architects, in this entirely successful adaptation of their style—in this case a variation of the Libby House of 1905. This house "is built entirely of wood on a foundation of field stone. Both purlins and rafters [are] exposed. Cypress is the wood used for the exterior of the house, but it is used in various forms. The weather-boarding and shingles are thick and broad so that the angle of their projection upon each other is deep enough to cast a shadow, and thus, even at a distance, the walls retain the rugged character of their construction. The roof is of low pitch with a projection of four feet at the eaves. The lower story and part of the second is covered with eight-inch weather-boarding, seven-eighths of an inch thick. This surface is varied by two belt courses of four-inch boards, laid flat, and stained a darker color than the rest of the house. Between the upper belt course and the eaves, rived shingles are used. In the gable, narrow V-jointed boards are laid vertically, with a flat band matching the belt courses in color, forming the finish between the vertical boards and the shingles, and running around the house at the line of the eaves. The effect of these three parallel courses of a darker color is to take away from the height of the house and give it a low, bungalow-like look in spite of its three stories. The windows all over the house are much the same, each

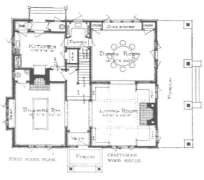

one protected by a hood; the large windows are made with a stationary panel, on either side of which a single casement opens outward. The smaller windows have a casement placed beside a stationary panel of the same size. When the window is open it gives the effect of a double casement with one half closed. By the use of a casement adjuster, it is possible to open the window and keep it open at any distance desired without raising the screen.

"The entrance door is paneled, with a group of square lights at the top, and opens upon a small porch built of

stone, with stone posts at either side of the steps. Large wooden pillars stand upon these posts and support the roof that protects the porch. Instead of a parapet, two wooden seats are built along the sides. As it is always the Craftsman idea to make a porch practically an outdoor room of the house, and not a public entrance, the large living porch is at the side of the house and opens with French doors from the dining room.

"From the entrance door one enters through a small vestibule into a hall, the end of which is raised by two

edge so that the effect of a balcony is given. From the landing the stairs continue to the second story behind a partition of spindles, which arrangement makes them a part of both the living room and hall and a really valuable asset when a large number of people are being entertained, as well as turning a most necessary feature of the house into a most artistic one."

The interior of the house (above) is filled with warm medium-brown-stained chestnut woodwork on both floors, and appears to be as planned, although the staircase landing was closed off to the dining room, where the sideboard appears to be specially built to fit in the space (the door, right, remains, but behind it is a shallow closet) and otherwise modified long after the home was built.

The second-story hall (left), with a bedroom through the door to the rear. Note the window in the wall of the center chamber allows cross-ventilation to the front room.

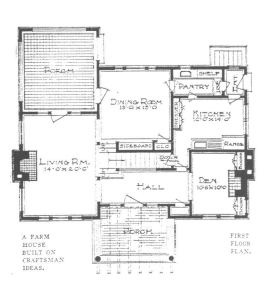

A FARM HOUSE BUILT ON CRAFTSMAN IDEAS.

FIRST FLOOR PLAN.

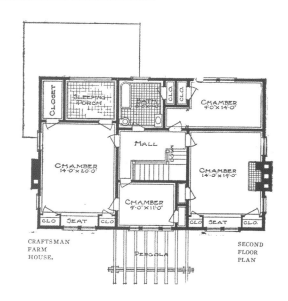

CRAFTSMAN FARM HOUSE.

SECOND FLOOR PLAN

Roof: Gable   *Bedrooms:* 3   *Baths:* 1   *Avery Plans:* 5 sheets (floor plans, sections, elevations, detail drawing, framing plans).

This low-slung bungalow type was gaining popularity and was frequently featured in publications like Henry Wilson's *Bungalow Magazine*. "The plans show the rooms to be conveniently arranged in such a way that although on the same floor, the bedrooms are completely separated from the kitchen and living room."

After several years of omitting them, Stickley offers decorating suggestions: "The decoration has been left to the Craftsman taste. The tones in hammered copper seemed best to sum up the light and shade that were needed in the rooms, and so, accordingly, our color scheme has resolved itself into an analysis of these shades. On the walls, the last coating of brown plaster has been smoothed with an iron trowel and left to dry with no finishing surface applied. Against this tone, are the girders, the built-in sideboard and all the stationary woodwork of chestnut, a wood showing a wide play of [brown] color under different light. It furnishes a transition from the light tone of the walls to the deep red-brown of the fumed oak furniture, upholstered in leather of the same shade. The wood furniture is varied by occasional pieces of brownish green willow, which again blends the brown of the furniture and walls with the green rug on the floor. The design in the rug is worked out in dull amber and red-brown and these shades are again repeated in the lanterns of hammered copper set with amber glass and suspended by chains from the

The house built by Roger Millan, a local photographer and weaver, in Hackettstown, New Jersey, ca. 1909–15 (center) closely resembles the concept drawing in *The Craftsman* (top). The article says that "we are at present building," so this could be constructed by the Home Building Company. However, there are four front columns instead of six, and the owner believes that the house was built about 1915. There are no Craftsman fixtures. A weaving studio still exists behind the main house. A Mr. Fletcher constructed another version of this home about 1910 (above), as one of the first homes in the "Craigmere" section of Mahwah, New Jersey, a development of homes built mainly in the Arts and Crafts style in a very rustic setting. Either at the time of construction or at some point thereafter, a large addition was added to the side of the house. It does have six columns, but they are square.

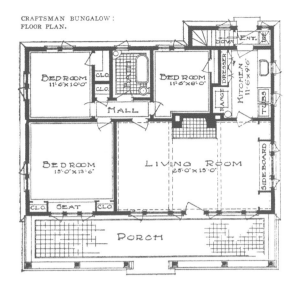

CRAFTSMAN BUNGALOW :
FLOOR PLAN.

girders. The china-closet doors have panes of this same glass and, like the sideboard, the trim is of hammered copper. In the matter of curtains and covers, in this room we incline to a curtain made of a soft silk that repeats the amber shade in the glass, and wherever covers are needed the darkest shade of Flemish linen would be in best harmony with the oak."

"The [living room] serves also as the dining room, occupying almost one-third of the whole bungalow (center left)." The Millan home interior is close to the plans, but the hardware is not Craftsman (above left). "The chimneypiece with its shelf of a thick oak board is of split field stone and the hearth is set with square, rough-textured tiles" (center right). "The bedrooms are completely separated from the kitchen and living room." A door to the left of the fireplace leads to the bedroom area (above right).

Miss H. M. Martin Commission, Ithaca, New York, September 1909

Roof: Clipped cross gable with shed dormers   *Bedrooms:* 7 (with 3 sleeping porches, a dressing room, and a billiard room)   *Baths:* 4
Avery Plans: None (partial set of blueprints are in possession of the current owner)

Of English/European influence, and similar to some published houses by Philadelphia architect Wilson Eyre, this house in upstate New York was designed for New York City resident Miss Harriet M. Martin, a student at Cornell University. The current owners say Martin used inheritance money to build the house. She lived off-and-on in the house, or in the nearby carriage house, all her life. When she was not there, the house was used as a sorority residence and later as apartments. Perhaps that explains the unique, apartment-like arrangement of the

The house is illustrated in an advertisement in the September 1909 issue of *The Craftsman* (top right). An emblem or device is plainly visible on the chimney. Mottos and quotes from literature are frequently found in Arts and Crafts architecture, particularly in the interior of a building, but this exterior design (above) is highly unusual on a Stickley house. The inscription "The Truth Shall Make Us Free" (surrounding a lit torch and the letters A and C) comes from the Bible (John 8: 31–36), but it was also the title of a famous speech on the principles of social freedom given in 1871 by Victoria C. Woodhall, an advocate of Free Love. The entrance to the house from the courtyard is a recessed door where the two wings intersect (center). An extensive garden south of the house (right) features a large bench inscribed with a poem by Goethe.

floor plans—Miss Martin intended it for use by a sorority or simply as backup income-producing property. More research still needs to be done on what relationship she may have had with Stickley.

The house is featured in an advertisement in the August 1909 issue of *The Craftsman* as a house designed by the Craftsman Home Building Company "carrying out the ideas of its client." While Stickley says "we do not call [this] house . . . a Craftsman House, because the building of it . . . is not, as far as we know, to be done by us, nor have we left to our own invention as to the plans. We have simply been asked by one who has seen and liked the houses we have designed and built in this town[59] to apply our trained knowledge . . . to make possible to her, her ideals of a house and home." The statement really makes very little sense, because

The north side of the house, and the real "front" elevation, faces a long bowling green built at the edge of a steep slope (below). A large pergola above a long porch frames the entrance to the house. The view is shown during construction (right) and in 2005 (above).

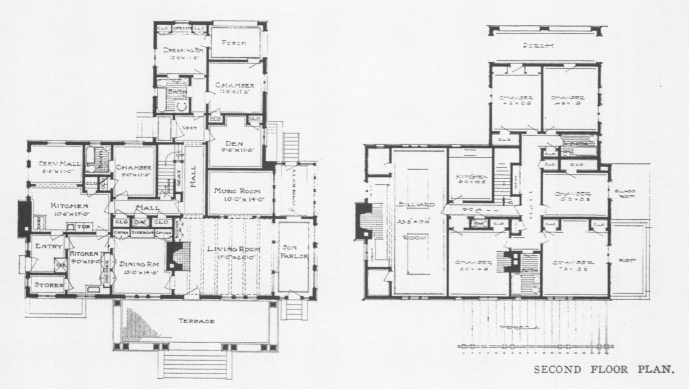

FIRST FLOOR PLAN.

SECOND FLOOR PLAN.

almost all the houses advertised by the Craftsman Home Building Company were built for clients who took an intense interest in what type of home they wanted. And the house most decidedly *is* a Craftsman Home, one of his finest designs!

Built in an L shape with two wings facing a courtyard, the house has two "main entrances," one a large door in a recessed porch where the two wings pictured in the drawing join, wrapping around the courtyard, and one framed by a large pergola above a porch on the opposite side of the main wing, the one to the right side of the drawing. The house is finished on the exterior with roughcast cement, the lower story being built with hollow tile block and the upper with metal lath. The color was left a natural gray. "The woodwork is all cypress chemically treated to achieve

a soft-grey brown. The roof is red Spanish tile." Large bold brackets are used to support the roof eaves instead of the traditional Craftsman use of large projecting purlins. The sprawling design is pulled together by a belt course marked by a deep indentation running around the building, "which causes a shadow and thus breaks the wall stretch and takes away from the height of the house. The big dormers broken from the roof also add to the low rambling effect of the structure, as does the blunting of the gables.

"The interior of the home has been essentially divided into four suites with certain living rooms in common, as can be seen in the floor plans provided." There are a total of three kitchens, although two are linked together (the smaller was a private libratory kitchen for the

owner's personal use and it could also be used as a very large pantry and serving preparation area), as well as a den, music room, and billiard room. The living room and music rooms have a spectacular view over the sun parlor and terrace to the lake in the distance. The living room has a beamed ceiling upon which the upper-story floor is laid.

By the time the house was actually constructed in 1911, the tile roof was done in green, not red, but the exterior woodwork was all cypress. The windows were solid cypress, and the doors were veneered with cypress on the exterior and chestnut on the interior. Stickley cabinet and door hardware, and lighting were used throughout. The interior woodwork is all flat-sawn chestnut that at some point was painted. The current owners have stripped it.

The existing blueprints indicate

Stickley may have worked with George Burnap, a well-known landscape architect in Washington, D.C. (most famous for planning the planting of cherry trees around the Tidal Basin in 1912), in planning the grounds. Burnap was working on his master's degree in the Cornell Rural Art program in 1910. He also was instrumental in setting up the school's landscape architecture program, all while serving as a lecturer. Whether the two men worked together or not, Burnap applied various design elements from the house to the garden structures. This included a large masonry bench with Moravian tile insets. Blueprints for the bench and other garden structures are dated July 16, 1909, so his work on the property is concurrent with Stickley's. The blueprints also show a sketch of the flat cap tiles on the garden wall, which probably influenced the choice

The fireplace area of the living room was photographed during restoration work in 1993 (top), and again when the restoration was complete in 2005 (above). The color of the plaster was replicated from the original color found during the restoration process (right). Some of the missing woodwork (mainly a frieze rail) indicated in the blueprints has not yet been replaced.

The hall and staircase form a central core to the floor plan. The hall is dominated by a huge bench seat (top left and above), behind which the staircase climbs to a landing and then up three more steps to reach each wing of the house (top right). The open front door and the newel post lamp were photographed while restoration was in progress in 1993 (top center).

The living room (above) is linked through post-and-panel partitions to a "music room" on the left, and with a step down, to an enclosed porch to the rear of the room. The living room is further defined by the beamed ceiling, which is absent from the two adjoining spaces. The porch (left) is linked by a door to a conservatory in the rear. The steps lead back into the living room.

of roofing tiles. Other gardens (courtyard, bowling green) were designed
after the house was built and date
from April 1912. Burnap was the one
who called the estate "Gipfelruh"
on all the plans. The name means
"hilltop" and the following poem—
on the back of the large garden
bench—is by Goethe:

WANDRERS NACHTLIED II

Über allen Gipfeln / ist Ruh,
In allen Wipfeln / spürest Du
Kaum einen Hauch.
Die Vögelein schweigen im
Walde;
Warte nur, balde
Ruhest du auch.

WANDERER'S NIGHTSONG II

On the tops of all the hills
there is silence.
In the tops of the trees, you feel
hardly a breath.
The little bird falls silent in the trees.
Simply wait. Soon you too
will be silent.
—translation by poet Robert Bly

Layers of paint were stripped from the interior to reveal magnificent woodwork. The dining room (top) features a
built-in sideboard and two china cabinets. The light fixture is not original to the house.

There was little information about the large billiard room (above) on the second floor above the kitchens that could
aid in the restoration of the space. A large fireplace with flanking benches dominates the room. Missing woodwork
has been replaced with sassafras. The ceiling may not be new; while the owners do not have the original plans for
the billiard room, they do have some plans used during later remodeling that give some clues about the room's
original built-in furnishings.

No. 76 October 1909

Roof: Gable with shed dormers   *Bedrooms:* 4 (with large sleeping porch)   *Baths:* 1
Avery Plans: 9 sheets (floor plans, sections, elevations, detail drawings, framing plans)

Commissioned by Fred W. Schultz in Maplewood, New Jersey, the Craftsman Architects prepared the plans, and the Craftsman Home Building Company may have built this house. Mary Ann Smith's research indicates that "after October 9, 1909, all receipt and disbursement records for the construction company terminated,"[60] but it appears that Stickley did continue to take on projects when clients paid his firm to "supervise" the construction of their home.

Built in Stickley's rustic bungalow style, the theme of this house is about living with the outdoors. The layout is that of a "camp" retreat or weekend and vacation house. Yet the house was built in an area that was being developed for year-round living, with typical suburban homes of the period. The plans presented in the October issue were changed when the house was built. Instead of double doors to the large main room, a less dramatic single door was installed. And there is no plaster on the finished lower floors; it is all wood, all finished at a high level.

The living room is designed to also serve as a dining room. "It is the plan of the owner to use the sleeping balcony on the second story during all sorts of weather, and a flight of stairs connects it directly with the chamber on the first floor; but it may also be reached from the living room. On either side of the sleeping balcony, which is protected by dormer roofs,

Matching the concept in *The Craftsman* closely (top), the Fred W. Schultz house sits in a rustic setting on the side of a hill, now surrounded by mature trees and plantings (center). Another version (above), built in a slightly modified form by W. W. Merriman in Los Gatos, California, was pictured in *The Craftsman* but has not been located. Merriman has been found listed as a San Francisco resident, and this house may have been built in the mountains west of Los Gatos as a retreat home. "The same materials—shingles with stone chimney—are used in the Western bungalow as in its first Eastern 'incarnation,' and with the exception of the windows and the openings of the big attic room, which have been slightly altered, the general appearance of the two is very similar."

When the Schultz house was built, the plaster ceiling and frieze pictured in *The Craftsman* (right) was not installed, leaving the second-floor joists exposed and finished as a beamed ceiling. To provide some surface to reflect light and relieve the admittedly unrelenting wood tone, panels were carefully and non-permanently inserted in the space between the massive joists to give the appearance of a plaster ceiling. Additional lighting in the Arts and Crafts style was added (above). The large french doors opening to the garden were also not installed—Schultz opted for a single door.

No. 78 Abraham Ackerman House, HoHoKus, New Jersey, built ca. 1910

This home sits far back from the street on a large property—the original lot was five acres. The exterior looks to have been built exactly from the plans sent by the Craftsman Architects, but the interior is not Craftsman at all. The floor plan was followed exactly, but, with the exception of the large fieldstone fireplace in the living room, it does not have a Craftsman-style interior. The woodwork is painted white and milled in a colonial style. The staircase balustrade has turned spindles. There is, however, a Craftsman-style door to the cellar. It has been impossible to tell if the home was built that way or was gutted and the interior totally changed at a later date. A rear addition was added in 1950.

The Abraham Ackerman house exterior (top) matches the plans, but the interior is not in the Craftsman style. The staircase (center) features turned spindles, but note the Craftsman door to the right rear, leading to the kitchen. The large fieldstone fireplace (above) was built in the living room. Newer pine paneling has been installed, hiding how the interior may have been finished. The dining room (right), as well as the rest of the house, does not feature Arts and Crafts detailing.

Charles H. Brockmeyer, the town pharmacist, built his home in this little Kentucky hamlet shortly after getting married. He later was a pilot after serving in the Army Air Corps in World War I. He and his wife lived their entire lives in the home. It appears to have been built according to the plans, with the room on the left of the porch added at a later date. Instead of the large round pillars in the plans, the front porch was built with four large square pillars made of brick. The house has aluminum siding.

No. 78 Unknown Client, Harvard, Massachusetts, built ca. 1912

This house was built with the plans reversed. Other minor changes were made as well. Instead of windows in the front, two sets of french doors open onto the porch. The interior was modified with an open kitchen and dining room combination.

Detail picture shows the front door and porch columns (left) with a cement floor laid over fieldstones.

No. 78 I. O. Jillison Home, French Gulch, California, built ca. 1910

I. O. Jillison built this house high in the mountains of northern California at the site of the famous Gladstone Mine. It was shoehorned onto a rock outcropping atop the steep slope of a ravine. The plans were altered so that the practical entrance was a side door leading into the dining room. The home was generally built according to the plans, but the details were not carried out in a totally "Craftsman" manner, as it was built totally from lumber milled on the site by the mine employees and engineers. Jillison must have liked his Stickley house, because he ordered a special commission in 1914 for another larger house further down the slope (see No. 186, page 479).

The Jillison house perches high above a ravine (above right). The fireplace is made of brick (right). The wall between the living room and the staircase (above) does not have the opening called for in the plans, and a portiere is hung to help seal off drafts.

The front porch (top left) has firewood stacked on it. The house is still heated partially by fireplaces. There is a steep climb to reach the front porch (above left).

The front entrance from the porch (top right) opens in to a foyer, with the hall and living room to the right and the dining room to the left.

The dining room sideboard was moved to the opposite wall in the French Gulch design so that french doors (above right) could be placed for access to the flat grade outside the house. These doors serve as the practical entrance to the home.

No. 78 Clarence Beckwith Home, Little Deer Isle, Maine, built ca. 1914

The Rev. Clarence Beckwith, a professor of theology, built this version of No. 78 as a summer home, and later used it as a full-time residence. The house is sited on a steep slope overlooking the Atlantic Ocean, which necessitated a large sweeping staircase to reach the front porch. The interior was built according to the plans, although the woodwork is now painted white.

The Beckwith home is shown as photographed in 1996 (top and left), and shortly after it was built ca. 1915 (above).

The current owners keep two old photos of Beckwith on a dressing table (above).

The Deer Isle hall/staircase (above left) is a close match to Stickley's concept.

The fireplace, built-in sideboard, and china cabinets were all done as Stickley planned in the dining room (center).

Brick instead of stone was selected for the living room fireplace (left).

No. 78 Unknown Owner, Mountain Lakes, New Jersey, built ca. 1914; Charles Hapgood, builder

Charles Hapgood is known to have used several Craftsman plans in constructing his suburban development not far from Stickley's Craftsman Farms. This house is a unique version, as it has been made about one third smaller by evenly reducing the floor plan but maintaining the proper height of the building.

Hapgood constructed a smaller version of Stickley's design (above).

Space was saved by opening up the staircase and making it part of the living room (center).

Fieldstone was used for the living room fireplace, but there is little wood trim in the living room and no beamed ceiling (right).

No. 78 Catherine Klyde Hassan and Charles T. Gaither, Boardman, Ohio, built in 1914

Catherine Klyde Hassan ordered the plans from Stickley as she prepared for her marriage to Charles T. Gaither in Youngstown, Ohio. They must have been a most interesting couple. She was the advertising manager for the *Youngstown Vindicator* and he had worked there beginning at the age of 15, where he quickly was placed in charge of the engines, machinery, and presses. Along with a partner, Gaither developed the photoengraving process when the *Vindicator* published the first photogravure on December 26, 1893. Gaither left the paper to design automobiles for the Fredonia Carriage and Manufacturing Company. A pioneer in auto design, he drove the Fredonia in the 1902 great endurance race from New York

to Boston and back. Upon the demise of the company he sold autos and ran repair facilities in the Youngstown area. The two appear to have lived their entire married life in the house, which was built of brick with large stone porch pillars. The house was torn down to make way for a large shopping mall.

The Hassan-Gaither home was pictured in a period directory for the area. It appears to be located on a large property facing a pond. In the rear of the house is what seems to be a matching two-car garage.

Kate and Henry E. Holmes ordered plans for No. 78 from Stickley in August of 1910. The house was one of several houses they built for their children, all located around their Victorian mansion in Seattle, Washington. This was the only Arts and Crafts–style house they built. It was a wedding gift for their daughter Ruth and her lawyer husband, Richard Huntoon; they lived there for the rest of their lives. The house faced east, taking advantage of a beautiful view of Lake Washington. Holmes was a partner in Stewart and Holmes Drugs, Seattle's first and later largest drug store. After spending time prospecting for gold in his youth, he was one of the pioneer founders of modern Seattle in the 1870s. The additional pergola porches and a "sun-room" were added much later, as was an addition to the rear. Thanks to the Huntoon's grandson, there is a wealth of historical images on this home and the people who lived in it.

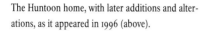

The Huntoon home, with later additions and alterations, as it appeared in 1996 (above).

The Huntoon home, photographed while under construction, next to the Holmes mansion at the left. This view (center) is of the rear of the house. Tax records indicate it was finished in 1910.

The Seattle house pictured shortly after it was constructed (right). The Holmes mansion is to the right. The Huntoon house was located on a ridge overlooking Lake Washington.

This wonderful photo (left) made in 1922 captures Ruth Huntoon and her four children in the living room of the house. Note the Arts and Crafts furniture and the built-in bookcases on the rear wall of the house. From left: daughter Ruth, Ruth holding daughter Isle, son David, and daughter Margaret.

The Huntoons sit on their porch with their grandchildren in 1957 (below left). If not the same, the furniture is similar to that shown in a 1922 photo on the porch.

Richard Huntoon is pictured (below) on the porch in February 1922 with his daughters Margaret, left, and Ruth. The porch floor is made of wood, but the current porch floor is tile on concrete.

The Moore house (top) has changed little over the years since it was first published in *The Craftsman* in 1910 (above).

Samuel J. Moore was a local boot and shoe merchant. He hired architect DuBois Carpenter, who used No. 78, simply substituting hollow tile block for "rived shingles." Built within a year of publication, the November 1910 issue of *The Craftsman* says, "The lines and proportions and interior fittings are identical with the original plans. The only marked variation is in the material used. The present house is of hollow tile, cement covered, with stone foundation, parapet and porch supports. The effect of the house is somewhat different, because of the variation in the site. The original Craftsman house rested on the crown of a slightly rolling bit of country, whereas the present house is definitely on the top of a small hillside. This naturally reveals much more of the foundation walls, but the proportion of the wall is nevertheless so perfect in relation to the house, and the wall itself so beautifully built, that it adds a picturesque touch to the building as a whole. The floor plans and the general arrangement of the interior are unchanged from the scheme of the original house."

Earnest L. Prior Commission, Maplewood, New Jersey, 1909

Roof: Cross gable with shed dormers   *Bedrooms:* 4 (plus sleeping porch)   *Baths:* 1   *Avery Plans:* None

This house was one of the projects of the Craftsman Home Building Company. "In this house, which was built for Mr. E. L. Prior at Maplewood, New Jersey, we see a most complete and consistent expression of the Craftsman idea, especially in the arrangement of the interior, which shows the built-in fitments such as book shelves and sideboard, and the structural effects which are now so well known all over the country. Our aim is always to make the house so interesting in itself that it will need very little furniture and almost no ornament, and the interior of Mr. Prior's house illustrates this idea as well as any we have built."[61]

The house features the typical mature Craftsman features of the wide-eaved roof supported by purlins, the shed dormers, chimneys of differing material (in this case stone merging into brick), and different siding materials for the first and second stories. The home survives today in beautiful condition and is being restored.

The E. L. Prior house was pictured in the September 1910 issue of *The Craftsman* (top) shortly after it was constructed. The Prior house as photographed in 1998 (above).

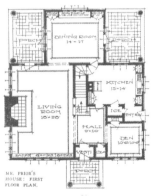

MR. PRIOR'S HOUSE: FIRST FLOOR PLAN.

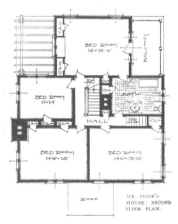

MR. PRIOR'S HOUSE: SECOND FLOOR PLAN.

The Prior house living room is pictured in *The Craftsman* shortly after the house was built (above) and in 2004 after a restoration that included stripping white paint off the fireplace (top).

The dining room pictured in *The Craftsman* article still awaits a dining table and chairs (facing below); in 2004 it was furnished with a Gustav Stickley table and chairs (facing above).

A detail shows a butterfly key joint linking boards of the frieze rail in the living room (below).

The wood trim in the den and a door is shown in this 1998 photograph (right).

The front door opens into a hall, with a den to the rear in this 1998 picture taken from the living room before restoration work was finished (bottom).

Frederick M. Hill Commission, Great Neck, New York, 1909

Roof: Gable *Bedrooms:* 4 (plus sleeping porch) *Baths:* 1 full, 2 half *Avery Plans:* None

Designed for Mr. Frederick M. Hill, of Great Neck, Long Island, this house "is an excellent example of the severer form of the Craftsman house. It has a good deal of the quiet conservative dignity of the old Colonial farmhouse, for the exterior shows not one superfluous feature and its beauty is entirely that of line and proportion, and the impression it gives of simplicity."

Hill was the General Secretary of the New York YMCA and knew Stickley from when they were neighbors in Syracuse. He paid $35 to have the plans of the Hicks house

The Hill residence is pictured in *The Craftsman* in a 1910 article (top) and as photographed in 1980 (above) after a number of alterations had been made in the intervening years.

(see page 265) modified for his use, and as can be seen the results were strikingly different. The Hicks house layout was reversed, and Stickley used a quite different pallet of materials.

The house has fared badly over the years, acquiring skylights, two additions, and a coat of stucco.

The living room of the home as shown in *The Craftsman,* probably before Hill occupied the house, given the empty interior.

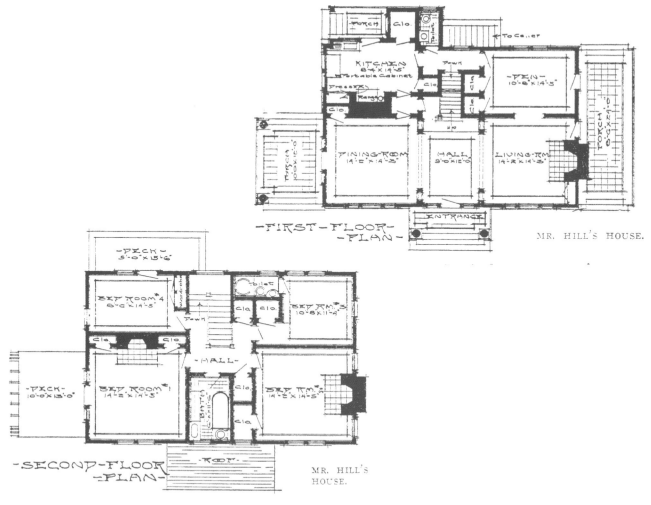

344

McKnight Realty Company Commission, Great Neck, New York, ca. 1909

Roof: Gable with shed dormers   *Bedrooms:* 4   *Baths:* 2 1/2   *Avery Plans:* 5 sheets (elevation drawings, floor plans)

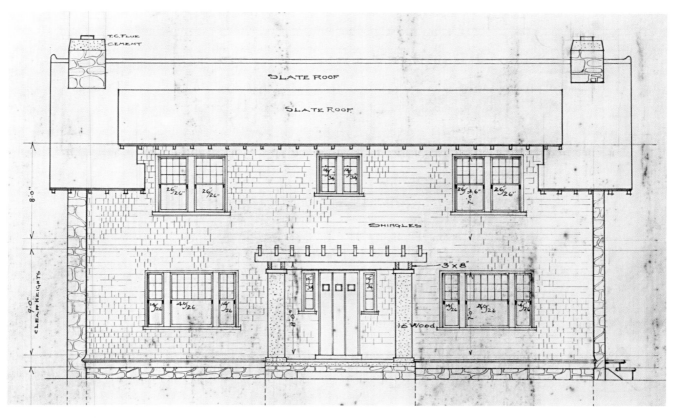

A set of drawings on linen of a handsome saltbox shingled bungalow exists in the Avery Library. The plans were drawn for the McKnight Realty Company of Great Neck, New York, the town where the Hill house (see page 343) was built. The house appears to be a design made for the company to use as a speculation home—one built to sell after it was constructed. It is similar in appearance to No. 74 of 1909, but the floor plan is closer to the Hill house. If the house was built, it has not yet been located.

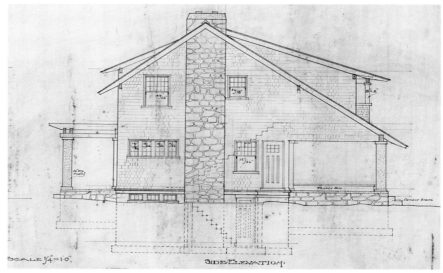

The front elevation is balanced and proportioned nicely (top). A side elevation drawing shows how the main roof sweeps low to the rear (above).

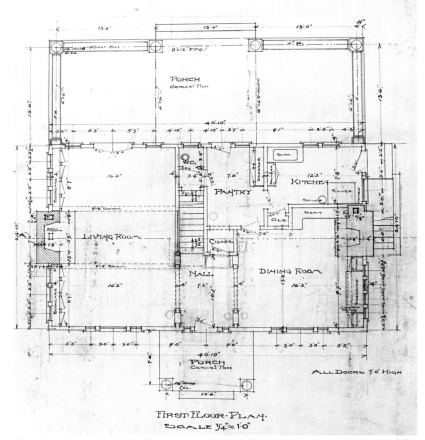

FIRST·FLOOR·PLAN·
SCALE ¼"=1'0"

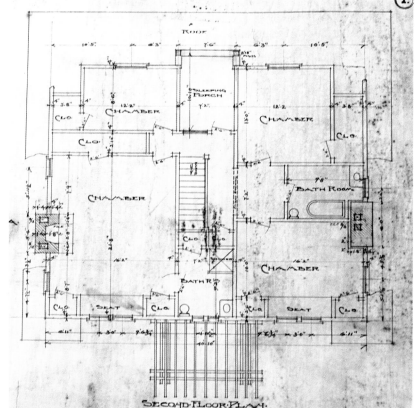

The floor plans of the
McKnight Realty Company
house are pictured as found
on linen drawings in the Avery
Library. It features a traditional
center hall arrangement.

SECOND·FLOOR·PLAN·

No. 84 February 1910

Roof: Gable with raised dormers *Bedrooms:* 4 *Baths:* 1 *Avery Plans:* 7 sheets (Elevations, plans, sections, framing, details)

This house is built of cement on metal lath on the first story and of shingles on the upper walls and roof. The roof profile looks back to the vernacular early Dutch homes found in the New York metropolitan area. The floor plans maximize the use of the space available. "A delightful color effect could be obtained by giving a rough, pebble-dash finish to the cement and brushing on enough pigment to give it a tone of dull grayish green, varied by the inequalities in the surface of the cement. It would pay to use rived cypress shingles for the upper walls, as these are much more interesting and durable than the ordinary sawn shingles, and possess a surface that responds admirably to the treatment with diluted sulphuric acid which we have found most successful with this wood. The roof could either be moss green or grayish brown, a little darker than the shingles of the upper walls. Four heavy cement pillars support the roof of the porch. . . . The [house] plan has purposely been made so that the construction shall be as inexpensive as is compatible with thoroughness and safety."

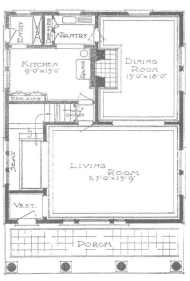

CRAFTSMAN COTTAGE OF CEMENT
AND SHINGLES: FIRST FLOOR PLAN.

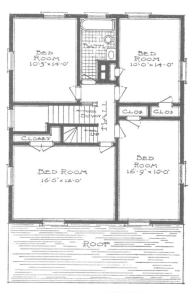

CRAFTSMAN COTTAGE:
SECOND FLOOR PLAN.

No. 85 March 1910

Roof: Gable *Bedrooms:* 3 (plus sleeping porch) *Baths:* 1 *Price:* $6,000 to $7,000
Avery Plans: 4 sheets survive from six originals (plans, elevations, framing, and a section through the house)

A variation of the chalet style, this house "has in it no element of pettiness, either in exterior effect or in the arrangement of the interior. The deeply recessed porch and the sleeping balcony above relieve the severity of the square. But for the rest the lines remain unbroken, and the plain surfaces depend for decorative effect upon the small hooded entrance and the design and grouping of the windows. The walls are built of cement on truss metal lath and the gables are sheathed with wide V-jointed boards, which form a pleasant variation to the plainness of the straight cement walls. The low-pitched roof, with its revealed rafters resting on heavy purlins that are also revealed, offers no corners or crannies to collect moisture and so rot under the action of the weather."

The cement should be "mixed with coarse brown sand and simply toweled on without any other finish, rough or smooth. A beautiful color effect would be gained by giving the cement a soft indeterminate tone of brown that would blend with the brown wood tones of the boards in the gable and the shingles on the roof.

"Owing to the arrangement of this house, the living room and dining room are more definitely separated than is usual in a Craftsman house. Both rooms are of the same size and are nearly square, and the arrangement of chimneypiece and bookshelves in the living room is repeated by the sideboard and china cupboards that occupy the whole of the corresponding side of the dining room."

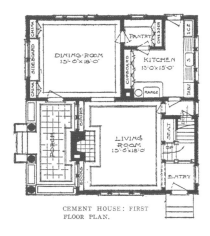

CEMENT HOUSE: FIRST FLOOR PLAN.

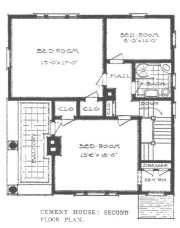

CEMENT HOUSE: SECOND FLOOR PLAN.

No. 85 John Fletcher House, New York City, 1910

The linen drawings at Avery Library for this home give every indication that this was a commissioned house. They are noted "Craftsman House for John Fletcher," and signed CHB Co. (Craftsman Home Building Company). The house itself exhibits all the features found in the better houses known to have been constructed by the Craftsman Home Building Company. For a small house it is very fine and very comfortable. The porches were enclosed many years ago and then recently restored, and the kitchen recently updated. Otherwise, the home has survived intact, with the exception of a replaced front door. The interior is chestnut woodwork and is stained the "standard Stickley" medium brown. His lighting fixtures and hardware were installed in the home.

A Stickley chandelier hangs in the Fletcher house dining room.

No. 85 Garlan Bowman House, "Hilkrest," Menomonie, Wisconsin, 1915

The Bowman house is both a testament to how people embraced Stickley's philosophy and how they could ignore some or all of the important details. In the April 1916 issue of *The Craftsman*, Bowman's wife, Alice, gives a detailed description of the building of their home.

Beyond the significant change of substituting narrow siding, mitered at the corners, instead of cement, some small modifications were made to room sizes. Mrs. Bowman wrote: "The pleasure in the use of the house has more than repaid . . . the unceasing vigilance which was necessary to get a "Craftsman" effect in its construction. Workmen in this section had little experience with the interior

woodwork of Craftsman type, and even after the woodwork came from the factory it was hard to keep them from cutting into it to make it conform to their notions." Still, the house does not compare in the small details to the Fletcher house (see page 353). The house was later enlarged significantly, moving the kitchen to the expanded porch and replacing the kitchen and pantry with a bedroom. It may have been converted for a time into two apartments.

Garlan Bowman, who built the house late in his life, was the principal of the Dunn County Normal School for eighteen years up to his death in 1922 at the age of 67. His particular interest was training

teachers to work in rural schools and he came to Menomonie for that purpose. He was recognized throughout the United States as an expert in that field.

A Unitarian, a Mason, and a lover of nature, he was a member and chairman of the town parks committee and was constantly in demand as a public speaker. He was "a philosopher and a student of life, a profound thinker, gifted with a fine command of language, and, above all, possessed with a magnetic and impressive personality." When he died the students and faculty "sat for 15 minutes in silent tribute to his memory and there were few dry eyes among those present."[64]

"This living room is wainscoted to the height of the frieze with wide V-jointed boards, and the staircase and all the interior woodwork are of the same wood. For a Craftsman house, as we build it, we are very apt to give the preference to chestnut for this kind of interior woodwork, as it is very interesting in texture and grain and takes on a beautiful color under the dull smooth finish of the surface. This wood is particularly desirable in a room because of its quality of mellow radiance, and the sturdy character which harmonizes so admirably with the rough sand-finished plaster of the ceiling and frieze." The Galliver home appears to have been built according to the plans, but the woodwork was more extensive. Broad horizontal boards replaced the plaster frieze and a beamed ceiling was added to the living room.

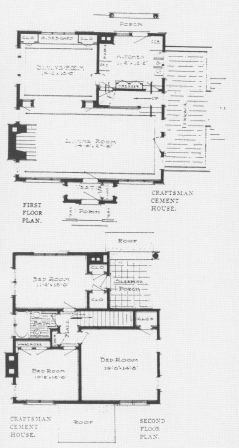

The living room features a typical Craftsman fireplace (above left). Large windows make the room bright.

Another view of the living room (left) shows the open floor plan with the dining room to the rear at the left, and the two-step landing of the staircase giving equal access to the kitchen or living room.

No. 92 June 1910

Roof: Gable *Bedrooms:* 4 (plus sleeping porch) *Baths:* 1 *Avery Plans:* None

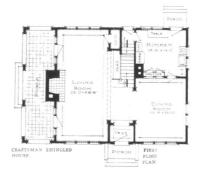

Stickley continues trying different designs that reflect the influence of the Swiss chalet without capturing any special character. The "house is of shingle construction and the whole of one end is taken up with the recessed porch and sleeping balcony above. A shingled hood supported on brackets shelters the small entrance porch, and small hoods appear over each of the windows that are exposed to the weather, and also over the openings at the ends of the upper and lower porches. The roof is of Ruberoid. The walls in both [living and dining] rooms are wainscoted to the height of the frieze with V-jointed boards, and the frames of doors and windows are so planned that they appear merely to emphasize the construction of the wainscot." In his introduction to both June houses, Stickley indicates that this home, like No. 91, was designed for a client.

No. 94 July 1910

Roof: Gable *Bedrooms:* 6 *Baths:* 1 1/2 *Cost:* $7,000 to $8,000 *Avery Plans:* None

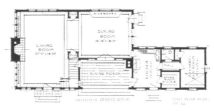

This is a less successful house than No. 93. There is a lack of balance in the massing of the second-story windows in relationship to the first story. The kitchen wing is a visual "tack-on" and throws the structure further in disarray. The exterior design is plainly driven by the interior arrangements.

"The cement house is considerably larger [than No. 93]. The walls are of cement on metal lath" and "the roof is made of red Ruberoid battened at the joints with thick strips of wood. The entrance door is entirely of glass and, with the windows on either side, forms the large group of windows that lights the front of the living room. A similar group appears at the back, and the whole side wall is occupied by casements set high over bookshelves on either side of the central fireplace. What little wall space remains is wainscoted to the height of the frieze with V-jointed boards."

No. 93 July 1910

Roof: Gable   *Bedrooms:* 2 (plus attic)   *Baths:* 1   *Cost:* $3,500   *Avery Plans:* None

After a number of uninspiring designs, this version of a rustic bungalow is one of his most successful designs and would make a great retirement cottage or a home for a small family. Even Victor Toothaker's rendering is done with more detail and refinement than most of the homes he has previously drawn for Stickley. In a September 1916 advertisement in *The Craftsman,* this plan is reprinted with the comment that it was "planned for a hillside site at Larchmont, New York. The walls are of rough stone blasted out in making the excavation." So here is another home designed for a client and originally offered without comment to readers. The interior woodwork and amber glass in the doors are proof that Stickley's company was probably involved in its construction.

The "split stone [is] carefully laid in darkened mortar with wide joints well raked out. The parapet and pillars of the front porch are of the same material. The porch itself is floored with cement, preferably red and marked off into squares. The gables are shingled with the split cypress shingles, and the roof also is shingled, with the rafters left exposed at the widely overhanging eaves. We would recommend that the shingles of the roof be oiled and left to weather. We find that the best treatment for the split cypress shingles of the gables is the sulphuric acid solution.

"The dining room is placed directly in front, with the two high windows

The Walter W. McCormick house (above) was built in Larchmont, New York, ca. 1911. The home, except for the dormer, is exactly like Stickley's concept (left). The handsome dormer has old but slightly different windows and casings—an indication that it was added soon after the house was built. Three more bedrooms were added under the raised second-story dormer, and a bath was added to the rear over the kitchen. A garage was built under the house in the basement at the time of construction. Another version (left) was built by a C. C. Prior in the mountainous frontier town of Priest River, Idaho, about 1912. Beyond the aluminum-sided exterior, little is left of the original home. The fireplace was removed following a damaging fire and replaced by a new one. The interior room walls and floors were altered. It is now impossible to determine if the interior ever followed Stickley's plans.

The Raymond Riordan house (top) was built on the shores of Silver Lake, near Rolling Prairie, Indiana, where he was superintendent of a boys' school during 1913. Prairie School architect George Washington Maher took the Craftsman design and modified it for Riordan. The house was abandoned and left to decay when the school closed after Riordan moved to New York. Only foundations and a large retaining wall built to the rear of the house remain (above). This house is an example of how Stickley's articles and plans were influencing other architects of the day.

The Riordan home inglenook (above) is quite different from that pictured in *The Craftsman* (facing above). It has more dramatic benches but lacks the post-and-panel separation from the living room and is certainly less rustic looking.

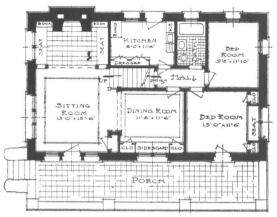

CRAFTSMAN HOUSE OF STONE AND
SPLIT SHINGLES: FLOOR PLAN NO. 93.

above the sideboard looking out upon the front porch. The room itself is small, but there is no feeling of being cramped because the wide opening into the sitting room makes it a recess in the larger room. The sitting room, with the large fireside nook at the back, occupies the whole end of the house. The fireside nook at the back naturally furnishes a most attractive gathering place for the family. Like the sitting room, it is wainscoted with chestnut to the height of the broad beam that marks the angle of the ceiling, so that the whole wall is of wood. This treatment is carried out in all three rooms, and the peculiar color quality of the chestnut, which under the right treatment has a soft mellow glow that seems to radiate light into the room, gives an atmosphere of warm rich color. The large chimney-piece is built of split fieldstone—indeed it is simply the chimney itself, which gives the same effect inside the house as it does on the outside. It extends to the ceiling without a break in the lines, and the recesses on either side are filled with bookshelves. The ceilings are of sand-finished plaster, tinted to a tone that harmonizes with the soft greenish brown of the chestnut."

The inglenook in the McCormick home (center) is almost a perfect match to Stickley's concept (above). The stairs to the second floor were not exposed when the house was built but were placed behind a doorway.

No. 95 August 1910

Roof: Hipped *Bedrooms:* 4 (plus 2 sleeping porches) *Baths:* 1 *Cost:* $8,500 to $9,500
Avery Plans: 12 sheets (plans, framing, elevations, sections, details)

This modified four square is absolutely in proportion and everything is balanced. Capping the structure, the wide-eaved roof pulls the entire design together. Note that heavy knee brackets are used to support that overhang instead of the traditional purlins. Despite all this, the house just doesn't seem to have what it takes to be exciting. Ruberoid is the roofing material chosen. The parapets of the balconies are high enough that Stickley feels they can be used as sleeping porches.

"The staircase, although it is apparently placed in the entrance hall, is really a part of the living room, which is divided from the hall only by the massive overhead beam that marks the boundary of the living room proper. The living room is very plain and simple as regards woodwork and other finish, but if the wood be properly selected and treated the room will have a greater beauty than could be given by a far more elaborate arrangement. The walls are wainscoted with wide V-jointed boards to the height of the frieze, and the big square chimneypiece of tapestry brick extends only to the same line, which thus runs unbroken all around the room. Above this line the chimneypiece is plastered like the ceiling and frieze with rough sand-finished plaster, tinted in any soft subdued tone that may harmonize with the woodwork. Large groups of windows light the room at both ends, and glass doors on either side of the fireplace lead to the porch and into the den."

The home of an unknown client in Kalamazoo, Michigan, ca. 1912. This home's interior appears to have been finished in the Craftsman manner but it is not accessible. The two important porch and balcony wings that make the original design successful were, apparently, never built.

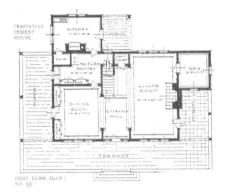

No. 96 August 1910

Roof: Gable with shed dormer *Bedrooms:* 2 (3 if den is used as bedroom) *Baths:* 1 *Cost:* $4,000 to $5,000 *Avery Plans:* None

CRAFTSMAN SHINGLED HOUSE: FLOOR PLAN: NO. 96.

A small economical bungalow, the design is not without merit and the drawing hardly shows the house to best advantage. "Split cypress shingles are used for the walls, and the foundation is of split field stone. A broad terrace open to the sky takes the place of a veranda in front. The roof, which has a very wide overhang, is made of Ruberoid battened at the joints, and its line is broken by the broad low dormer with its group of casement windows, a feature that adds greatly to the structural interest of the building. The living room is wainscoted to the height of the frieze, and the windows and door openings are so placed that the line around the room is unbroken. The top of the wainscot is finished with a square beam instead of a plate rail. There is only one group of windows in the living room, but that is so large that almost the entire front wall appears to be of glass."

No. 97 September 1910

Roof: Gable *Bedrooms:* 4 (plus sleeping porch) *Baths:* 2 *Avery Plans:* 8 sheets (details, elevations, framing, floor plans, sections)

CEMENT HOUSE: NO. 97: FIRST FLOOR PLAN.

NO. 97: SECOND FLOOR PLAN.

This handsome house surprises—it is larger than it looks. The footprint of this long rectangular low-pitched gable-roof home is about 36 by 50 feet. The low roof makes the second-story window height marginal, but it is a two-story home. This cement house has a roof "of Ruberoid stretched and battened down as usual, but instead of the roll at the eaves we have brought it down to the inside of the cypress gutter. The rafters are hollowed out, and the gutter let into the curve so that it forms a continuous trough, which serves the purpose of [draining] rain, and giving the decorative effect formerly obtained by the heavy roll. Above the pergola is a partly recessed sleeping porch, ending in a balcony that is supported on the extended rafters of the second floor." Stickley says that both September houses "are of dwellings we are now building."[66] So somewhere, hopefully, this house still survives.

No. 98 September 1910

Roof: Gable   *Bedrooms:* 5   *Baths:* 2   *Avery Plans:* 10 sheets (details, elevations, framing, floor plans, sections)

A wonderful home, No. 98 was designed for a Mr. Wilson, the engineer who designed the Cape Cod Canal, and sits on a prominent site overlooking the entrance of the canal almost exactly as the exterior illustration places it. "This rising ground curves around in a sort of flattened semicircle, and the house was built right at the edge of this terrace, with a walk following the line of the curve leading up from the street to the veranda. In consequence, the house is built on a side hill and is therefore higher in front than it is at the back. The rough stone parapet, with its massive irregular coping stones, rises about ten feet from the lawn below, affording ample room for a line of casement windows which give light to the billiard room that occupies the front of the basement. On the walls the usual proportions of the clapboards and shingles are reversed, the clapboards being carried much higher than ordinary in order to emphasize the low broad effect of the building. The grouping of the windows and the low pitch of the roof tend to increase this effect still more, the position of the house on a height demanding it."

Here is an example of the tragedy that can befall old houses that are not understood or cared for. The Wilson house, called "Hillport," near Sandwich, Massachusetts, has survived with much of its character but is badly defaced. The house was intact until the 1980s, when the front pergola and one bedroom were removed and an inappropriate Palladian window was installed. The removed bedroom was turned into an interior atrium space. The original Stickley lights disappeared. Skylights were added to the rear of the roof. The current owner is trying to restore the house. A pergola has been added to the front, restoring needed balance to its appearance. While Stickley implies in the article that the home has been built, it was not constructed until 1911—and not exactly as described in the article—the plans were reversed and the large fireplace was built with fieldstone, not tapestry brick. In the 1950s the house was a bed-and-breakfast, still owned by the Wilson family.

"The highlight of the interior is a unique design of the big chimneypiece (top left) at the back of the square living hall between the living room and the dining room. This chimneypiece, which is built of tapestry brick, extends clear to the ceiling of the second story. The heavy cement mantel shelf is placed at the level of the high wainscoting in the living hall, and a recess in the brickwork above breaks the monotony of the plain surface. On one side of this fireplace is the landing of the staircase, which runs up behind the chimneypiece to another landing, which also serves for the kitchen stairs and from which the main staircase goes on up to the second story."

This photo from the bed-and-breakfast brochure (above) shows the interior with its hanging Stickley fixtures intact and the ceiling still in place. The living hall and fireplace with the staircase to the rear is pictured in 2004 (top right). A view of the upper hallway (center right) shows a detail of the newel posts and balustrade in the second-story hall. This 1991 photo (right) shows the sweep of the two-story fireplace and chimney cut through the center of the house. The inscription "Hillport" is cut into the stone above the fireplace mantel in the Arts and Crafts custom of naming a home.

The dining room (top left) features a built-in sideboard and china cabinets along one wall.

One of the two built-in china cabinets is pictured in the dining room (top right).

The living hall (above right), photographed showing the entrance door of the home, with the large Palladian window installed above the door in the 1980s.

A detail of the post-and-panel divider between the living hall and dining room (above). The woodwork in the Wilson home is southern pine stained dark.

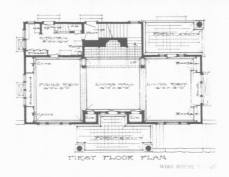

FIRST FLOOR PLAN

WOOD HOUSE NO. 98.

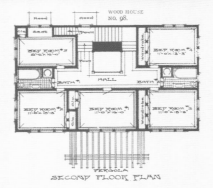

WOOD HOUSE NO. 98.

PERGOLA
SECOND FLOOR PLAN

No. 104 Edward Warren Vaill Jr. House, Oradell, New Jersey, built in 1911

This house is another example of what happened when the owners and builders received the plans and then went their own way. While Mr. Vaill and his wife, Helen, built a solid and substantial home, they did cut some corners to save money. Vaill was 41 years old and a patent attorney in New York City when he purchased the land in August 1911 to build the house from the Oradell Heights Land Company. The deed indicates the house cost $4,000 to build. By December, the Vaills and their two children, Amy and Edward, had moved into their new home. After service in the Army Corps of Engineers in World War I, Vaill sold the property in 1919, shortly after he started his own firm in the city. He was a Mason and a member of the Appalachian Mountain and Green Mountain Clubs.

"Natco" brand hollow tile block faced with a smooth cement exterior was used instead of the suggested brick, and this was carried up the side walls so there is no handsome gable of V-joint vertical boards that add interest to the exterior. However, ivy was planted on the north side and it adds to the charm of the home. The cement was left in a natural state until the 1950s, when it was painted bright yellow. Later, a sand mixture in gray paint was spray-applied. This application began to fall off in sheets in the 1980s. The cement was power-washed, but traces of the bright yellow paint could not be removed, so the original cement color was matched as close as possible with Kiem Granital masonry paint from Germany. This paint has lasted more than twenty years. Instead of red slate, the roof is red Ludowici Spanish interlocking tile—not the best roof to have on a property that now has twenty-seven mature trees overhead.

Generally the living room was constructed according to Stickley's design. Vaill made a change in the visually balanced windows on either side of the entrance door—a casement was installed on one side instead of a matching double-hung window, so that the family upright piano could be placed on that wall. Elsewhere in the house, standard woodwork from the local mill was used, but Stickley-style doors were used throughout. The living room features chestnut paneling and trim, and

This photo (above) was made in 1913. There was a circular drive that turned near the end of the porch. The large step that allowed someone to alight from a carriage or automobile is visible. The upstairs windows had uncharacteristic shutters—Stickley homes were not designed with them. A photograph made during the Depression (above right) shows the house unchanged but overrun with wisteria. At some point a garage was constructed and is visible to the rear of the property. The Vaill home in 2003 (right).

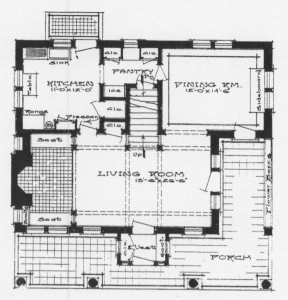

CRAFTSMAN HOUSE: NO. 104: FIRST FLOOR PLAN.

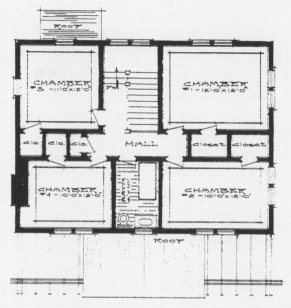

CRAFTSMAN HOUSE: NO. 104: SECOND FLOOR PLAN.

Stickley Plans

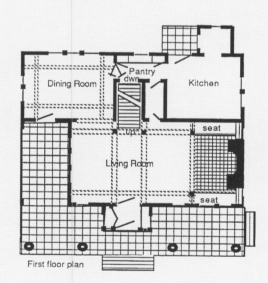

First floor plan

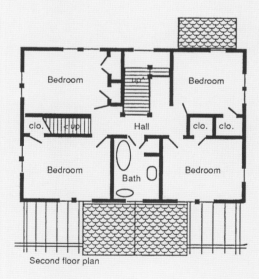

Second floor plan

Vaill House Plans

The Vaills reversed the plans so that the house could be sited facing east on a rise with a view of the Oradell reservoir and distant Manhattan, and so the dining porch could be on the south side of the house—thus the house does not face either of the streets that border its corner lot. Vaill wisely changed the number of doors that opened into the living room—in Stickley's design there are four—preventing it from becoming simply a very large passageway. The door to the dining porch was eliminated, as was the door to the kitchen. Where the closet was planned, he placed an equally impractical passageway to the pantry. Later this space was closed off to create a closet for the living room and a powder room off the pantry—a very practical solution. The added staircase to the attic reduced the bedroom sizes.

the ceiling beams are cypress. The dining room had a handsome beamed ceiling added; the thickness of the beams is smaller than those in the living room, so that although the ceiling heights are the same, the ceiling in the dining room appears higher. The rear porch was slightly expanded to include a "mud room" entrance to the kitchen.

Vaill's daughter, Amy Vaill Kelly, recalled that it was a wonderful home to grow up in. She noted that the light fixtures were very "medieval" looking—an indication that Stickley fixtures were used. When purchased by the author, those fixtures were gone, so reproduction lamps have replaced them. The woodwork had also been painted, although the panels in the living room had been "pickled" to look like natural wood. We stripped and stained all the woodwork, and missing details were replaced (the inglenook had been removed in the 1970s). A stained-glass set of windows has replaced the double-hung ones that faced the dining porch, as that room had been enclosed in the 1950s. The decision was made to expand the dining porch into a large sunroom, since it had already been historically compromised.

Major Edward Warren Vaill Jr. (above), during service in WWI. He may be standing at the wall to the rear of the property.

Edward Vaill III and Helen May Vaill on the Gloucester hammock hung at the edge of the dining porch under the pergola, about 1915 (above). Amy Vaill sits on the rocking chair to their right.

The den (one of the four bedrooms) was redecorated in 2004 (above) using a grass cloth similar to that used at Craftsman Farms, but in a deep red. The stencil is adapted from one found in an early issue of *The Craftsman*.

Baby Nina's room in 1988 (left). The frieze was painted by a friend of the family based on an English wallpaper frieze of the period, with some flights of fancy. The woodwork in the second-story bedrooms and bath appears to have always been painted.

The chimney was constructed inside the side wall instead of externally, thus there is less room in one bedroom, and more importantly, the fireplace projects into the inglenook several feet, destroying Stickley's design and making the seats of the inglenook less useful. The inglenook, as called for in the plans, is floored with red quarry tile. Stickley's design (above left) is matched in 2004 in the restored house (above).

The living room looking south (above). The dining room is through the portiere on the right. The stained-glass windows are not original, but replaced the double-hung windows to screen the enclosed porch on the other side of the glass. The cattail stencil is from the pages of *The Craftsman*. The rug is a Morris design "mead moss" from Nature's Loom Carpets.

The dining room details had to be completely reconstructed (above left). The idea for the plate rail corbels came from those found in the Parker house (No. 157). The swinging door on the left leads to a passage through a narrow pantry to the kitchen. The stencil is from a Helen Foster design.

One would think that the Vaills must have had Stickley furniture, because the hall at the top of the stairs (above right) was slightly enlarged by putting the entrance doors to two rooms at an angle, thus making it easy to turn the corners with large pieces of furniture. The chandelier is period, by Handel.

View through the portieres separating the dining room from the living room (left). The Vaill's piano once was placed below the casement window. The portieres are a Stickley design re-created by Dianne Ayres of Arts and Crafts Textiles.

While it is not the intent of this book to present a "how-to" restoration guide, these photos can serve as an example of the author's twenty-year journey in seeking the proper interpretation and décor for a Craftsman Home. We purchased the Vaill home, seeking an Arts and Crafts–style home to house our collection. We knew it had potential under layers of paint, but we had no idea what we would discover.

The living room (above), photographed on the day we took possession in 1986. We didn't know there had been an inglenook, but we did know the carpet, draperies, that awful fireplace mirror, and layers of paint had to go. We hired a small firm that did stripping and they worked five days a week for six weeks. Once the carpet had been removed, we realized something was odd about the fireplace area. Why was the tile on the floor so expansive, and why did it not reach as far as the wall. As stripping began it revealed clues (center). What were those horizontal dark marks on the wall near the bookcases? Two 6-by-6-inch-square sections that had never been stained were found on the low cross-beam. Why? And the beam itself, why was it there? Quite by accident we found the answer when we bought a copy of Stickley's *More Craftsman Homes.* My wife noticed the similarity of the fireplace

illustration for House No. 104 and we finally realized that we had purchased a Stickley-designed house! And behind that mirror (made just to fit that space) we found a painting carefully hidden away. We think it dates from the 1920s when the Churchills, a very artistic family, owned the home. It probably depicts a scene along the Oradell reservoir. The painting is shown (right) after it was restored.

After the woodwork was stripped, it was stained and varnished to match some of the Craftsman furniture finishes we had seen (above). Stripping the fireplace brick was a nightmare; we had to put down layers of paste stripper and then use high-pressure water jets to wash it off (we built a plastic "room" to contain the water, draining it into the basement through holes in the floor where we knew the inglenook post and panels would go some day). Other discoveries were made: the last two stair steps were not original. Later evidence from Amy Vaill Kelly told us there had been a large landing, with a railing, the final two steps at a 45-degree angle ending beside the passageway to the pantry. There had been a plate rail, a built-in china cabinet, and a built-in window seat in the dining room—

all gone, but the stripping revealed the bare wood where the plate rail had been (top left) and the missing vertical battens were revealed by the discovery of carpenter's pencil marks under a mismatched piece of wood frame beneath the window sill.

We rebuilt the inglenook (top right), but the interior still did not look right. It was too plain and too severe. The warmth of the wood needed to be supplemented. The painting was interesting but not very good, and it conflicted with our pottery collection displayed on the mantel. We began to read as much as we could about the colors, linens, and rugs found in Arts and Crafts homes.

The kitchen (above) was another nightmare. There was nothing left of the original kitchen to restore. In the 1920s and '30s the house had been operated as a coffee house/restaurant and a commercial-type kitchen had been installed.

We reused existing white cabinets (above) and replaced the doors. We have tried to create an Arts and Crafts "feel" for the kitchen, but some day we will redo the kitchen again.

The bathroom (right) also needed to be replaced. The day we took possession we began to strip off the wallpaper. Nothing remained of the original bathroom except evidence that the plaster had been scored in 6-inch squares to resemble tile. Even the linen closet had been torn out. The attempt has been to have a modern bathroom (above) with an Arts and Crafts flavor. The cabinets have Arts and Crafts touches in the detailing, and the walls feature a William Morris "Weeping Willow"-design wallpaper.

1911

The firm produced twenty-two homes in 1911, with four houses in March and none in October or November. The overall quality of the designs is outstanding, but Stickley is reworking earlier floor plans and ideas. The homes continued to be aimed at the middle- and upper-middle-class. There were also several more commissioned homes completed. Numbers 105, 106, and 112 stand out as exceptional homes. Stickley begins to push his readers to buy and install his Craftsman fireplace-furnace, and almost all the designs feature the device prominently. While the illustrations are all unsigned, those for the first three months are still in the style of Victor Toothaker, bearing a look like they were originally watercolor renderings. In April a more detailed style done in line drawings begins to appear. For unknown reasons there were no Craftsman Homes published in October and November. In December they resumed without comment but under a feature titled "Among Craftsmen."

No. 105 January 1911

Roof: Cross gable   *Bedrooms:* 6   *Baths:* 1 1/2   *Avery Plans:* None

"A three-story bungalow is unusual," yet this Craftsman house "shows a distinctly bungalow form of construction . . . ." Nominally, the bungalow is a story-and-a-half-type house, with at least one bedroom on the ground floor. Stickley achieves this but in a grander way—similar to the scale of the homes being produced by a number of California architects of the period. The design manages to borrow from the chalet style as well. While the house "does not look very large" there is a great deal of room hidden away. The home has a full basement containing a billiard room

Oscar Carrabine, Teddy Roosevelt's orthodontist, according to local legend, built this home (above) about 1915 in New Rochelle, a Westchester County suburb of New York City. The house is sited at a location similar to that pictured in the original article in *The Craftsman,* which leads to speculation that it was actually the prototype of that home. It was rare for Stickley to feature a garage attached to a house, and this one fits into the site, further indicating that this house is the one pictured in the magazine. Still, if this is the prototype, it took Carrabine four years to actually build the house. Carrabine may be the fellow standing in front in this ca. 1920 photo.

The home (left), which in 2000 still had its original kitchen and lighting fixtures, recently underwent extensive "renovations" that altered the rooms throughout the house, including the removal of walls, with only the living and dining rooms being preserved in their original state. The color photographs were made in the early 1990s and show the house before any major changes were made.

In an article on the Craftsman Building, a photo appears in *The Craftsman* of a model of No. 105 exhibited in the home exposition hall. This view is of the rear of the house (below).

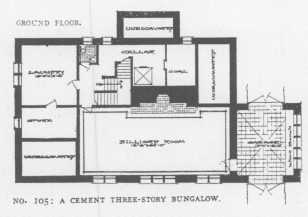

GROUND FLOOR.

NO. 105: A CEMENT THREE-STORY BUNGALOW.

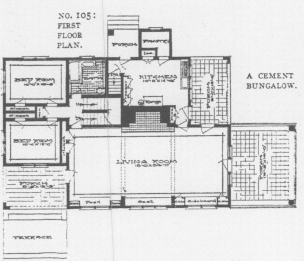

NO. 105: FIRST FLOOR PLAN.

A CEMENT BUNGALOW.

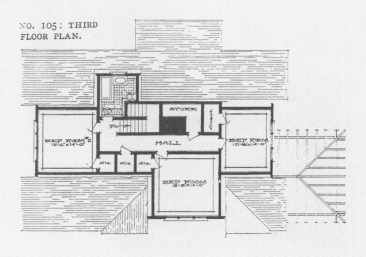

NO. 105: THIRD FLOOR PLAN.

and access to a built-in garage, placed under a pergola porch opening off the dining room. "The cement walls would of course be given a sand finish, and would look best in a soft greenish or brownish tone that would harmonize with the stones of the foundation and with the cypress boards that sheath the gables. The roof is covered with roofing slates which come in beautiful tones of dull red, mossy green and a strange dull shade of grayish purple. These slates, of course, are absolutely durable and fireproof, and are as interesting as tiles or hand-riven shingles. The ridge poles are finished with tiles of the same color as the roof."

In the interior, "a large fireplace, with a massive chimneypiece, occupies the center of the inner wall space, the staircase being placed on one side and the door leading to the kitchen and the dining porch upon the other. The entire front of the long room, although treated as a unit, contains three separate built-in features. In the center is a large window seat occupying the space below the main group of windows. At one side of this is a large built-in writing desk, with book shelves on either side and double windows above, and on the other side, in the part of the room that is meant to be used as a dining room, is a built-in sideboard with china closets.

Treated in this way the whole end of the room is made interesting and decorative, while it serves all purposes of utility and convenience. There is opportunity for a generous display of woodwork, and the line of wainscoting that runs around the whole room is preserved unbroken by the tops of the book shelves, china closets and the high ends and back of the window seat."

This inglenook is central to the design of the interior. The house features all the typical Stickley woodwork, but there is an additional layer of medieval-style scrollwork added to the beams in the living and dining rooms and in the billiard room. While it does match the wood color, it is hard to say if the woodwork was placed there when the house was built, or added later (above). While there is no way to be certain, David Cathers believes that the copper fireplace hood (left) may be from the Craftsman Building in New York, where a similar hood with the motto "Where young men see visions and old men dream dreams" existed. The fixtures from the Craftsman Building were auctioned around the time the house may have been built.

Sexton Wilkerson Commission, Roanoke, Virginia, ca. 1911–12

Roof: Hipped with hipped dormer   *Bedrooms:* 4   *Baths:* 2   *Avery Plans:* None

A catalog and brochure published by Stickley to promote Craftsman fireplaces in September 1913 gives a rare glimpse into a number of homes that had Craftsman fireplace-furnace systems. Not all the houses featured are Craftsman Homes and none are identified specifically as Craftsman houses, but several obviously are. While this house is unique, there are design references to the later Frederick J. Wagner house built in 1912 and featured in *The Craftsman*. A study of the interior confirms the home is a Stickley design.

Sexton Wilkerson house, Roanoke, Virginia, 2004 (top). After a number of years of neglect, the home has recently been restored to its former glory (above). Many years ago the dining porch on the right was converted to an extra room, and that has remained. More recently, the stucco has been painted a more appropriate olive green.

The fireplace catalog offers a view of the fireplace facing the entrance door shortly after the house was built (above). The fireplace has been painted and there is a new tile hearth, but otherwise little has changed, as seen in the same view photographed in 2004 (left). There is a unique feature to this house—a curved staircase leads to the second floor, and the stair railing is a welded wrought-iron chain. The dining room is beyond the stairs to the right.

The dining room (top left) features built-in cabinets and sideboard.

The living room (center left) opens off the fireplace inglenook/entrance hall to the left side of the house, and there is a study through the broad opening toward the rear of the living room.

1912

Taken as a whole, the 1912 designs may not be Stickley's finest, but they are almost all handsome homes, well-planned and appointed, and generally aimed toward the upper-middle-class customers he probably now realized were his base. He continued to push his Craftsman fireplace-furnace for almost every home, and experimented with different construction materials. The individual descriptions of each house are now minimal, and generally describe the obvious to anyone who studies the floor plans. Twenty-four house plans are produced, and at least seven commissions are completed.

No. 127 January 1912

Roof: Saltbox with shed dormers   *Bedrooms:* 4   *Baths:* 1   *Avery Plans:* None

No. 127 is another classic Craftsman bungalow with the roof sweeping low over the porch to disguise a two-story home. "A view of the dining room of this little home is shown with vista of stairway through the wide door leading from the hall." The view of the living room "includes the decorative use of a high seat between the windows and low bookcases. As this seat faces the open fire, it will prove especially comfortable for pleasant hours. . . . This house is built of shingles with double-hung windows. No particular shingle is mentioned, because there are several kinds equally suitable. . . . The pillars that support the porch are of rustic logs, squared so that the curve of the tree is kept as rounded corners. A pillar hand-hewn in this way is extremely suitable for shingled houses."

HOUSE NO. 127: FIRST FLOOR PLAN

HOUSE NO. 127: SECOND FLOOR PLAN

An example of No. 127 (above) is the third Craftsman Home built in Lyons, New York, probably by William T. Johnson, about 1913 as a "spec" home. The home appears to follow the Craftsman plans (top), although the windows are changed on the upper story.

No. 128 January 1912

Roof: Saltbox *Bedrooms:* 3 *Baths:* 1 *Avery Plans:* None

No. 128, is similar to No. 127 but the roof sweeps down to the rear porch, leaving a two-story face in the front. "This house is also of shingles with double-hung windows, recessed porch and brick chimney running up the outside of the house. A distinguishing feature is the placing of the trellis up both sides of the windows and across the full face of the house." Stickley sells this house and the previous No. 127 idealistically: "When the word 'home' is spoken or read, the picture that passes before the mind is generally, of some cozy little house with vines clambering over it, flowers encircling it, trees in the yard, a little orchard nearby, perhaps, and, above all, an open fire with the members of the family gathered around it, chatting of the events of the day, plotting wonderful things for the future, reading aloud, telling stories or sitting quietly and letting the leaping flames and floating smoke and singing logs bear the mind to the delightful land of daydreams and hopes and memories."

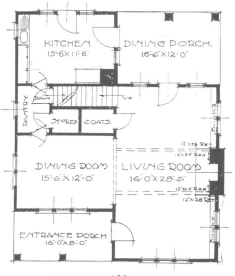

HOUSE NO. 128: FIRST FLOOR PLAN.

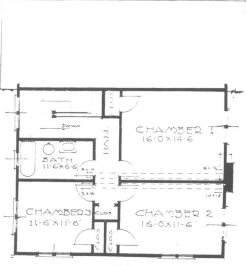

HOUSE NO. 128: SECOND FLOOR PLAN.

No. 129 February 1912

Roof: Cross gable   *Bedrooms:* 4   *Baths:* 1 1/2   *Avery Plans:* 9 sheets (floor plans, elevation drawings, details)

Stickley presents a huge article on the desirability of these homes and how to build them. Both the exteriors and interiors are built of brick with, of course, some Craftsman woodwork and the Craftsman fireplace-furnace. In both these homes and the ones the following month, Stickley is influenced by several popular California-based bungalow plan books, such as those published by Henry Wilson, even though he indicates the houses are designed for the eastern part of the country. It must also be said that these designs, while not completely original, are better than those found in the plan books. "Brick is undoubtedly advancing in favor as a building material for houses. . . . [T]he wood supply of the country is becoming a matter for serious consideration, and some material must be found to take the place of wood which is equal or even more satisfactory. The walls of these bungalows are made by erecting two four-inch walls, side by side, leaving a two-inch air space between. These walls are tied together by metal

Around 1912, George Clark built this home (center) in Delaware City, Delaware, as a wedding present for his daughter when she married the local banker.

The interior (above) was designed to be constructed almost completely of brick or plaster-covered brick, with only doors, windows, beams, and post-and-panel dividers built of wood.

No. 130 February 1912

Roof: Cross gable *Bedrooms:* 4 *Baths:* 1 1/2 *Avery Plans:* 8 sheets (floor plans, details, elevation drawings)

tie straps inserted every few courses. The partitions of these houses are of brick, the wall at the baseboard, side and head casings being eight inches thick, while the panels between are only four inches thick. These panels are plastered on both sides, leaving a reveal between the plastered panels and casings of about one and one-quarter inches. Doors and windows are hung on jambs only, expensive frames and trim being thus saved. The main walls only of these houses have been planned to be built of brick, but where partitions are only suggested—as between the living and dining rooms and inglenook of the first bungalow, No. 129—we have used the post and panel construction in wood."

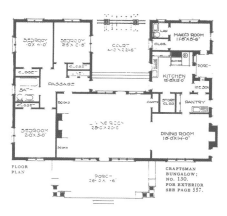

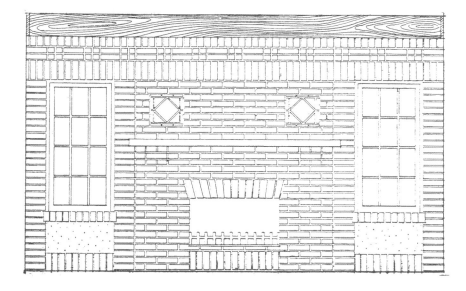

This elevation drawing (left) of the interior of No. 130 shows the details of the dining room fireplace—integrated with the walls that are also made of brick.

No. 131 March 1912

Roof: Cross gable   *Bedrooms:* 3   *Baths:* 1 1/2   *Avery Plans:* None

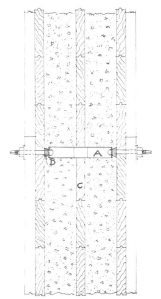

Illustrated section of the wall (above), showing how it is constructed and how the tie-rods are placed.

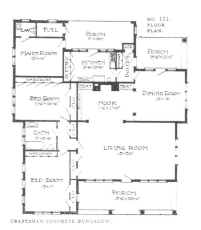

CRAFTSMAN CONCRETE BUNGALOW.

In a rare use of the first person, Stickley introduces the two March houses: "I am presenting here two Craftsman bungalows embodying a practical and economical idea in concrete construction. I believe that this new method, which is illustrated with perspective views and working drawings, will mean a reduction in cost and an increase in efficiency over the methods hitherto used, and so will be of interest to architects, builders and all who are considering the problem of building a home. I have worked upon the theory that the most satisfactory form of concrete wall is one which can be cast with a continuous vertical air space, or other insulation, between two thicknesses of concrete, yet built in such a way as to necessitate only the simplest, fewest and least expensive forms possible. I have decided, therefore, to use wooden forms, which cost much less than metal ones and can be put up right on the building site by any car-

No. 146 October 1912

Roof: Saltbox *Bedrooms:* 4 (plus sleeping porch) *Baths:* 1 *Avery Plans:* None

This house could be a rethinking of the design for the cement farmhouse No. 74 of 1909 (see page 302), although the interior is quite different because the hall has been rotated to extend the full depth of the house from front to back. This home "is planned for a wider [60-foot] lot. Here we have shown concrete on a field stone foundation, with shingled roof, stone pillars at the entrance porch, stone and brick combined in the chimney. If fieldstone is not found [locally] the foundation could be of concrete, with concrete pillars for the front porch. The brick chimney, however, will in any case give a note of variety to the materials of the exterior."

No. 147 November 1912

Roof: Gable *Bedrooms:* 2 *Baths:* 1 *Avery Plans:* 8 sheets (floor plans, elevation drawings, details)

This house is a rethinking of the two-bedroom bungalows No. 123 and No. 124 offered in 1911. "This one-story cottage, while confined to the limits of a narrow lot, is so planned as to give reasonably large dimensions to the various rooms. It is shown here developed in cement, but other material may also be used with good effect. The exterior of this unpretentious little dwelling is pleasing because of the window grouping and spacing—square panes also seem best for the small house—and of the low, gently sloping roof. The foundation is of fieldstone. Brick is used for the chimneys, porch floor and steps." The house is heated by a Craftsman fireplace-furnace.

W. B. Smith Commission, Worcester, Massachusetts, ca. 1912

Roof: Gable *Bedrooms:* 2 *Baths:* 1 *Avery Plans:* 7 sheets (floor plans, elevation drawings, details)

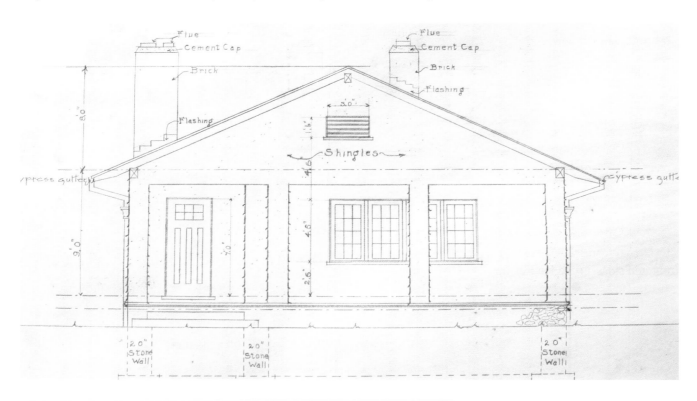

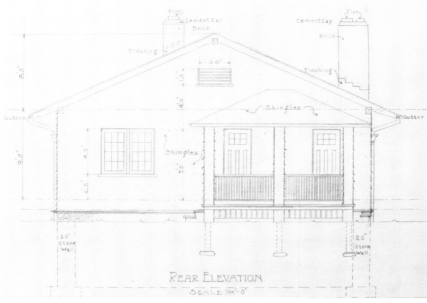

Plans exist in the Avery Library for a shingled modification of the No. 147 cottage (see page 427), designed for a W. B. Smith in Worcester, Massachusetts. The main change was the extension of the roof to allow the addition of a front porch to the house. The drawings are all on tracing paper and unnumbered. The home may have been a proposal that was never finished. The house has not been located, if it exists at all. Drawings show the front (above) and rear (left) elevations.

No. 148 November 1912

Roof: Cross gable *Bedrooms:* 3 *Baths:* 1 *Avery Plans:* 9 sheets (floor plans, elevation drawings, details)

The use of the large cross gables in the roof arrangement allows the space for three bedrooms on the second story, and therefore more space for the common rooms downstairs, compared to No. 147. This house "has shingle walls and roof, the gables of the latter permitting the development of the half story [for a second floor]. The living room, 25 x 18 feet, with its ample fireplace, cheerful groups of windows on the front and sides, broad landing to stairway, and wide arches into nook and dining room, is more generous than might be expected in a small house, and creates a sense of comfort and ease." The house is heated by a Craftsman fireplace-furnace.

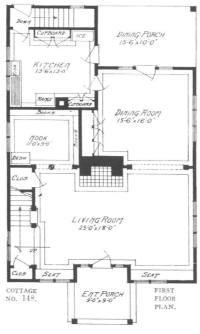

COTTAGE NO. 148. ENT. PORCH 9'-0"x9'-0" FIRST FLOOR PLAN.

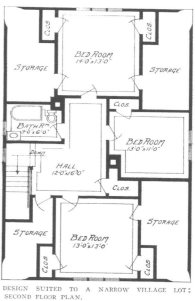

DESIGN SUITED TO A NARROW VILLAGE LOT: SECOND FLOOR PLAN.

No. 149 December 1912

Roof: Saltbox *Bedrooms:* 4 *Baths:* 1 *Avery Plans:* 11 sheets (floor plans, elevations drawings, details)

This house is a variation on a number of previous houses that feature the low shed dormer behind a porch extending along the front of the structure. This model is particularly successful, with the banded windows and arched openings creating interest under the wide eaves with voids and spaces that break the flat expanse of concrete. "House No. 149, however, is so well adapted to the material chosen here—stucco on metal lath—that we would suggest that the builder keep to either this or concrete. The edges of the porch and front steps are emphasized by brick laid in header courses—a little touch that will give an interesting variation against the plainness of the stucco walls, and will add a note of warm color to the building. The porch floors may be of cement, and here again a decorative effect can be obtained by introducing red brick as a border. The front wall of the dormer as well as the parapet is covered with shingles, while the walls of the balcony may be lined with either shingles or boards, and the floor covered with canvas made waterproof by paint." (Note that Craftsman houses are rarely pictured as they would look in the winter, but this December both houses are shown surrounded by snow, and with the evidence of happy home life as the children frolic in the yard.)

The Chauncey O. Garrett house (above) in Wellesley Hills, Massachusetts, shortly before completion in 1912. Stickley spells the name Garrett, but town records indicate that his name could have been Garritt (although other records say he was Chauncey C. Garrett), and he was a local decorator. The house, a wedding gift from his wife's parents, was built with few changes—the main one being the addition of a bay window to the living room. The home was fitted with a central vacuum cleaning system and featured Grueby tiles around the fireplace. This photo was published with a short article on the house in a 1913 issue of the *The Craftsman*.

The Chauncey O. Garrett house as photographed in 2003. New owners built a large addition in the rear in the 1920s, and at some point the distinctive roof overhang was removed, the upstairs porch enclosed, and the dormer pitch altered by enclosing the balcony.

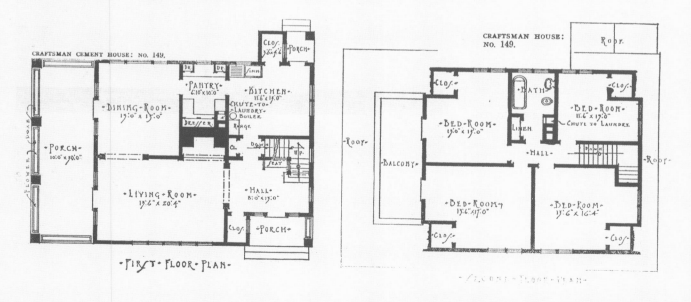

No. 150 December 1912

Roof: Cross gable *Bedrooms:* 2 *Baths:* 1 *Avery Plans:* 6 sheets (floor plans, elevation drawings, details)

In this little well-thought-out home, "shingles are used for roof and walls, with a foundation of stone, V-jointed boards in the gables, rough-hewn pillars for the porches, a wood pergola above the entrance and brick in the porch steps and chimneys. The first impression upon stepping into the living room is the sense of spaciousness—an unusual feature for so small a home. For instead of breaking up the plan into separate living and dining rooms the two are combined in one. As a study of the plan reveals, a partition [which may be about six feet high] has been placed at the further end of the room, so that the portion on the left, with its bookshelves and desk, may serve as a den or library, while that on the right, being next to the kitchen, can be used for dining purposes. The long seat built against the wall not only helps to simplify the furnishing but also permits the seating of more people than would be possible with chairs—a useful feature when guests increase the meal-time gathering."

Unknown owner, Tenafly, New Jersey, ca. 1913. This home was built according to the plans and featured the Craftsman fireplace-furnace. The structure has original Arts and Crafts–style lighting but not by Stickley. This house is an example of what can happen to small houses on large lots in today's crowded suburbs. The dining porch was enclosed in the 1950s to make a third bedroom, and recently, a second story and an addition were added. The current owners have tried to be sympathetic to the home's history while wishing to remain in the community and to accommodate their growing family. Earlier, they had removed the ugly asbestos siding to reveal the home's original siding, still in good shape in this 2000 photograph (right).

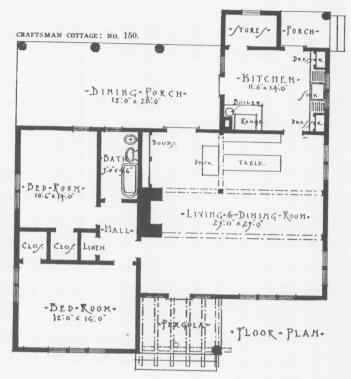

CRAFTSMAN COTTAGE: NO. 150.

FLOOR PLAN

The house in 1992 featured a combined living and dining room (above). The light fixtures are original to the house but are not Stickley designs.

The Craftsman fireplace-furnace (top) retains its original fixtures, including a screen with "The Craftsman" embossed on it.

Miss Caroline B. Freeman Commission, Gales Ferry, Connecticut, 1912

Roof: Gable with shed dormer   *Bedrooms:* 3   *Baths:* 1   *Avery Plans:* None

This home (top), built for Caroline B. Freeman in Gales Ferry, Connecticut, may be an expanded and rearranged version of No. 77 of October 1909.

The house was featured in a promotional brochure for the Craftsman fireplace-furnace, with which it was heated. The photo (above) must have been made soon after the house was built, as it appeared in the advertising brochure in 1913.

Caroline B. Freeman built this home in Gales Ferry, Connecticut. Freeman, an instructor of music from Mt. Vernon, New York, built the home for herself and her parents on a one-acre plot. They occupied the house in December 1912. Freeman and her brother Casper spent their vacations with their parents in the home, named "The Bowrie," where roses climbed over the cedar fence and the arbor entrance to the property. By 1914 both parents had died and the home was used as a vacation residence; in 1916 Freeman left Mt. Vernon to live in the house permanently. Freeman became an active participant in local and social activities and was a popular piano teacher. She passed away in 1944.

John H. Cobb Commission, Juneau, Alaska, ca. 1912

Roof: Not known *Bedrooms:* not known *Baths:* not known *Avery Plans:* None

There can be little doubt that the interior of the Cobb house in Juneau, Alaska, was designed by the Craftsman Architects, based on the photo above that was used in a promotional brochure for Stickley's Craftsman fireplace-furnace. Since the house has not been visited or photographed, it is difficult to determine if the entire house was carried out in the Craftsman style. The author has misplaced a set of photos sent to him in 1995 and cannot rely on memory. Cobb lived in Juneau from 1902 to 1908 and from 1913 to 1917 while serving as Territorial Counsel. After his government service, he returned to Juneau, where he practiced law until 1923. He died in Santa Barbara, California, in 1924.

John V. Bacot Jr. Commission, Camden, Maine, 1912

Roof: Gable with hipped dormers   *Bedrooms:* 4   *Baths:* 2   *Avery Plans:* None

This site, on a point jutting out into a lake, demanded a unique design, and Stickley's architects provided one quite unlike any other home designed by the firm (above). The main part of the house has a large living room with a recessed porch wrapped around two sides of the room. A dining room extends off the living room parallel to the porch, with french doors opening onto the porch. The bedrooms are on the second floor, which extends over the living room, porch, and dining room.

A service wing extends at a 90-degree angle to the left of the front of the house and contains a large kitchen (facing top left).

John V. Bacot Jr. was the son of a prominent New Jersey and New York lawyer whose firm (Bacot and Record) had offices in Manhattan and Morristown, New Jersey. Bacot Sr. was also the developer of several water companies—including the East Jersey Water Company, which provided water for about forty communities in northern New Jersey. Bacot Jr. asked Stickley to design a vacation home for him in Camden, Maine, and paid him $220 for the special

plans, which were delivered on July 22, 1911. Bacot bought the land for the house in October 1910, and paid Stickley in three separate payments, with the final payment in August 1912. The house was probably constructed in the spring of 1912. In 1919 he sold the property for $8,000.

A very early color photograph of the house (above), probably made in the 1920s, is in the collection of the current owners.

A fieldstone fireplace dominates the large living room (above), which is finished in light-stained pine. The staircase at right leads to the bedrooms on the second floor. Note the cutout designs on the staircase stringers. The dining room is to the left of the fireplace. There is evidence that the house was originally furnished with Stickley furniture.

Arthur G. Martin Commission, Fairmont, West Virginia, ca. 1912

Roof: Gambrel *Bedrooms:* 3 *Baths:* 1 *Avery Plans:* None

This house was built in Fairmont, West Virginia, and its interior has all the hallmarks of a design from the Craftsman Architects, including the use of Stickley hardware, Grueby and Rookwood tiles, and a large fireplace hood. The exterior is more questionable, but the sense of proportion and use of materials indicates the entire house is probably by the firm. Stickley produced at least one gambrel-roof design similar to the Martin house (No. 202 of February 1915, see page 500). The house sits on a steep hill and the design is certainly site-related. The floor plans from Home No. 51 of 1907 (see page 229) were modified and the upstairs arrangement was altered significantly, reducing four bedrooms to three. Arthur G. Martin, who served two separate terms as mayor, and his wife, Mary, are first shown occupying the house in the 1913 city directory. The local businessman was at times a stenographer; sold books, paper, and cigars at retail; was County Clerk; and sold real estate and insurance.

The exterior of the Martin house is not typical of Stickley designs. But he did design a few gambrel roof homes, and this house uses the mixed material of brick for the first story and shingle above (right). There was a large side porch on the right side, but that was enclosed to create another room many years ago.

The living room (above), viewed from the staircase, features a large fireplace faced with Grueby tiles (above and left). Most of the lights are reproduction Arts and Crafts style or found period lighting. The staircase and entry (below), as viewed from the living room.

The dining room (above and left) features a metal fireplace hood (probably brass) and built-in cabinets and sideboard with Stickley hardware.

J. C. Bolger Commission, Queens, New York, 1912

Roof: Gable with shed dormer   *Bedrooms:* 3   *Baths:* 1
Avery Plans: 8 sheets (blueprints, floor plans, elevation drawings, details on tracing paper

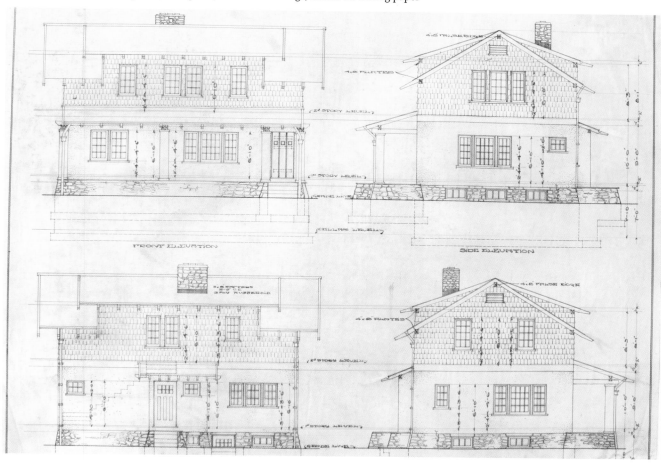

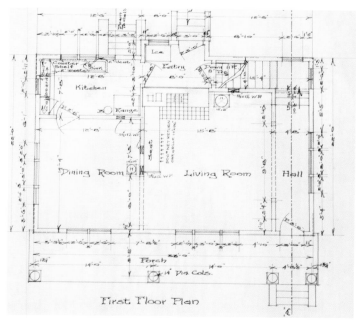

First Floor Plan

This commission is a variation on the standard shingled, Stickley bungalow-style house with raised shed dormers to create a second story. According to local legend, the house was originally built in New York's Queens borough on a prominent hill with spectacular views, but in the 1920s the city decided to build a water storage tank on the site and the house was condemned. To save this house, the owner had it cut into three sections and moved down the hill to a standard lot that was available. The author has not been able to ascertain if this is true, and the house has not been located.

F. J. Wagner Commission, Smithtown, New York, 1912

Roof: Gable with shed dormer   *Bedrooms:* 4   *Baths:* 2   *Avery Plans:* None

The Wagner home as pictured in *The Craftsman* (top), shortly after it was built. The home (above, photographed in 1996) is now the parsonage for a Catholic church. The upper balconies have been enclosed, but it still sits on a large property and can be viewed as Stickley meant it to be seen.

This home, built by Frederick J. Wagner in Smithtown, New York, in 1912, has some stylistic similarities to the Sexton Wilkerson home in Roanoke, Virginia, but is built on a much larger scale. Note the perfect balance of the various structural elements. Still, this is not a great design; the two wings and the pergola-covered sleeping porches do not help relieve the plain design. Stickley says Mrs. Wagner herself supervised much of the construction. The house was built with the Van Guilder system of dual hollow concrete walls. The concrete was in a light gray color and the roof and trim were green.

442

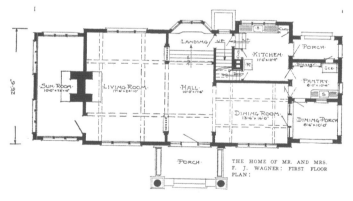

THE HOME OF MR. AND MRS.
F. J. WAGNER: FIRST FLOOR
PLAN:

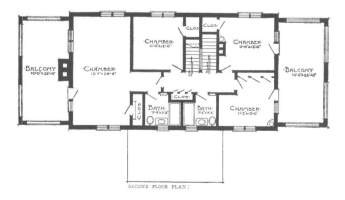

SECOND FLOOR PLAN:

The living room has since been painted and cork-like
ceiling panels installed (top).

The main staircase (above). Much of the house needs
repair and restoration.

Edgar F. Schiebe Commission, Cambridge, Massachusetts, 1912

Roof: Gable with shed dormers   *Bedrooms:* 3 (plus a huge dressing room and a maid's bedroom, 3 balcony/sleeping porches)   *Baths:* 2 1/2
Avery Plans: None

Stickley published an extensive article in *The Craftsman* on this special commission for E. F. Schiebe in Cambridge, Massachusetts. The building permit was issued in October 1911 and the construction cost was listed as $6,000. Stickley charged $200 to design the home. Built of stucco and stone, the house featured Stickley lighting, hardware, a Craftsman fireplace-furnace, and Craftsman furniture. In the second-floor hall area, a pipe organ was installed, with the pipe chamber extending into the attic. Schiebe is listed in city directories as mechanical engineer. It appears that he sold the house in 1918 and later became the president of a glass manufacturing company bearing his name.

E. F. Schiebe house, Cambridge, Massachusetts, from a photograph in *The Craftsman* (top) and as photographed in 2004 (above).

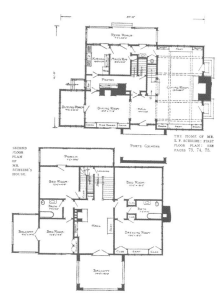

The stone fireplace (above left) pictured in *The Craftsman* eventually was resurfaced or replaced with brick and later painted white (left), along with the woodwork.

A pipe organ was installed (below) in the second-floor hall of the house, with the larger pipes extending into the third-floor billiard room. All trace of the instrument has disappeared from the house.

House at Craftsman Farms, Parsippany, New Jersey, ca. 1912

Roof: Gable   *Bedrooms:* 4   *Baths:* 1   *Avery Plans:* None

The house at Craftsman Farms has beautiful proportions, with a stone first floor and shingle second floor capped by a low-pitched wide-eaved roof.

This is Gustav Stickley's mystery house. Built at Stickley's Craftsman Farms, in Parsippany, New Jersey, it is never mentioned or photographed in any of the articles on Craftsman Farms in *The Craftsman*. It is a substantial building, and an excellent example of Stickley's low-pitched, gable-roof, mixed-material homes. Stickley did publish an article on the proposed Home No. 159 (see page 458) as a home for his daughter and son-in-law, but it was never built. This may have been built instead. The finish of the interior, however, indicates that it may have been the home of the manager of the estate, or perhaps living quarters for several key employees. It does not have the refined interior of most Stickley homes—

the woodwork is minimal, and the doors are the vertical V-grooved plank doors often seen in Stickley's cabin designs. The interior, however, may have been heavily modified after it was built. It has a lower floor consisting of a living room with a fireplace, dining room, and kitchen, and an upper floor with four bedrooms and a bath. There is no basement. The house is privately owned and is not part of the museum property.

1913

With twenty-six offerings, his largest number yet, this is the year of the roof in Stickley homes! Previously the predominant Craftsman Home has variations of the gable roof, but by mid-1913 Stickley begins to feature homes blending different roof styles, often clipping the corners at the ends. These houses appear to be influenced by design trends in other publications of the period, where the concrete or stucco home was gaining popular favor. Rooflines are often used to disguise the simpler home underneath. The illustrations often try to make the houses look inviting and "homey." While many of these homes are still designed with the Craftsman fireplace heating system, Stickley merely mentions it and does not dwell on the subject. While these houses really feature no more windows than in previous years, there is a constant emphasis on the brightness of the rooms, their airiness, and how the plans bring in the outdoors and vice-versa. Based on the number of these houses that have been found, these designs failed to attract readers compared with the years between 1909 and 1911. They are, as a group, less distinctive looking. But many of these designs also blend better into the fabric of neighborhoods, just hiding and waiting to be discovered.

No. 151 January 1913

Roof: Cross gable with saltbox influence and hipped dormers *Bedrooms:* 4 (in each living unit) *Baths:* 1 (in each living unit)
Avery Plans: 7 sheets (floor plans, elevation drawings, details)

This is a beautiful home with a strong Voysey influence (look at Voysey's "Homestead" of 1899) and could also be influenced by "Ragdale," the summer home of Voysey admirer and architect Howard Van Doren Shaw, in Lake Forest, Illinois. It is hard to believe that this house was not built in various locations and is just waiting to be "discovered." While Stickley claims this is his first semidetached house, he did design an upper/lower two-family home for a client in Brooklyn in October 1907 (No. 52, see page 235). "There is no reason why the semi-detached building should not be as satisfying as the single house. It is more economical in construction, [and] needs less fuel for its heating. While brick could be substituted if desired, the general form and lines of the structure seem to lend themselves best to concrete or stucco construction, with shingled roof. The symmetrical arrangement of the exterior combined with its solid and well-balanced proportions gives the place an air of dignity without being at all severe; while the inviting shelter of the recessed entrance porches and those on each side, the tiny dormers that break the slope of the long roofs, and the little sunken balconies to which the dormer windows give access, all contribute to the homelike appearance of the building."

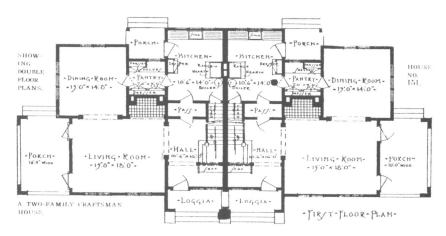

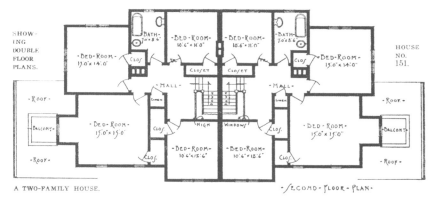

Roof: Cross gable with hipped dormers   *Bedrooms:* 3   *Baths:* 1 1/2   *Avery Plans:* 8 sheets (floor plans, elevation drawings, details)

The second offering for January uses the same materials but is a smaller home designed for one family. Intended for a corner lot, the entrance porch with its small pergola is on the side. The design is a little awkward, marrying the gable roof to the rear—and a mixed cross gable and shed roof, with a hipped dormer thrown in! It is in the English country house/Voysey style, and may also be influenced by the work of Philadelphia architect Wilson Eyre. "An interesting feature of this plan is the fact that the living room and dining room are combined in one, thus eliminating the cutting up of the floor plan into smaller spaces. If desired, of course, portieres or a screen could be used to separate the farther end of the room (used for dining) from the living portion. Breakfasts and other

meals may be served in the kitchen. With this idea in mind we have planned the latter room large, light and cheerful. The house is especially adapted to the Craftsman [fireplace heating] system, for the fireplace is so centrally located that the warm air could be carried to the various rooms with very little piping."

Living in a small Iowa farming community, Leslie Ray French, the son of a lumberyard owner and town mayor, took his pencil to the floor plans on the page of *The Craftsman* and redesigned the rear of No. 152 to accommodate another bedroom and bath. He also moved the kitchen (with a full-width pantry) and created a dining room where the kitchen had been planned. He moved the basement stairway to the new kitchen wing, and placed a half bath under the staircase in the hall. The house (left) appears to have been built from plans modified by Stickley's firm in 1913.

cessed sufficiently to emphasize its sense of cosiness, yet not enough to shut it off from the rest of the room. Glass doors open onto the porch which is so well protected from sun and rain that it will prove a popular place for outdoor living.

The dining room, which is comfortably large and lighted by pleasant window groups overlooking the garden, communicates with a small pantry equipped with dressers and shelves. By placing the pantry window rather high in the wall, room may be left below it for the ice-box, which may be filled through a door accessible from the kitchen porch. The kitchen is also fairly large and from it the cellar stairs descend below the main staircase.

The second floor comprises four bedrooms and bathroom, all opening out of the central hall and being provided with fair-sized closets. The small sunken balcony referred to before will afford a place for ferns or flower-boxes that will add a note of cheeriness to the outlook from the large

it may help light the hall.

In the second house, No. 152, which is planned merely for one family, the same materials — concrete and shingles — are shown, a touch of variety being added by the wood pergola roof and post in the small entrance porch. While this building is intended primarily for a corner lot, it could be readily adapted to a middle one by changing the steps of the entrance pergola to face the street.

The small vestibule opens into a hall with a coat closet directly opposite, and the well-lighted staircase winds up on the left beside a recessed seat. On the right is an opening into the large living room with its fireplace nook and tiled hearth. How light and airy this room will be, is evident from the windows in two opposite walls and the glass doors which open onto the long sheltered porch. The latter has flower-boxes between the pillars and steps at each end leading to the garden.

An interesting feature of this plan is the fact that the living room and dining room are combined in one, thus eliminating the cutting up of the floor plan into smaller spaces. If desired, of course, portières or a screen could be used to separate the farther end of the room (used for dining) from the living portion. In any case, the absence of a partition will help to lighten the house-

This is a page from a 1913 issue of *The Craftsman* (above), where Mr. French made his pencil markings on how he would change the plans. The plans for both floors appear below.

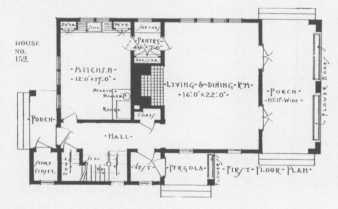

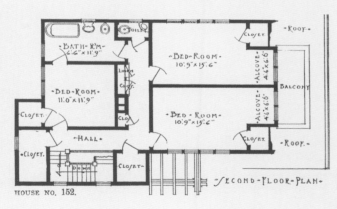

No. 157 April 1913

Roof: Gabled with shed dormers   *Bedrooms:* 4 (plus sewing room)   *Baths:* 1   *Avery Plans:* None

This asymmetrical structure shows Stickley's eye for balance and proportion. This is a fine house, one of his best, rich in interior design and very interesting on the exterior. "The stone and shingle house shown here was designed to be built on a plot of several acres in New Jersey, about thirty miles from New York. As the owner was particularly fond of fieldstone and had plenty of it on his site, he naturally decided to use it for the first story. The walls are 20 inches thick, except on the inside of the recessed entrance porch, where a wood partition is used with a stone veneer. For the walls above this it seemed best to use large shingles or shakes laid about 10 inches to the weather. These, when placed somewhat irregularly, help to carry out the rustic effect. The house is practically two and a half stories high, for a good-sized attic is provided, lighted by double windows in the gables and dormers at each side. This attic later on might be finished off as one large room or several small ones . . . we have managed to keep the appearance of the house comparatively low, partly by the extension of the side porch with its widely overhanging roof, the gradual slope of which repeats the

Col. William C. Parker house, Morris Plains, New Jersey, 1913. Col. Parker was a friend of Stickley and was the local photographer in Morristown. Stickley also designed the interior of the Parker Studio, and he must have been closely associated with the planning and construction of this house, only several miles from Craftsman Farms. The house must have been built after the article in *The Craftsman*, because further changes were made in the plan. An extra window was added to the right bedroom and that balances the three-window group on the left of the house. The porch was a bone of contention: "In planning this porch we wanted at first to have it run entirely across the side of the house; but the owner objected. He said he preferred to have it as shown here, so that it would leave a little sheltered southern corner where he could plant flowers and vines. Also, he thought the irregularity in the outline of the building would add considerably to its charm. Naturally, we are more than pleased when the owner takes such a personal interest." In the end the porch roof was also altered from Stickley's carefully proportioned plan, where it mimicked the shed dormers in the roof, and it was built as a balcony/sleeping porch, accessed by french doors from two of the bedrooms. In later years the sewing room was converted into a second bathroom, the kitchen pantry was removed, and the upper stories were sheathed in aluminum siding. Otherwise the home (left) remains in its original condition.

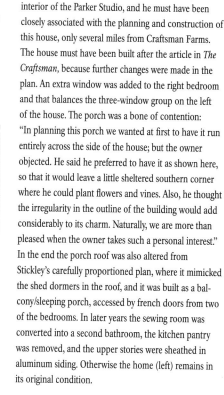

lines of the dormers. Another point that gives the place a somewhat 'bungalow' effect is the use of different materials for the lower and upper stories. The grouping of the windows . . . helps to accentuate the horizontal lines of the house. Most of the windows are outward-opening casements, and their small panes add to the interest of the rooms and of the outside walls. The only exceptions are the large groups in the living and dining rooms, which consist of a stationary picture pane in the center, two small-paned casements on each side and a transom above. This house was planned for a western exposure, so that the living porch at the side would face the south." In the interior, "as we have indicated in the plan, a post and grille might be used to screen part of the landing from the hall, and this corner would be just the place for a telephone stand. If the owner happened to possess a tall clock, it could be placed against the wall beside the window, and being visible from both stairs and living room, it would add to the interest and usefulness of the landing. Both living and dining room have glass doors opening onto the side porch, thus ensuring plenty of light within. This porch may be glassed-in during the winter for a sunroom, if desired. As the second floor plan shows, we have indicated a place for an electric light bath in one corner of the bathroom, and a clothes chute beside the staircase going down to the laundry in the basement."

The living room has a large fieldstone fireplace (above). It was not the Craftsman heater type.

The cozy entrance foyer and staircase as viewed from the living room (top). There is also a built-in window seat.

The dining room (top center) has a large fireplace that backs to the living room one, sharing the chimney. On the common wall with the pantry and kitchen is a built-in china cabinet.

The upstairs hall (above center) features gumwood trim and a large linen closet. The bedrooms (above, for example) are all spacious and most have access to a sleeping porch.

No. 168 August 1913

Roof: Gable *Bedrooms:* 3 *Baths:* 2 *Avery Plans:* None

This cottage has "the walls covered with shingles, the roof with composition sheet roofing, while field stone is used for the foundation and end pillars of the front porch, as well as for the chimneys. For the pillars on each side of the entrance, however, we have used wood, for this forms an intermediate

link between the textures of the rough stonework and smooth roof. Wood pillars are also used for the pergola porch at the side, . . . the shingled walls are stained light golden brown and the roof is olive green. The trim and flower-boxes may also be green and the sash cream or white." Inside,

a fireside seat is built in on one side of the chimneypiece, and "this end of the room will naturally be furnished as a general living room, while the dining table and sideboard will be placed over toward the right, near the kitchen. The pergola porch at the side will be a convenient place for outdoor meals."

No. 169 September 1913

Roof: Mixed gambrel and gable elements *Bedrooms:* 4 (plus sleeping porch) *Baths:* 2
Avery Plans: 8 sheets (floor plans, elevation drawings, details))

This is a fairly clumsy marriage of gambrel and gable roofs. The illustration shows that the rear of the house should be as "inviting" as the front. "We are showing a rear view of No. 169, with the garden path winding up to the back entrance porch. An inviting seat is placed against the outside chimney,

which breaks up the plain surfaces of wall and roof, . . . there is nothing about it to suggest that this corner of the building is in any way inferior to the front." This house is stucco on either hollow tile or metal lath, and shingles are used for the roof and across the gables. "If the stucco is left in its natu-

ral grayish tone a touch of warmth may be added by staining the shingles for the roof a rich mossy green, and using golden brown for those in the gables and in the extension that shelters the kitchen windows. Brown or green might be used for the door and window trim, with white sash."

No. 170 September 1913

Roof: Cross gable *Bedrooms:* 2 (plus maid's room and sleeping porch) *Baths:* 2 1/2 *Avery Plans:* None

This house looks like a version of an L-shaped plan, but it could be considered an adaptation of the typical four-square. There is an odd mismatch of cross gable and shed-roof types, the shed sweeping low to cover the recessed porch. It has been designed to be built of stucco on either hollow tile or metal lath, and shingles are used for the roof and across the gables. As to color, "it would be a good plan to use terra cotta for the roof and olive green for the door and window trim and window boxes. If the house was built near the shore or in some open section of the country where there were not many trees, paler tones would be more appropriate, for they would blend better with the blues and grays of sea, sky and distant hills." Stickley does not tell much about this interesting house, other than to describe the floor plan.

No. 171 October 1913

Roof: Hipped with gable dormer *Bedrooms:* 4 (plus sleeping porch) *Baths:* 2
Avery Plans: 9 sheets (floor plans, elevation drawings, details)

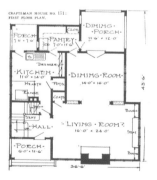

This is one of Stickley's awkward looking houses, as the gable dormer does nothing to help the design. The dormer around the chimney throws the proportion and balance off. In the description of the house, *The Craftsman* disagrees: "The roof we have shown covered with asbestos shingles, and the outside chimney of the living room is carried up in concrete through a gable extension, ventilated by louvers, as shown in the drawing—a construction which results in a more substantial and pleasing appearance than if the chimney were carried up above the main roof without any support." The house is of stucco or concrete construction. "While the house is very simple in construction, the exterior does not look too solid or plain. The walls are pleasantly broken by the recesses and projections of the porches, and the roof lines have sufficient variety to be interesting from whatever angle."

No. 172 October 1913

Roof: Saltbox and gable *Bedrooms:* 5 (plus sleeping porch) *Baths:* 2 *Avery Plans:* 5 sheets (floor plans, elevation drawings, details)

This home is also not one of *The Craftsman*'s better designs—it too does not marry the saltbox and gable-roof styles well. This is essentially a foursquare house that Stickley has tried to disguise with the roof. "This house is shown with shingled walls and roof, and while the exterior is comparatively simple, the construction of the porch and sleeping balcony, the grouping of the windows and angles of the roof lines give it a certain architectural interest. It will be noticed that we have arranged no entrance to this porch from the garden. The owner can, of course, provide one at the front or side if it seems desirable; but our idea in omitting it was to secure greater privacy for the family, who might otherwise he disturbed by callers whom they would rather receive indoors, or by strangers who might mistake the porch steps for the main entrance."

No. 173 November 1913

Roof: Cross gable with clipped corners *Bedrooms:* 4 *Baths:* 1 *Avery Plans:* 7 sheets (floor plans, elevation drawings, interior details)

The article for the November homes begins "'If you ever intend to build,' wrote a friend of ours when describing in another publication the making of his home, 'look up the work of Gustav Stickley. It is from his magazine that I got the idea for our house.' Naturally we were pleased to read this apprecia-tive statement, to know that its writer was not only satisfied with the home which our plans had helped him to evolve, but eager to have others profit by our experience and aid." A variation on the bungalow theme, Stickley works out the idea under a gable roof, but he clips the corners to make the roof look hipped in this lovely home. "The irregularity of outline—the result of planning the rooms for a maximum of light and ventilation—makes a rather interesting exterior, for the nooks and angles of the walls and the shadowed recess of the living porch break up the sides of the building pleasantly, giving the place an air of cozy seclusion. The walls are stucco on metal lath, and the roof is composition fireproof shingles. . . . [W]e suggest shingles of a soft grayish green, the same color for the door and window trim and other exposed woodwork, white sash, and a warmer note of terra cotta in the cement floors of the porches."

No. 174 November 1913

Roof: Cross gable *Bedrooms:* 5 *Baths:* 2 *Avery Plans:* 8 sheets (floor plans, elevation drawings, interior details)

 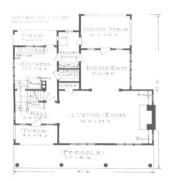 

The perspective drawing does not present this home well—it looks too tall and boxy and the cross-gable roof perches awkwardly in the middle. Perhaps if the view from the other side of the house were shown, a different opinion of the exterior would result. But even though it is balanced and symmetrical, the sum of its parts is an unattractive house. Stickley disagrees: "Both in size and contour the building lends itself to concrete construction with shingled roof, although brick walls and slate roof can be substituted. A southern exposure will ensure the morning sunlight for the dining room, while the living room, having windows on three sides, will get the sunshine practically all day. While the house is very simple in design, it is saved from severity by the pergola, the recessed entrance porch, the other porches and the sleeping balcony, and the outside chimney."

No. 175 December 1913

Roof: Hipped, with clipped gable dormer *Bedrooms:* 4 *Baths:* 1 *Avery Plans:* None

 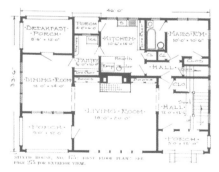 

"As a low roof, wide eaves and dormers give a homelike, bungalow effect, we have kept the roof lines low, and given headroom to the upper story by means of dormers which break up the large roof area and give variety of both contour and materials. . . . [A] single perspective view can give only a limited impression of these stucco houses, for the angles and nooks formed by the porches and dormers result in an irregularity of outline which makes the buildings interesting from whatever point one sees them." Note the warm glow of the windows welcoming home the breadwinner as he trudges through the snow after a long day at the office in this rare night view! After several months of presenting awkward looking homes, this house is pleasant and well proportioned. The symmetrical cross-shaped upper story is quite different from most Craftsman Homes.

No. 176 December 1913

Roof: Gable, with clipped corners and large clipped shed dormers *Bedrooms:* 4 *Baths:* 2 *Avery Plans:* None

With large clipped corner dormers and downward sweeping roofline, Stickley creates a new variation to his long rectangular house design theme. "No. 176, with its solid, compact outline and its hood-like roof, suggests the cottage rather than the bungalow type. The small-parted casement windows that peer out from the stucco walls below the steeply sloping eaves, the recessed entrance porch that shelters the front door, the dormer-like gables breaking up the roof on each side, and the stucco chimneys that suggest the hospitality of the fireside within—while necessary features of an economical form of construction, have all been planned so as to contribute to the homelike, sturdy air of the exterior.

"A point worth noting in this interior is the symmetrical way in which the spaces and vistas have been planned. The big open fireplace in the center of the living-room wall is directly in line with the opening in the hall, while the group of front windows is in line with the dining room opening. This gives an opportunity for a very interesting use of ceiling beams as well as handling of wall spaces. Upstairs four bedrooms are provided, opening out of the central hall, and in addition there is a small room or alcove next to the bathroom. This little room may be used as a sewing nook, storeroom, linen room or tiny nursery, or it may be turned into a bathroom and either used with the bedroom or made to open from the hall."

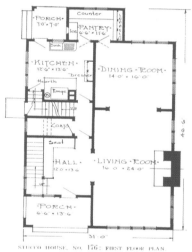

STUCCO HOUSE, NO. 176: FIRST FLOOR PLAN

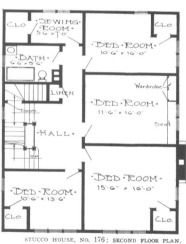

STUCCO HOUSE, NO. 176: SECOND FLOOR PLAN.

C. L. Knight Commission, Sacramento, California, ca. 1913

Roof: Hipped with eyebrow dormer *Bedrooms:* 4 *Baths:* 2
Avery Plans: 20 sheets (floor plans, elevation drawings, plumbing sections, site plans, interior details)

C. L. Knight ordered plans from the Craftsman Architects to build this home in Sacramento, California, about 1913. This is a most interesting commission, as Knight made a number of exterior and interior changes to the house after getting the plans but maintained most of the details inside. The changes can best be seen in comparing the drawings from the Avery Library with the photograph of the home. It may be that these Avery plans were revised by Stickley for Knight, and that the newer plans have not survived. Knight was the engineer responsible for the construction of the deepwater shipping canal that linked Sacramento to San Francisco Bay, opening up commerce for the entire region. He lived in this house until he died in the 1970s.

The exterior design built is far less successful than the original concept was.

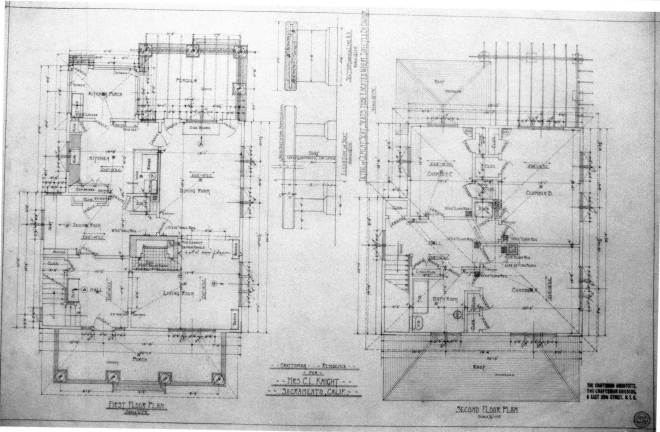

The original front and side elevations (top) and the floor plans (above), from the Avery Library. When the house was built, there were some alterations, including the extension of the kitchen and the elimination of the sewing room. The built-in sideboard was relocated to the side of the dining room. The bathroom was enlarged to extend over part of the staircase.

The house was designed to be heated by the Craftsman fireplace heating system, and in the mild climate of Sacramento only some auxiliary heaters have been required to be added. The staircase to the upper floor is to the left, and the dining room is to the right beyond the fireplace. These photos were made in 1994.

A view of the dining room, showing the Craftsman built-in sideboard and china cabinets. The room was not painted originally.

Some of the original fixtures remain in the bathroom, as well as the original stained woodwork.

The upstairs hall (right), now painted, has extensive and detailed woodwork.

No. 187 May 1914

Roof: Saltbox with shed dormer   *Bedrooms:* 4 (plus sleeping porch)   *Baths:* 1 1/2
Avery Plans: 9 sheets (floor plans, elevation drawings and details)

After producing 186 houses, does the inspiration run thin? Probably. Looking at this house, the term "standard Stickley" comes to mind. It is a nice house—there is nothing wrong with it—but it has been done before, it is just another version. The description in *The Craftsman* is "standard Stickley" too—it has all been said before. The floor plans and knowledge of other Stickley designs is all one needs to know to understand this house.

No. 188 May 1914

Roof: Crossed hipped   *Bedrooms:* 3   *Baths:* 4   *Avery Plans:* None

This house is confusing with its zigzag roof, a far cry from the simplicity of earlier designs. Stickley reverts to hyperbole to sell this design: "The exterior of this cottage, while most unpretentious, has a certain sheltering, cozy air due to the recessed porches, the wide eaves and the tiny balcony sunken in the front roof and edged by a low wooden rail; while the projecting roof that covers this little nook reminds one of the mothering wing with which a hen protects her little chicks. For this cottage an eastern exposure would probably be the most satisfactory: although if the lot happened to face south it would be better to reverse the plans bringing the living and dining rooms over on the right or east."

No. 189 July 1914

Roof: Gable with shed dormers *Bedrooms:* 2 (plus large sleeping porch) *Baths:* 1 *Avery Plans:* None

The exterior of this design is similar to No. 180 from February 1914 (see page 474). It is a beautifully proportioned and well laid out home. "Designed for a site in Palos Park, Illinois, it is to be built in the center of a five-acre woodland lot, three hundred feet from the roadway. The construction is stucco on hollow tile, with shingled roof, and the interior is, as the owner said, 'snug and compact for winter, but arranged for plenty of outdoor living in the summertime.' The perspective view of the front and one side of the house gives an inadequate idea of the interest of the exterior; for in addition to the recessed porch and hooded entrances, the pleasant window groups, the dormer effect in the roof, and the openings of the upstairs sleeping porch on the right, there is a big porch projecting from the house at the opposite side which is barely seen.

"Above this porch is a balcony, which can be picturesque with flowers and vines set around the parapet. The pergola construction suggests a delightful form of semi-shelter between the entrance porch and the flower garden. The interior embodies an original and unusual scheme, one that is not only especially convenient for the family for whom it was planned, but may be readily adapted to the needs of others." The use of large heavy brackets instead of purlins is rare in a Craftsman Home, but they do appear in several other houses, including the Harriet Martin house of 1909 (see page 306).

George B. and Evelyn Hart Ward owned a photography business in Chicago when they built their home, which they called "Brookwood," in 1914 on a parcel opposite a forest preserve just outside the borders of Palos Park, Illinois, a village south of Chicago. Mrs. Ward created magnificent gardens on the property and was active in the Wildflower Conservation Movement. In the 1920s the home was a popular restaurant. After her husband passed away in the late '30s, Evelyn began to sell off parts of the property, and when she died in 1950, the new owners subdivided it even more. But even in 1994 when the author visited, there were several acres surrounding the house in a magnificent, if overgrown, setting. The pergola had long since fallen into disrepair and had been removed, but the house appeared in fine shape, if a little worn around the edges. This is an example of what tragedy can befall these little-understood homes. John and Pat Goes owned it for fifty years and treasured it as a special place. Its history was known to the community, but shortly after Mrs. Goes sold the house in 1998, believing it would be preserved, the house was razed. Before anyone in the community could do anything about it, a large "MacMansion" was built it its place.

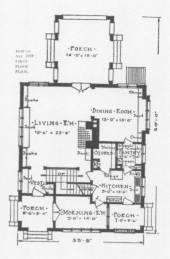

The living room (above left). Almost all the woodwork had survived with perhaps an extra coat of varnish, and while the walls were dark, the interior was filled with light even on a gray day. The only major change was a resurfacing of the Craftsman fireplace-furnace with inappropriate white stonework—the owners said that the fireplace had caught fire and had to be rebuilt in the '60s—but the heating vents remained.

The staircase at the end of the living room (center). The spectacular woodwork inside the home shows that even in 1914 Stickley was designing detailed Craftsman interiors—and his homes were beautiful when built according to the plans.

The dining room (left). Notice the heating vent from the rear of the fireplace. No Stickley hardware was used in the house.

No. 190 July 1914

Roof: Gable with shed dormers *Bedrooms:* 2 (plus large sleeping porch) *Baths:* 1 *Avery Plans:* None

The Craftsman Architects were also called upon to design a simpler house on a smaller scale "for a site in Sycamore, Illinois, and as in the first case, the drawings and specifications were specially prepared from sketches and suggestions sent us by the owner." Brick is used for the main walls, chimney and porch parapet, pillars and steps, shingles being chosen for the main roof as well as for the sides and roofs of the dormer. "The most satisfactory exposure for the house is facing south or southwest, insuring plenty of sunshine for the dining room, living room and porch. The second floor comprises two good-sized bedrooms, bathroom and sleeping porch, the latter sunk into the back roof and sheltered by a dormer similar to that in front."

The house was designed for local physician Orville Thompson, in Sycamore, Illinois (top), and a photo postcard made in 1924 (above) confirms that it was built pretty much as planned. Dr. Thompson chose not to build the house of brick but finished off the exterior with a pebble-dash stucco finish in this western Illinois farming community. The dormers and porch roof sides were finished in wood shingles as called for in the plans. The home that was built does not look quite as good as the drawing, but it is a good example of Stickley's refinement of the bungalow design. In later years the front porch was enclosed to create another room, and an addition in the rear was built (faced with clapboards) to add bedrooms and a garage.

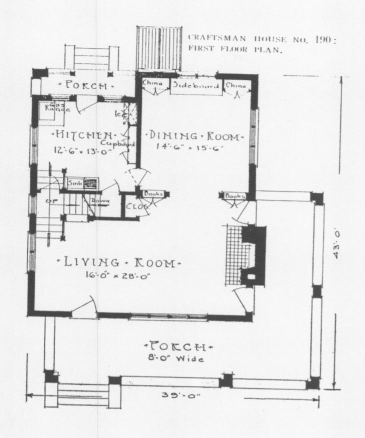

CRAFTSMAN HOUSE NO. 190:
FIRST FLOOR PLAN.

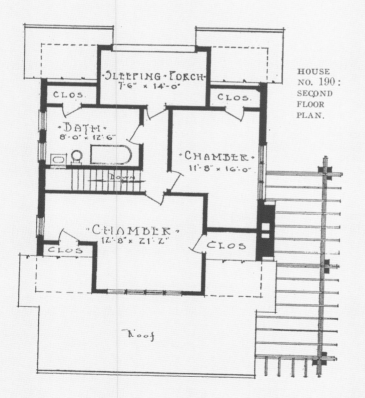

HOUSE
NO. 190:
SECOND
FLOOR
PLAN.

A careful restoration was undertaken in 1994 when these photos were made; all the woodwork was carefully removed and refinished, and the badly deteriorated beaverboard was replaced with Sheetrock. Thompson appears to have followed the plans closely, but there must have been a limit to his finances, so some interesting decisions were made. Stucco was generally cheaper than brick and was used on the exterior. Inexpensive "beaverboard" composite wall panels were used instead of lath and plaster in the interior. Pieces of the original composite flooring in the kitchen were found, as well as a signature on the back of a piece of beaverboard dating the construction of the house: "Otto Klemmedson Carpenter Sept 17th 1914."

Yet in contrast, expensive tapestry brick was used in the fireplace, and the home had expensive Stickley lighting fixtures.

The staircase features spindles and had a newel post lamp. Smaller than the contemporaneous home built in Palos Park, it is interesting to compare the application of the woodwork in the two homes. The Palos Park house (see pages 482–83) had extensive chestnut boards lining the walls, while this house uses woodwork—gumwood, not oak or chestnut—sparingly in an open floor plan to give the rooms a sense of spaciousness.

No. 191 August 1914

Roof: Cross hipped   *Bedrooms:* 6 (plus 3 servants' bedrooms in basement)   *Baths:* 3 (plus 1 servants' bath in basement)
Avery Plans: None

This house shows Stickley's sense of proportion in a large-scale home, one that hopefully was built and survived. Like No. 25 of 1905, this is another large home based on a center hall H-type plan. This is the last house that Stickley claims in *The Craftsman* that he designed for a client. Looking at the drawings and style of building, some assumptions can be drawn as to its possible location. While any location in a warm climate is possible, the home mimics vernacular features present in the Southwest and in California. The client is obviously wealthy, and the location has developed streets and is hilly with a view, according to the article. The fireplace will be needed in winter, so the location is in an area that has at least moderate temperature changes. A guess would be that the house might be located in the San Francisco–Sacramento area; Los Angeles; Santa Fe, New Mexico; Flagstaff, Arizona; or Austin, Texas.

"A short time ago one of our subscribers asked us to prepare special plans for a three-story home, to be built upon a sloping lot that ran from one street through to another. The dip in the land was considerable, and he wanted to adapt his design accordingly, so as to avoid unnecessary excavation, to get plenty of light for his basement rooms, and to take advantage of the view. The drawings show, moreover, an unusually interesting embodiment of Craftsman ideas on a large scale—

for the present design includes not only spacious rooms and outdoor living places for the family and guests, but also convenient accommodation for several servants, chauffeur and an automobile. In planning the house, it was natural to have it face the highest street, for this allowed the servants' quarters and garage to be built at the back of the basement with plenty of windows. It also permitted the erection of a big living porch and balcony above the garage, where one could overlook the garden from a pleasant height. The dining room has also been placed at the rear, in the southeast corner, where it will get ample sunshine, and this brings the kitchen to the front—an unusual but in this instance satisfactory arrangement."

"The two perspective drawings of this house give one some impression of its appearance from different points. The surfaces of the concrete or stucco walls are broken by the recesses and projections of the various porches and balconies, while the roof of flat tiles, with its various angles and ridges, presents an opportunity for a note of warm color—moss green or terra cotta— against the more neutral tone of the walls. The front and back of the building are symmetrical in design, unlike the sides, which follow the lines of the hill, and there is a suggestion of the Mission effect in the arches, balcony parapets and tops of the façades. These architectural features give the house a certain decorative air . . . and when the garden is planted and vines trained against the walls, the building will seem quite to belong in its surroundings."

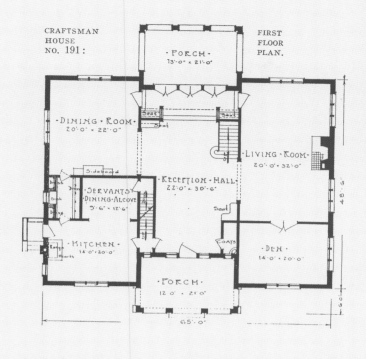

CRAFTSMAN
HOUSE
NO. 191:

FIRST
FLOOR
PLAN.

· PORCH ·
13'-0" × 21'-0"

· DINING · ROOM ·
20'-0" × 22'-0"

Seat

Seat

Seat

· LIVING · ROOM ·
20'-0" × 32'-0"

Sideboard

· SERVANTS ·
DINING · ALCOVE ·
9'-6" × 12'-6"

· RECEPTION · HALL ·
22'-0" × 30'-6"

Seat

· KITCHEN ·
14'-0" × 20'-0"

Range
Hearth

COATS

· DEN ·
14'-0" × 20'-0"

· PORCH ·
12'-0" × 21'-0"

48'-6"

65'-0"

CRAFTSMAN
HOUSE
NO. 191:

SECOND
FLOOR
PLAN.

· BALCONY ·
15'-0" × 21'-0"

· BED · ROOM ·
17'-6" × 20'-0"

· BED · ROOM ·
13'-0" × 20'-0"

· BATH ·
8'-0" × 11'-6"

CLO

HALL

· HALL ·

CLO

· BATH ·
6'-0" × 11'-0"

CLO

CLOS

CLOS

· BED · ROOM ·
11'-0" × 15'-6"

Roof

· BED · ROOM ·
20'-0" × 20'-0"

· BED · ROOM ·
12'-0" × 17'-0"

CLOS

· BATH ·
6'-0" × 11'-0"

CLOS

CLOS

· BED · ROOM ·
12'-6" × 20'-0"

· BALCONY ·
12'-0" × 21'-0"

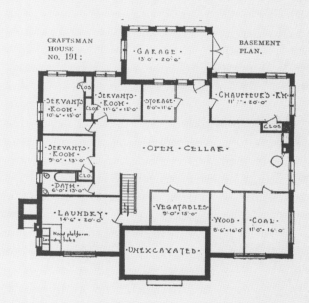

CRAFTSMAN
HOUSE
NO. 191:

BASEMENT
PLAN.

· GARAGE ·
13'-0" × 20'-6"

CLOS

· SERVANTS ·
ROOM ·
10'-6" × 15'-0"

CLO

· SERVANTS ·
ROOM ·
11'-6" × 12'-0"

· STORAGE ·
8'-0" × 11'-6"

· CHAUFFEUR'S · RM ·
11'-0" × 20'-0"

CLOS

· SERVANTS ·
ROOM ·
9'-0" × 13'-0"

CLO.

· OPEN · CELLAR ·

· BATH ·
6'-0" × 13'-0"

· LAUNDRY ·
14'-6" × 20'-0"

· VEGETABLES ·
9'-0" × 15'-0"

· WOOD ·
8'-6" × 16'-0"

· COAL ·
11'-0" × 16'-0"

Wood platform

Laundry tubs

· UNEXCAVATED ·

No. 192 September 1914

Roof: Cross gable with gable dormers *Bedrooms:* 0 *Baths:* 2 *Avery Plans:* None

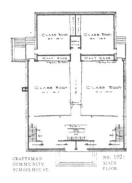

CRAFTSMAN COMMUNITY SCHOOLHOUSE. NO. 192: MAIN FLOOR.

CRAFTSMAN COMMUNITY SCHOOLHOUSE, NO. 192: PLAN OF TOP FLOOR.

NO. 192: BASEMENT PLAN. CRAFTSMAN COMMUNITY SCHOOLHOUSE,

Stickley revisits the schoolhouse, but times have changed and this is no simple one-room schoolhouse like the two he published in July 1911 (Nos. 119 and 120, see page 402). This is a handsome building and well thought out for a school of the period. A number of school boards across the country, probably as financially strapped then as now, must have jumped at the chance to get free working drawings to build this, thus saving an architect's fee. Surely this rare Stickley public building must have been built somewhere.

No. 193 September 1914

Roof: Saltbox *Bedrooms:* 2 *Baths:* 1 *Avery Plans:* None

CRAFTSMAN BOAT-HOUSE COTTAGE NO. 193: SECOND FLOOR PLAN.

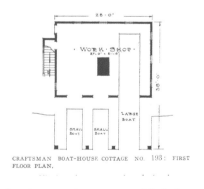

CRAFTSMAN BOAT-HOUSE COTTAGE NO. 193: FIRST FLOOR PLAN.

This may be the structure with the widest overhanging eaves in all of Stickley's designs. It is almost over-the-top but these overhangs are surely practical. "While we have shown this building beside a lake in a mountainous and wooded country, it would also be suitable in design for either sea shore or river bank. In the present case the shingled covering and the long slope of the roof are particularly in keeping with the woods and hills among which it is set. This little building is really more than a boat-house. For in addition to the accommodation downstairs, sleeping quarters are provided above, so that the place will serve as a summer camp if desired."

488

No. 194 October 1914

Roof: Cross hip with eyebrow dormers *Bedrooms:* 4 (plus maid's room) *Baths:* 3
Avery Plans: 12 sheets (plans, elevations, interior, construction details)

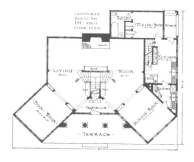
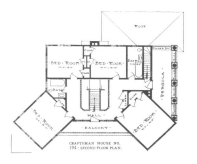

This is a radically different design, south facing, with the two wings projecting at 45-degree angles from the center. Stickley's sense of proportion and balance show through but this house does not have some of the typical Craftsman features, such as exposed purlins. The house is a unique attempt to address the problem of how to position the house for the best light and air and to get good views. "We have developed an interior full of possibilities for a decorative handling of structural woodwork and furnishings. The exterior, with its various angles, its window groups, porches, balcony and pergola, holds decided architectural interest. The construction is stucco, left in its natural grayish tone, on brick, with roof of flat tile, the round pillars and the beams of front porch and side pergola being of wood."

No. 195 November 1914

Roof: Sort of cross hipped *Bedrooms:* 3 (plus maid's room) *Baths:* 2 *Avery Plans:* None

Stickley revisits the U-shaped house with this attractive bungalow that features an interesting plan. "The main idea was to provide a central, glassed-in living place that would be sufficiently protected for use all the year round, and would have windows all along one side which could be thrown open during warm weather. Around this, the living rooms, kitchen and servant's quarters and the family sleeping rooms were to be grouped in such a fashion that each section would be separated from the others. The bungalow, which is shown here of stone with slate or shingle roof, is intended to face the east, as this will insure morning sunlight for kitchen and dining room as well as library and living room, and the latter will also receive sunshine later in the day through the glass doors and roof of the covered garden at the rear."

No. 196 Rustic Cabin, December 1914

Roof: Gable   *Bedrooms:* 0   *Baths:* 0   *Avery Plans:* None

The following three structures (Nos. 196, 197, and 198) are an indication that Stickley was still interested in promoting ideas, even though he was in the midst of trying to save his firm from financial ruin. While it is a stretch to call a playhouse and a doghouse Craftsman Homes, he did give them house numbers, so they are placed in the official canon. And why not, for he was putting the youngsters, if not the pets, on the proper path to an "Arts and Crafts" lifestyle!

Stickley writes a detailed description of how to build this little cabin and the techniques needed. He is passionate about this structure, as he finishes the article by making an offer to provide the materials from his Craftsman Farms. "The cost of the materials would be about $400. For those who wish to build one, we have prepared complete working drawings, details and specifications, as well as a lumber bill, which can be obtained from our Architectural Department. Moreover, as we have more timber than we can use on Craftsman Farms . . . our plan is to utilize it for the building of rustic cabins like the one shown here. We will therefore ship, to any one who wishes to build from this design, the requisite number of slabs for the walls and logs for the porch posts, cut and trimmed the right lengths, all ready for building."

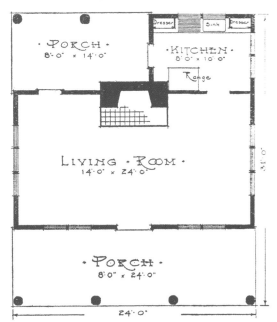

FLOOR PLAN OF THE RUSTIC CABIN.

No. 197 Playhouse, December 1914

Roof: Gable *Bedrooms:* 0 *Baths:* 0 *Avery Plans:* None

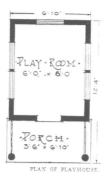

PLAN OF PLAYHOUSE.

"We are also showing here the plan and perspective view of a children's playroom, which would be particularly in keeping with the rustic cabin just described. There are few things that afford greater delight to children than a tiny house of their own, and there are few forms of construction that appeal to their active imaginations more keenly than the rustic cabin. It suggests pioneers, Indians, and deep shadowy woodlands; about its logs still clings the mystery of the forest in which they grew. For these reasons, we think the little playhouse with its slab walls and roof and latticed porch will appeal to many children. It can be easily and cheaply put together. The simplest way to build it would be to set the slabs upright about an inch apart with tar paper and sheathing inside. The playroom is 6 by 8 feet, and would really be large enough to hold a cot and use as an extra sleeping room if one needed another bedroom at any time."

No. 198 Dog House, December 1914

Roof: Gable *Bedrooms:* 1 *Baths:* 0 *Avery Plans:* None

"The dog kennel is also of log construction, and for this either slabs or solid logs might be used."

Charles B. Evans Commission, Queens, New York, 1914

Roof: Hipped with eyebrow dormer   *Bedrooms:* 4   *Baths:* 2
Avery Plans: 20 sheets (floor plans, elevation drawings, plumbing sections, site plans, interior details)

When Charles B. Evans asked the Craftsman Architects for a home for a location in Queens, New York City, in 1913, the plans for Craftsman Home No. 8 of August 1904 (see page 124) were resurrected. The exterior was done in stucco with brick trim and modifications were made, particularly with the addition of a den/porch to the rear of the living room, the enlargement of the kitchen, and a reduction in size of the dining room. The first-floor plans (right) from the Avery Library show the changes.

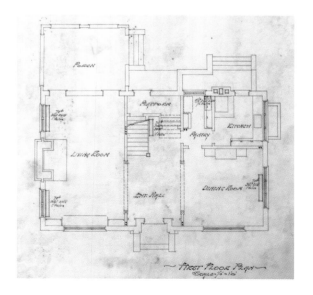

Nathanial R. Bronson Commission, Middlebury, Connecticut, 1914

Roof: Gable with hipped dormer *Bedrooms:* 4 *Baths:* 1
Avery Plans: 24 sheets (floor plans, elevation drawings, details, preliminary sketches, plan revisions)

In March 1914 the Craftsman Architects began to design a home for Nathanial R. Bronson, an attorney in Waterbury, Connecticut, who wanted a weekend retreat in nearby Middlebury. The hipped dormer is out of character with most Craftsman bungalow designs, which feature a shed roof.

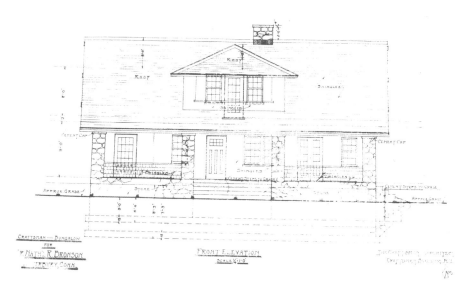

The side of the Bronson bungalow as photographed in 2000 (above). The front elevation from the Avery Library (right).

Mrs. J. A. Ives Commission, Marengo, Iowa, 1914

Roof: Hipped with gable dormers *Bedrooms:* 3 (with sleeping porch) *Baths:* 1 *Avery Plans:* 15 sheets (floor plans, elevation drawings, details)

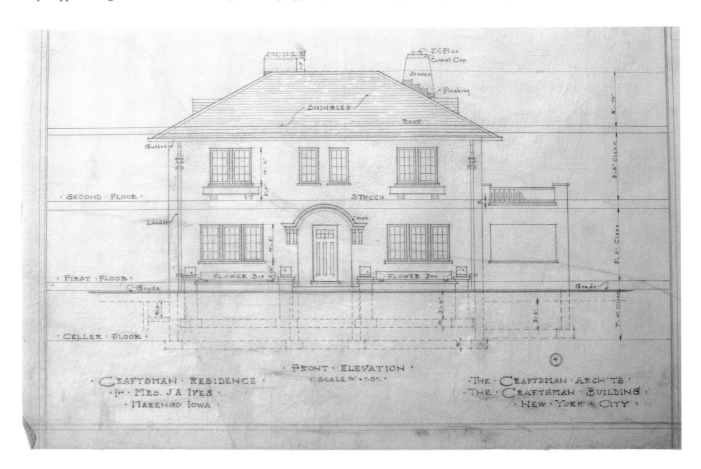

This very English Arts and Crafts stucco house was designed for a Mrs. J. A. Ives in the Marengo, Iowa, area. The semicircle with wings over the front entrance is very unlike a Craftsman Home, but is pure Voysey (see his Holly Mount of 1905). The form is vaguely reminiscent of the Prairie School style in silhouette. The integrated planters and stair plinths create a base for the building, which also speaks of the Prairie School. There is a little bit of Wright and a little bit of Voysey combined in a rather timid center hall design. The house has not been located, if it was built.

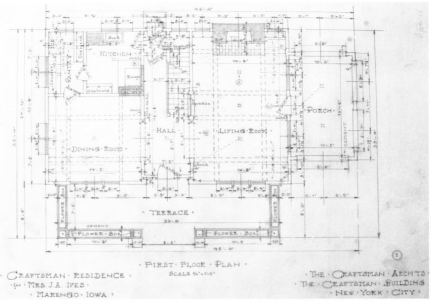

Front elevation (top) and first-floor plan (above), from the Avery Library.

494

I. R. Williams Commission, Ossining, New York, 1914

Roof: Cross gable   *Bedrooms:* 4   *Baths:* 1   *Avery Plans:* (floor plans, elevation drawings, details, also modifications and proposals)

Mr. and Mrs. I. R. Williams of Ossining, New York, asked Stickley to revise an earlier Craftsman design (No. 116 of May 1911, see page 397). Mrs. Williams "was a dedicated Craftsman reader who felt that she had to have a real Craftsman house when the time came for the family to build on a newly opened street . . . ." After they had chosen the floor plan they liked, she "is said to have taken scissors in hand and cut through it to enlarge the house with space for an additional bedroom and bath to the right of the living room."[67] Making the porch smaller and roofing it with a cross-gable roof that changes the entire appearance of the house from No. 116.

I. R. Williams home in 2003 (above). It is strongly influenced by the bungalow designs being built in California during the period.

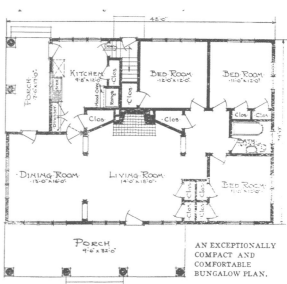

The I. R. Williams house floor plan (see page 495) and a drawing of the interior (above) appeared in *The Craftsman* as an example of "an exceptionally compact and comfortable bungalow plan," but no mention was made that it was designed for a client and was a Craftsman Home.

The living room was photographed in 1991 (right). The house still has a Craftsman fireplace heating unit.

Post-and-panel dividers separate the living room from the dining room (below).

1915

These ten homes are the last of the pure Stickley designs. While not very inventive, they are solid practical homes with appealing exteriors that integrate easily into suburban neighborhoods and with interesting, and sometimes creative, floor plans. Most of these homes are now of concrete or stucco construction.

Looking at these homes, it would be hard to tell that by now the "Craftsman Empire" was in bankruptcy and that Stickley was losing control of his company. The familiar "Als ik kan" inside the joiners compass trademark of Stickley disappeared from the drawings in April and May. Perhaps that is why in June of 1915 the houses ceased to be published, with no word of explanation.

No. 199 January 1915

Roof: Cross gable with saltbox influence and a shed dormer. *Bedrooms:* 3 (plus sleeping porch) *Baths:* 1 *Avery Plans:* None

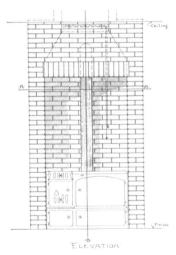

This illustration shows the special construction of the ventilating hood over the kitchen range in Craftsman cottage No. 199 and Craftsman bungalow No. 200.

The Stickley Museum at Craftsman Farms has the original drawing for this home in its collection. It is a pen-and-ink drawing with some watercolor added to the snow and sky. This is a nice design as the variations in the roof break up a square pattern. It features shingled walls and roof, and a brick chimney. "The cottage would be interesting if the shingles up to the line of the gables were stained a rich golden brown, and those above a darker tone, with a mossy green for the roof." The door and window trim should be painted green with white sash, and a touch of red brick in the chimney will contrast nicely. "[A]lthough the house is a small one, the great living room with its wide window groups, central fireplace and long bookshelves gives one a sense of spaciousness as one steps inside from the porch. The kitchen is a big, light, airy place, with windows on three sides and a door at the back leading out to the garden."

This pen-and-ink with watercolor illustration of No. 199 (above), from the The Stickley Museum Collection at Craftsman Farms, indicates that many of the illustrations for *The Craftsman* may have had some color.

498

No. 215 September 1916

Roof: Crossed hipped   *Bedrooms:* 3   *Baths:* 1   *Avery Plans:* None

This home might be a vague shadow of No. 78 of 1909 (see page 317). It is a pleasant home but does not look Craftsman at all. The magazine shills it as "a small but roomy farmhouse . . . beautiful enough for erection on any town lot or for any suburban residence. If this house be painted white, with silver gray roof, apple green blinds, with flowering vines clambering over the trellis, it surely would radiate that sweet, simple home atmosphere every one wishes to secure in their own home and love to see in the home of others."

No. 216 September 1916

Roof: Cross gable *Bedrooms:* 2 *Baths:* 1 *Avery Plans:* None

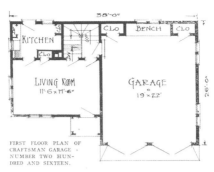

FIRST FLOOR PLAN OF CRAFTSMAN GARAGE · NUMBER TWO HUNDRED AND SIXTEEN.

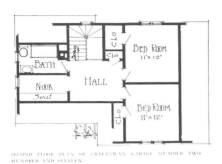

SECOND FLOOR PLAN OF CRAFTSMAN GARAGE · NUMBER TWO HUNDRED AND SIXTEEN.

"Since garages are an important part of all farm life nowadays, we have designed a garage to be used in connection with this house (No. 215). Servant's quarters have been arranged in this building, so that if desired the farmhouse can be entirely closed in the winter and the farmer's overseer or caretaker can live comfortably in this garage. Another use could be made of this garage if so desired—that of a studio. The great doors [could have] faced north, and provided with larger glass would give splendid light for this room. This garage even would serve as a good model for a small house. Instead of the garage, would be living room, instead of the garage doors a row of casement windows; entrance could be provided by a door immediately to the right of the entrance door. Thus with a little adjustment a small sized farmhouse or summer cottage could be made from this plan."

No. 217 October 1916

Roof: Cross gable with hipped dormers *Bedrooms:* 4 *Baths:* 1 *Avery Plans:* None

First floor plan of Craftsman House Number Two Hundred and Seventeen.

SECOND FLOOR PLAN OF CRAFTSMAN HOUSE NO. 217.

This house copies a simple English country cottage, and is designed for a small family. If there are stones in the neighborhood, then the foundation and the stairway should be of stone. "The railing of the stairway should be very wide, built hollow, filled with earth and planted with flowers. The treatment of the roof is distinctive, the roll edge gives softness and the cut in the roof (to permit the dormer), with its box of flowers adds color and variation. Composition shingles are advised not only because they are fire-retarding, but because they can be curved at the edges more easily." Stucco is suggested, as it is the cheapest form of construction, but the "design could be carried out in brick, stone or concrete. For this small house we suggest that the walls be soft cream, the woodwork stained warm brown, window sash painted white. The roof should be a soft, rather olive, green."

John Bryan, his longtime associate Jan Toftey, and the staff at Crab Tree Farm gave me access to his memorial to the genius of Harvey Ellis—the amazing re-creation of Ellis's 1903 Bungalow—and to his research into the colors and stains that may have been used. What a magnificent achievement!

Janet Parks, curator of drawings at the Avery Architectural and Fine Arts Library at Columbia University in New York City, and her staff have been gracious and helpful over the years. And thanks to Virginia Kurshan, who compiled the excellent drawing index in September 1980.

Gibbs Smith and Suzanne Taylor saw the potential and gave me the opportunity to submit this work to the public; project editor Madge Baird, art director Kurt Wahlner, designer Rudy Ramos, copy editor Linda Nimori, and production editor Melissa Dymock have put up with numerous missed deadlines and allowed this project to grow into a larger book so that every known Stickley house design could be featured. Their commitment to this project has been magnificent.

My thanks to all my colleagues at The Craftsman Farms Foundation, with special thanks to Frank and Susan Finkenburg for their discovery of a Craftsman Home in New Mexico; David W. Lowden for the loan of books and other critical material; and to Foundation president Mark Hewitt, AIA, and Ed Heinle, AIA, for a detailed and intense review of the drafts and criticism of the house designs. Their comments and criticisms have educated me and enriched the final product immeasurably.

Nancy Strathearn, the foundation's late executive director, gave me great encouragement and support, and located one home all on her own. I greatly miss her. I miss the late Paul Fiore, too. His strong support for Craftsman Farms was an inspiration to me, and his encouragement and enthusiasm pushed me to begin this book.

Former Craftsman Farms trustee David Cathers has supported me and shared his knowledge on Stickley, even before publishing it in his own book, the recently published and now definitive *Gustav Stickley*. A number of the homes pictured in this book were located as a result of his research, and his discovery of the papers of the Jud Yoho trademark infringement interference yielded important information. He has been a truly wonderful colleague.

Dr. Mary Ann Smith wrote the first definitive biography on Gustav Stickley and recognized how significant the homes were to the overall picture of his life, and the Arts and Crafts movement in America. She has shared her knowledge, her thoughts, and her time unselfishly, including a review and edit of my text, and I thank her deeply for her support.

Joe Farmarco, who manages the modern crafts part of the annual conference and show at the Grove Park Inn, is one of the most interesting people I have ever met. He has been my sidekick on a number of house-hunting trips and has kept me from dozing off behind the wheel and ending up in a ditch—or worse—more than a few times. We have had some great adventures together. For instance, we drove sixteen hours through a blizzard listening to Mahler's Resurrection Symphony at top volume to keep awake in order to photograph the home in Presque Isle, Maine, before its light fixtures were removed and sold at auction.

Franklin Piccirillo, who works for the city of Cleveland in historic preservation and is restoring his own National Register–eligible home, has been my muse as well as occasional traveling companion. Many of the well-turned phrases in this book are Frank's, as we have discussed its plot and direction over many miles of traveling, and his red ink notations all over my drafts smoothed my awkward sentence structure. His keen eye spotted a number of Craftsman homes, whose pedigree I questioned, and I was proved wrong. The color charts used in the book are from his collection. Thanks for all the time and effort to guide me, and for spending all that vacation time helping make this book possible!

Finally, my wife, Ula Ilnytzky, who makes a living as an editor, made the final edit, smoothing over the remaining bumps. And she, and my daughters Nina and Vika, put up with me for three years while I read and wrote and ducked household chores and family time to finish the book. Nina, who at the age of nine, located a Craftsman Home in western New Jersey from a block away, did the massive job of scanning the illustrations from *The Craftsman* for the book. I thank them all for their love, patience, and support from the bottom of my heart.

Bibliography

Anderson, Timothy J., Eudorah M. Moore, and Robert W. Winter. *California Design 1910*. Salt Lake City: Peregrine Smith Books [Gibbs Smith, Publisher], 1980.

Ayres, Dianne, Timothy Hansen, Beth Ann McPherson, and Tommy Arthur McPherson II. *American Arts and Crafts Textiles*. New York: Harry N. Abrams, Inc. 2002.

Ayres, Dianne. *Arts and Crafts Period Textiles: Past and Present*. Berkeley, California: Private Printing, 1990.

Baillie Scott, M. H. *Houses and Gardens: Arts and Crafts Interiors*. London: George Newnes Ltd., 1905.

The Bankmule. Official Publication of the Van Lear Ky., Historical Society 4, no. 4 (December 1987).

Barrett, Helena, and John Phillips. *Suburban Style—The British Home 1840–1960*. London: Little, Brown and Company, 1993.

Bartinique, Patricia A., ed. *Gustav Stickley: His Craft*. Parsippany, New Jersey: The Craftsman Farms Foundation, 1992.

Bosley, Edward R. *Greene & Greene*. London: Phaidon Press, 2000.

Bragdon, Claude. "Plaster Houses." *Architectural Review* 11 (December 1904).

Cathers, David. *Furniture of the Arts and Crafts Movement*. Rev. ed. Philmont, New York: Turn of the Century Editions, 1996.

_____. *Genius in the Shadows—The Furniture Designs of Harvey Ellis*. New York: The Jordan-Volpe Gallery, 1981.

_____. *Gustav Stickley*. New York: Phaidon Press, 2003.

_____, ed. *Gustav Stickley's Craftsman Farms—A Pictorial History*. Parsippany, New Jersey: The Craftsman Farms Foundation, 1999.

_____, and Alexander Vertikoff. *Stickley Style—Arts and Crafts Homes in the Craftsman Tradition*. New York: Simon and Schuster, 1999.

Clark, Michael, and Jill Thomas-Clark. *The Stickley Brothers*. Salt Lake City: Gibbs Smith, Publisher, 2002.

Congdon-Martin, Douglas, ed. *The Gustav Stickley Photo Archives*. Atglen, Pennsylvania: Schiffer Publishing Ltd., 2002.

The Craftsman (selected issues from 1901–1916).

The Craftsman on CD-ROM. New York: Interactive Bureau, 1998.

Cumming, Elizabeth, and Wendy Kaplan. *The Arts and Crafts Movement*. New York: Thames & Hudson, Inc., 1991.

Duchscherer, Paul, and Douglas Keister. *The Bungalow—America's Arts and Crafts Home*. New York: Penguin Studio, 1995.

_____. *Outside The Bungalow—America's Arts and Crafts Gardens.* New York: Penguin Studio, 1995.

Dumblane—The Suburban Estate of S. Hazen Bond. Private Printing by S. Hazen Bond, ca. 1914.

Durant, Stuart. *C. F. A. Voysey.* London/New York: Academy Editions/St. Martin Press, 1992.

Fish, Marilyn. *Gustav Stickley—Heritage and Early Years.* North Caldwell, New Jersey: Little Pond Press, 1997.

_____. *Gustav Stickley—1884-1900.* North Caldwell, New Jersey: Little Pond Press, 1999.

_____. *The New Craftsman Index.* Lambertville, New Jersey: The Arts and Crafts Quarterly Press, 1997.

France, Jean R., Roger G. Kennedy, Black McKelvey, and Howard S. Merritt. *A Rediscovery—Harvey Ellis: Artist, Architect.* Rochester, New York: Memorial Art Gallery of the University of Rochester, 1972.

Freeman, John Crosby. *The Forgotten Rebel: Gustav Stickley and His Craftsman Mission Furniture.* Watkins Glen, New York: Century House, 1966.

Gebhard, David. *Charles F. A. Voysey, Architect.* Los Angeles: Hennessey & Ingalls, 1975.

Gill, Brendan. *Many Masks—A Life of Frank Lloyd Wright.* New York: Da Capo Press, 1998.

Good Housekeeping (selected issues 1901-1914)

Hering, Oswald C. *Concrete and Stucco Houses.* New York: McBride, Nast and Company, 1912,

Hewitt, Mark Alan. *Gustav Stickley's Craftsman Farms—The Quest for an Arts and Crafts Utopia.* Syracuse, New York: Syracuse University Press, 2001.

The History of Dunn County (1925).

Hitchmough, Wendy. *C. F. A. Voysey.* London: Phaidon Press, 1995.

Hooper, Carol. "All True Work is Sacred—The Influence of the Arts and Crafts Movement in Washington, D.C." Master's thesis, School of Architecture, University of Virginia, 1989.

The House Beautiful (selected issues 1902–1910).

Interference in the United States Patent Office—Gustav Stickley vs. Judd Toho. Interference No. 35725, July 1913.

Kaplan, Wendy, ed. *The Art that is Life—The Arts and Crafts Movement in America 1875-1920.* Boston: Museum of Fine Arts, 1987.

_____, ed. *The Arts & Crafts Movement in Europe & America— Design for the Modern World.* New York: Thames & Hudson, Inc., 2004.

Kardon, Janet, ed. *The Ideal Home 1900-1920—The History of Twentieth-Century American Craft.* New York: American Craft Museum, 1993.

Kinsler, Carolyn. "Creating a Vernacular: Gustav Stickley and The Craftsman Magazine." Master's thesis, 1989.

Kornwolf, James D. *M. H. Baillie Scott and the Arts and Crafts Movement.* Baltimore. Maryland: John Hopkins University Press, 1972.

Kreisman, Lawrence, and Larry E. Johnson, A.I.A. "Bungalows in the Ravenna Neighborhood." Research paper, n.d. Seattle, Washington: Seattle Architectural Foundation.

Kurshan, Virginia. *Catalogue of Drawings of the Craftsman Homes by the Craftsman Architects 1904-1914.* New York: Avery Architectural and Fine Arts Library, Columbia University, n.d.

Lang, Robert W. *Shop Drawings for Craftsman Interiors.* Bethel, Connecticut: Cambium Press, 2003.

Livingstone, Karen, and Linda Parry, eds. *International Arts and Crafts.* London: V&A Publications, 2005.

Ludwig, Coy L. *The Arts and Crafts Movement in New York State, 1890s-1920s.* Hamilton, New York: Gallery Association of New York State, 1983.

MacCarthy, Fiona. *William Morris—A Life for Our Time.* New York:

Alfred A. Knopf, 1995.

Maston, Bruce, M.D. *An Enclave of Elegance*. Schenectady, New York: The Schenectady Museum/ G. E. R. P. A. Publications, 1983.

Michels, Eileen Manning. *Reconfiguring Harvey Ellis*. Edina, Minnesota: Beaver Pond Press, Inc., 2004.

Muthesius, Hermann. *Das Englische Haus: Entwicklung, Bedingungen Anlage, Aufbau, Einrichtung und Innenraum [The English House]*. 3 vols. Berlin: Ernst Wasmuth, 1904.

O'Gorman, James F. *The Architecture of Frank Furness*. Philadelphia: Philadelphia Museum of Art, 1973.

Sanders, Barry. *A Complex Fate— Gustav Stickley and the Craftsman Movement*. New York: John Wiley & Sons, Inc., 1996.

Schweitzer, Robert. *Bungalow Colors—Exteriors*. Salt Lake City: Gibbs Smith, Publisher, 2002.

Smith, Bruce, and Alexander Vertikoff. *Greene & Greene Masterworks*. San Francisco: Chronicle Books, 1998.

Smith, Bruce, and Yoshiko Yamamoto. *The Beautiful Necessity—Decorating with Arts and Crafts*. Salt Lake City: Gibbs Smith, Publisher, 1996.

Smith, Mary Ann. *Gustav Stickley— The Craftsman*. Syracuse, New York: Syracuse University Press, 1983.

Sparrow, W. Shaw Sparrow, ed. *The British Home of Today—A Book of Modern Domestic Architecture & the Applied Arts*. New York: A. C. Armstrong & Son, 1904.

Stevenson, Katherine Cole, and H. Ward Jandl. *Houses By Mail— A Guide to Houses from Sears, Roebuck and Company*. Washington: The Preservation Press, 1986.

Stickley, Gustav. *Craftsman Fabrics and Needlework*, n.d.

_____. *The Craftsman Fireplace— A Complete Heating and Ventilating System*, September 1913.

_____. *Craftsman Furnishings for the Home*, October 1912.

_____. *Craftsman Homes*. New York: The Craftsman Publishing Company, 1909.

_____. *Craftsman Houses—A Book for Homemakers*, 1913.

_____. *More Craftsman Homes*. New York: The Craftsman Publishing Company, 1912.

_____. *24 Craftsman Houses*, 1912.

_____. *What is Wrought in the Craftsman Workshops, a brochure published in the interests of the Homebuilder's Club*, 1904.

The Touchstone (1916–17).

Trapp, Kenneth R., ed. *The Arts and Crafts Movement in California— Living the Good Life*. New York: Abbeville Press, 1993.

Turgeon, Kitty, and Robert Rust. *Arts and Crafts*. New York: Friedman/Fairfax, 1997.

_____. *The Arts and Crafts Home*. New York: Friedman/Fairfax, 1998.

Varnedoe, Kirk. *Vienna 1900—Art, Architecture & Design*. New York: The Museum of Modern Art, 1986.

Winter, Robert, and Alexander Vertikoff: *American Bungalow Style*. New York: Simon & Schuster, 1996.

Photo Credits

Avery Architectural and Fine Arts Library, Columbia University: Gustav Stickley original plans and drawings, throughout.

Nina Stubblebine: All images from *The Craftsman* magazine.

Ron Frehm: 204-10 (Craftsman Home No. 40).

The Craftsman Farms Foundation: xiii, xvi, 2, 3, 56 (bottom), 59 (top), 63 (bottom), 65.

Page 4—Courtesy of Barbara Fuldner.

Page 6—Period fireplace photo courtesy of Carole Harper.

Pages 7 (center)—Baillie Scott, M. H.: *Houses and Gardens: Arts and Crafts Interiors;* 8—(top and bottom) Voysey illustrations from *British Home of Today*, edited by W. Shaw Sparrow.

Page 8—from *Houses and Gardens*, by Baillie Scott.

Page 12—Dietrich color drawing courtesy John Spencer of Riverow Bookshop, Inc. Owego, New York.

Page 18—Voysey illustration from *The British Home of Today*, ed. W. Shaw Sparrow.

Page 39—Courtesy of David Cathers.

Page 40—Courtesy of Larry Kinsman.

Page 49—Courtesy of Decorative Arts Photographic Collection, Winterthur.

Page 72—Photos by Ian Hunter.

Page 73—Courtesy of Mac Morrow.

Page 76 (top)—Courtesy of Glenn and Mary Anne Barbie.

Page 82—Photos by Raymond Lauenstein.

Pages 83, 84, 86, 87—Paint charts and image courtesy of Franklin Piccirillo.

Page 99—Blueprints courtesy of Victor Nee.

Page 102—Blueprint courtesy of David and Roberta Griffiths.

Pages 115, 116—Photos by Harvey Kaplan; period photo courtesy of Silver City Museum.

Pages 121, 122—Period photos from *Good Housekeeping*, June 1906.

Page 129—Period photo from *Das Englishe Haus*, by Hermann Muthesius.

Page 135 (top)—Photo by John Ellington.

Page 147 (right)—Photo by Susan Keller.

Pages 155, 156—Acly house photos scanned by Jim Bourg; courtesy of William Acly.

Page 173—Photos courtesy of Brian Mack.

Pages 243-247—Photos by Jim Heuer; postcard courtesy of Jeff Newenhof.

Page 276 (bottom)—Courtesy of The Bankmule, Official Publication of the Van Lear Ky. Historical Society.

Page 293 (top)—Courtesy of Randy and Sue Froehlich.

Page 295 (bottom)—Courtesy of Mac Morrow.

Page 299—Interior photo courtesy of the Fort Worth *Star Telegram*.

Pages 307, 310 (top right), 312 (bottom)—Photos by and courtesy of Melissa Pollock.

Pages 322, 323—Photos by and courtesy of Ramona Larramendy.

Page 327—Courtesy of Franklin Piccirillo.

Pages 328 (center and bottom), 329—
   Courtesy of Peter Buck.
Pages 354, 355—Photos by and
   courtesy of John M. Russells.
Page 366—Photo by Sharon Ferraro.
Page 369 (center left)—Courtesy of
   Mary Margaret Smith.
Page 376 (top left), 378—Vaill house
   1913 and Vaill family photos
   courtesy of Amy Vaill Kelly.
Page 376 (top right)—Oradell Public
   Library.
Page 386 (bottom)—Courtesy of
   Thomas Murray.
Pages 407 (bottom), 408—Photos by
   Lori Hafner.
Page 409 (bottom)—Photo by
   Steve Claris.
Page 422 (bottom)—Courtesy of the
   Larchmont Historical Association.
Page 437—Courtesy of Priscilla Sadler.
Page 449 (bottom)—Photo by
   Linda Hughes.
Page 450 (top)—Courtesy of
   Nelson T. French.
Pages 453, 454—Period photos
   courtesy of Frank N. Sollitto.
Pages 479, 480—Photos by and cour-
   tesy of Ramona Larramendy.
Page 484 (bottom)—Courtesy of
   Martin Olsen.

Craftsman Homes Web Site

Visit the site for more information on Craftsman Homes and the latest discoveries. There is an exclusive members area for readers of this book.

http:/www.craftsmanhomes.org

Think you have found a Craftsman Home?

E-mail Ray Stubblebine with any information and photos:

ray@craftsmanhomes.org

Or mail to:

Ray Stubblebine
863 Midland Road
Oradell NJ 07649

Information should also be forwarded to:

Executive Director
The Craftsman Farms
Foundation, Inc.
2352 Route 10 West - Box 5
Morris Plains, NJ 07950

Index

Phillips, W. H. home, 252
Plaster, 96
Price, William, 5
Prior, C. C. home, 363
Prior, Ernest L. home, 42–43, 335–38
Purcell, William, 5

R

Rand, George D., 222
Recker, Carlos home, 172–73
Reconfiguring Harvey Ellis, xii
Red Gables, 47
Reichbacht, Catherine home, 292
Richards, Dr. Mary E. home, 290
Riordan, Raymond home, x–xi, 364
Robbins, R. L. home, 192
Roberts, George home, 229, 232–34
Roberts, Mary Fanton, 34
Roosevelt, Theodore, 386

S

Sailer, Carl, 27
Sander, Barry, xii
Sargent, Irene, 5, 28
Schiebe, Edgar F. home, 41, 444–45
Schlager, Jacob, 1
Schultz, Fred W. home, 313–15
Scott, M. H. Baillie. *See* Baillie Scott,
    M. H.
Sheppard, G. Harry home, 477
Shrimpton, Louise, 27
Simonds, Elgin, 3
Smith, Dr. Mary Ann, xii, 80
Smith, W. B. home, 428
Smyth, J. Gordon home, 277–78
Soiland, Albert home, 129
Spaid, Dr. John M. home, 248, 250–51
Spencer, Robert, 135
Stevens, C. W. home, 230, 234
Stevens, John Calvin, 110
Stickley, Barbara: on Gustav Stickley's
    design process, 47

Stickley, Eda Simmons, 3, 4
Stickley, Gustav: furniture career of,
    1–4; architectural career of, 4–10;
    Syracuse home of, 44–51
Stickley, Marion, 3
Stickley Brothers Company, 83
Story, Oliver J., 27, 28
Strickler, Dr. A. F. home, 126
Stucco, 96
Sullivan, Louis, 5, 144
Syracuse home, 44–51

T

Tannahill, Robert, 133
Taylor, Alfred T., 27
Taylor, B. A. home, 339–42
Tenafly, New Jersey home, 432–33
Thompson, Orville home, 484–85
Toothaker, Victor, 360, 385

U

Unwin, Raymond, 5, 9, 290
"Urban House", 14–15

V

Vaill, Edward Warren Jr. home,
    374–84
Van Duyn, Walter S. home, 74, 78
Voysey, C. F. A., 7, 9, 12–13

W

Waite home, 423
Ward, George B. and Evelyn Hart
    home, 482–83
Ward, Ward Wellington, 28
Warner, LaMont, 27, 28, 47
Watts, E. L. home, 425
Werkstadt, Wiener, xiii
White, Joseph and Minnie home, 8,
    79–80
Wiles, Barbara, 2

Wilkerson, Sexton home, 409–10
Wilkinson, Henry Wilhelm, 5–6, 10,
    28, 47
Wilkinson, Marshall F. home, 260–62
Willeke, Leonard home, 153
Williams, I. R. home, 495–96
Williams, Ruth Anne, 27, 28
Wilson, Henry, 304, 414
Wilson home, 368–70
Windy Gap home, 73
Winslow, William, 123
Woodhall, Victoria C., 306
Wright, Frank Lloyd, 123, 142, 144

Y

Yoho, Jud, 38–43